T0287905

BEER AND REVOLUTION

TOM GOYENS

Beer and Revolution

THE GERMAN ANARCHIST MOVEMENT IN NEW YORK CITY, 1880–1914

UNIVERSITY OF ILLINOIS PRESS
URBANA, CHICAGO, AND SPRINGFIELD

First Illinois paperback, 2014

∞ This book is printed on acid-free paper.

The Library of Congress cataloged the cloth edition as follows:
Goyens, Tom, 1972–
Beer and revolution : the German anarchist movement
in New York City, 1880–1914 / Tom Goyens.
p. cm.
Includes bibliographical references and index.
ISBN-13: 978-0-252-03175-5 (cloth : alk. paper)
ISBN-10: 0-252-03175-X (cloth : alk. paper)
1. Anarchism—New York (State)—New York—History
—19th century. 2. Anarchism—New York (State)—New
York—History—20th century. 3. Germans—New York
(State)—New York—Political activity—History. 4. German-
Americans—New York (State)—New York—Political
activity—History. 5. Most, Johann Joseph, 1846–1906.
6. Subculture—New York (State)—New York—History.
I. Title.
HX846.N7G69 2007
320.5'70893107471—dc22 2006100923
PAPERBACK ISBN 978-0-252-08046-3

It is worth while to know what the Anarchists among us think, for, though few in number, they indicate a tendency of the time.

—*Springfield (Mass.) Republican*

Thu' des Maul nit unnütz auf, Red' was Geistreich's oder sauf.

[Don't open your mouth idly, say something witty or drink.]

—From an ad for Justus Schwab's beerhall, *Freiheit,* 15 June 1898.

It is easy to say that Anarchist ideals are impractical, but as I look back and think of friends of mine who have lived by those ideals for half a century, I am not so sure.

—Lucy Lang, *Tomorrow Is Beautiful*

Anarchists are people who make a social and political philosophy out of the natural and spontaneous tendency of humans to associate together for their mutual benefit.

—Colin Ward, *Anarchy in Action*

Contents

Acknowledgments

This book originated with my graduate studies at the University of Leuven, Belgium, and the College of William and Mary in Williamsburg, Virginia. Without the help of the staff and history faculty of both institutions, this book would not have been possible. I thank Louis Vos, my advisor, who made this project possible from the start. When I suggested German anarchists as a topic, he was instantly enthusiastic, and he has remained a constant promoter of my project. Ronald Creagh has been an invaluable companion in my search for order and insights into this topic. I truly appreciate his targeted feedback and kind encouragement.

I was fortunate to have benefited from the comments of some of the leading scholars in the field. What more could I ask than to have Paul Avrich, Paul Buhle, Heiner Becker, and Dirk Hoerder provide me with priceless feedback? I must also thank Robert Helms for sharing information from his research on Philadelphia anarchists. I thank Carlotta Anderson, Timothy Gilfoyle, Kenneth Jackson, Terje I. Leiren, and Dirk Philipsen, all distinguished historians with whom I shared my thoughts or on whom I relied for a quick answer to a vexing question.

I most emphatically thank Heather Harvey for her unremitting companionship throughout this endeavor. She has edited countless pages and provided creative feedback, and she also created the digital maps. Let me also thank other friends and family who have supported me in this effort. Many, like James Spady, Tim Barnard, and Matt Cohen, have significantly contributed ideas that ultimately found their way into this work.

I am also indebted to the professional help of dozens of librarians and archivists. I thank Julie Herrada of the Labadie Collection at the University of Michigan; Mieke Ijzerman, Monique van de Pal, and Ella Molenaar of the International Institute of Social History in Amsterdam, who assisted my research (and helped with mountains of copies); Jenny Spurrier of the Southwest Collection at Texas Tech University; Marilyn Pettit of the University Archives at Columbia University; the people at the DadA website; Sigrid Woeste of the Bibliothek des Ruhrgebiets, Ruhr Universität Bochum; and the staff and colleagues at the Colonial Williamsburg Foundation's Research Division. I further thank Marie Lopez for translating a crucial document from Spanish into English.

This book would not exist without the people at the University of Illinois Press. I thank in particular Laurie Matheson for her assistance throughout the editing process. The book is much better than the original manuscript because of her guidance.

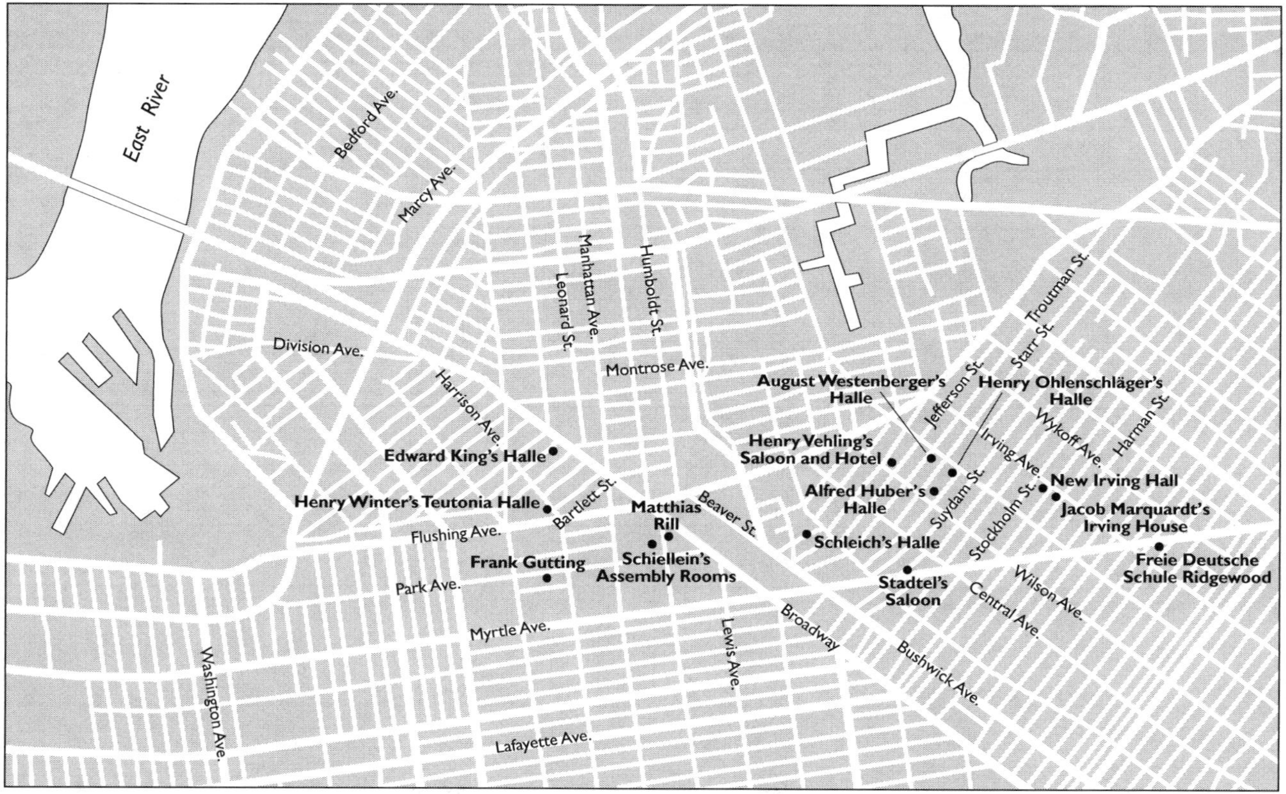
East River
Bedford Ave.
Marcy Ave.
Manhattan Ave.
Leonard St.
Humboldt St.
Division Ave.
Montrose Ave.
Harrison Ave.
Troutman St.
Starr St.
August Westenberger's Halle
Jefferson St.
Henry Ohlenschläger's Halle
Harman St.
Wykoff Ave.
Irving Ave.
Henry Vehling's Saloon and Hotel
Edward King's Halle
New Irving Hall
Alfred Huber's Halle
Suydam St.
Stockholm St.
Jacob Marquardt's Irving House
Henry Winter's Teutonia Halle
Bartlett St.
Matthias Rill
Beaver St.
Flushing Ave.
Schleich's Halle
Frank Gutting
Schiellein's Assembly Rooms
Stadtel's Saloon
Freie Deutsche Schule Ridgewood
Park Ave.
Wilson Ave.
Central Ave.
Myrtle Ave.
Broadway
Bushwick Ave.
Lewis Ave.
Washington Ave.
Lafayette Ave.

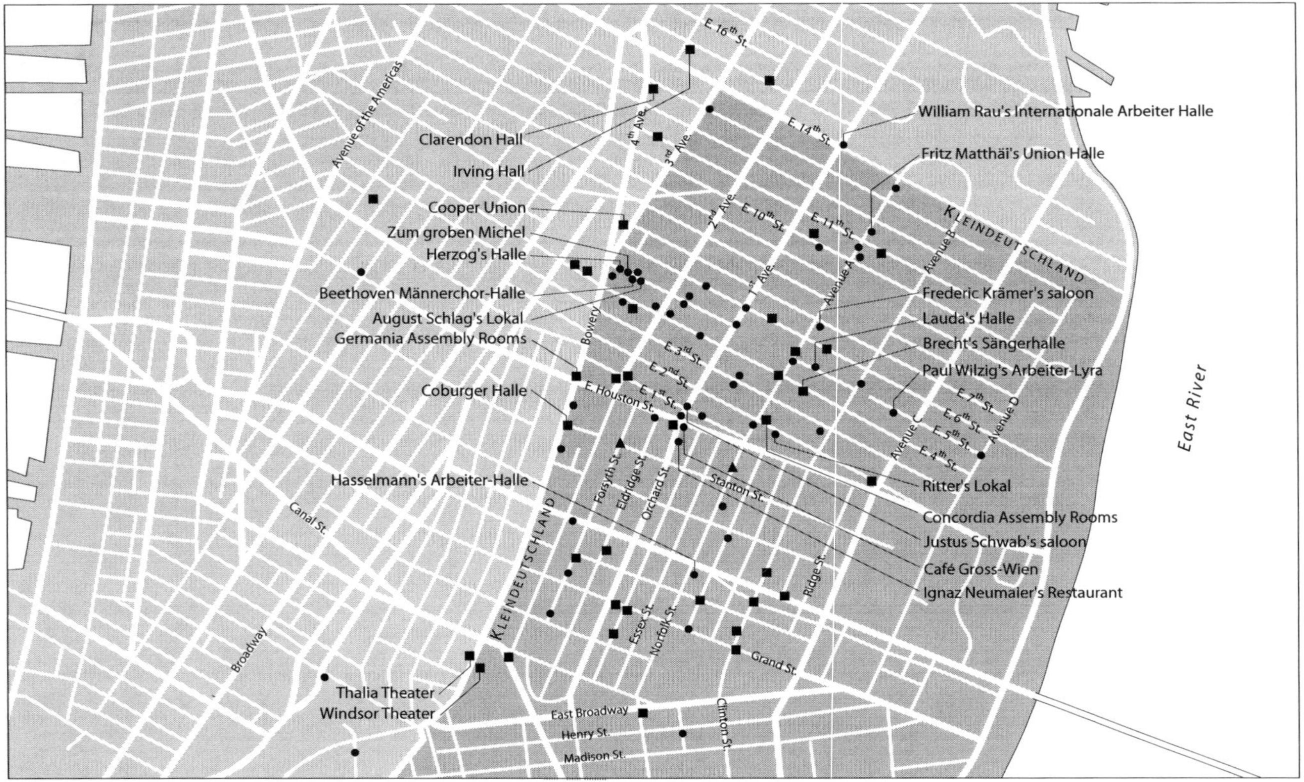

Key:

- ● = Saloons or Bierhalle owned or frequented by German anarchists
- ■ = Lecture or assembly halls used by German anarchists
- ▲ = Printers or editorial offices affiliated with the German anarchist movement

BEER AND REVOLUTION

Introduction

A modern visitor to New York City who is interested in radicalism may want to venture to Allen Street on the Lower East Side. There, at number 172, is the Bluestockings Radical Bookstore, which labels itself as an "activist center" that strives to "create a space that welcomes and empowers all people." They "actively support movements that challenge hierarchy and all systems of oppression."[1] This modern anarchist infoshop is one of many that comprise the contemporary anarchist movement in the United States. It is remarkable that Bluestockings is located only two hundred meters south of what was once the best-known radical hangout in Lower Manhattan during the 1880s and 1890s, Justus Schwab's beerhall at 50 First Street. At the time, each of the streets surrounding Schwab's place, extending for several blocks, counted at least one saloon where anarchists regularly met. Johann Most, a central figure in the movement, once lived at 198 Allen Street. In the 1870s and 1880s, this neighborhood—Manhattan's Seventeenth Ward—was the heart of German New York.

German-speaking anarchists were the first to fashion a revolutionary anarchist movement in the United States. In New York, the country's largest and culturally most diverse city, socialism had been almost exclusively a German affair since the 1850s. These German socialists made up a tiny fraction of the millions of Germans who disembarked in New York. Nonetheless, they forged a community all their own. From 1880 on, dissident or revolutionary socialists carved out their own subculture, rooted in working-class saloons of New York, Brooklyn, Newark, Paterson, and several smaller towns. Anarchists (as the revolutionaries came to be called) went out of their way to differentiate themselves from socialists, even though they shared a common past. Not only did they form separate clubs and singing societies, they also created a unique anarchist image, complete with its own rhetoric, humor, symbols, and rituals—a renegade persona that was bolder and more provocative than your average armchair socialist willing to work within the system. Nothing illustrates this better than the way these radicals inscribed anarchism in a radical, urban space—a space that was hidden, but not secret; ideologically circumscribed, but remarkably integrated in the city's own patchwork of geographies. By mapping the anarchist movement's geopolitical space, by understanding what they believed in, and by examining cultural expressions, it will become clear that German anarchists were no freak phenomenon but rather a small component of the larger immigrant fabric spun across America's largest urban region. The men and women who made up this movement lived and worked in cities and towns along the Hudson, Passaic, and East Rivers. They were politically aware, class-conscious, ideologically committed, and seldom afraid of confrontation. What instilled fear and loathing in the minds of respectable Americans was the assumed lawlessness and anti-institutionalism of the anarchist ideology and the occasionally threatening language that went with it.

This book focuses on New York City, but it also ventures outside its city limits. Surrounding towns were inevitably pulled into New York's magnetic field, and some—like Brooklyn and Queens—eventually became part of the city by consolidation in 1898. Newark, Elizabeth City, Paterson, and the localities within Hudson County along the Hudson River—all working-class towns in New Jersey—housed enough Germans for clusters of anarchists to emerge that developed into energetic communities linked to what was brewing in Lower Manhattan. Hoboken in 1890, for instance, was, after Milwaukee, the most German city in America with nearly 55 percent of its population German.[2] The movement in New York and northern New Jersey was not unique but rather part of a network of German anarchist groups spread across the northeastern and midwestern United States. But the size and diversity of the city combined to make the movement there a hub of radical activity. Since the 1850s, the city on the Hudson had been home to thousands of German families huddled in one of the largest ethnic communities in nineteenth-century America: Little Germany on the Lower East Side. The history of this enclave is well documented, except for a small but vocal minority: the anarchists. This book seeks to fill the gap. It was not inevitable that German anarchist immigrants would settle among other German Americans, but they did. There was no anarchist neighborhood per se, only clusters of anarchist meeting places sprinkled across the larger German district.

There are several reasons the presence of a German-language anarchist movement in New York should not be a surprise. First, there was the renewed appeal of anarchist ideas among disaffected workers and artisans in the 1880s and 1890s, linked to the success—and for some, staleness—of Social-Democratic parties in Europe. Secondly, a community like Little Germany provided a relatively safe living space for radical compatriots. In other words, it would be surprising if there had been no anarchists active in the hive of Gilded Age and Progressive New York.

The German anarchist movement in New York was part of the broader history of international radicalism, making it an American, a German, and a transnational movement. Immigrant anarchism in the Americas constitutes an episode in the broader phenomenon of transatlantic Jacobin radicalism that began at the end of the eighteenth century. This current opposed not only the ancien régime but also the new ethos of bourgeois capitalism that emerged during the early nineteenth century. Revolutions and upheavals on both sides of the Atlantic between 1775 and 1914 reveal a surprising degree of cross-fertilization. Thomas Paine, for instance, traveled to the American colonies, Benjamin Franklin charmed Parisian royal society as ambassador of a popular republic, and the forty-eighter Friedrich Hecker moved to America to become an antislavery Republican. The marketplace of ideas ignores national borders. Jacobin, socialist, and anarchist ideas spread easily through travel, correspondence, and an increasingly transnational radical press. Especially important for this study is the phenomenon of exile or immigrant radicals, who became the vehicle for the spread of revolutionary ideas.

Contemporaries were not blind to parallels between seemingly disparate struggles for liberation. The American Civil War, for instance, was as much a battle against a slaveholding aristocracy as it was a war to preserve the political integrity of a nation. Similarly, the German revolution of 1848 and its suppression are linked to the emergence of German social revolutionaries thirty years later and consequently to the appearance of a German American anarchist movement. Several veteran forty-eighters became radicalized once more during the 1870s and 1880s, and a good number of them already resided in America. The 1848–49 radicals and the anarchist club members of 1890 in New York were skilled workers and artisans who despised the aristocracy as well as the bourgeoisie who imposed their rule by way of free-market exploitation. The prospect of working for wages under an employer drove these craftspeople into the streets of Berlin, Paris, and New York. For a time, the radicalized artisans perceived America as a model free republic of small producers. This would change during the Gilded Age, when anarchist artisans viewed the fight to restore the independence of the worker as a lost cause.

Anarchism in late nineteenth- and early twentieth-century America was one among a maelstrom of competing and conflicting ideas, loyalties, and expectations within a rapidly altering society. A barrage of change overtook this society, unhinging the stability of different social groups almost simultaneously. The country was plunged into an uncontrolled "search for order," as the historian Robert Wiebe has summarized it.[3] Farmers and workers rebelled on a national scale, clashing with the promoters of a new economy and leaving religious and political leaders to witness what the historian Howard Zinn has called "the other civil war."[4] By the mid-1890s, the economic and political elite succeeded in curbing the tide of protest by implementing a politics of exclusion, drawing "a line around the good society and dismissing the outsiders."[5] The anarchists became outsiders—recreant undesirables. Their exclusion was based on the alleged danger of depraved humans and turned out to be an excellent tool of control and containment for the privileged. The historian Martin Duberman observed that "it allows them to insist that our current institutions—purportedly the wise embodiment of past experience—must be preserved intact against misguided agitators who assail them in the name of some unachievable egalitarianism."[6]

Anarchists in the nineteenth century were predominantly viewed as unsettled malcontents—violent, mentally impaired, probably foreign, and fanatical. While a few individuals may have fit that description, the majority of anarchists were loath to commit acts of violence. That popular image, which lingers to this day, is largely a distortion, resulting in what one anarchist paper termed "anarchophobia."[7] It has become necessary for serious scholars of anarchism to debunk the myth of the cloaked, bomb-carrying anarchist. German anarchists used inflammatory language laced with threats to peace, order, and property, but their utterances pale in comparison to the ubiquitous violence against marching or striking workers, or the belligerent tone of popular newspapers, or even the frightening omnipresence of "ordinary" crime in cities like New York and Chicago. With the exception of Alexander Berkman's attempt on the life of a robber baron, no anarchist-inspired acts of deliberate violence have been committed by a self-identified anarchist in the United States. If anarchists spoke of arms, it was in the context of self-defense. Anarchists saw brash posturing as a form of resistance, as when bawdy irreverence during a carnival could pack a punch at the rich and powerful. Johann Most, an influential character in the movement, was a master of the invective. In his writing and speechmaking, Most employed biting sarcasm—often tongue-in-cheek—to assail his adversaries, not dissimilar from the irony and bluntness of 1970s punk culture. It is therefore essential to be sensitive to the nature of anarchist language and semiotics to understand the dynamics between it and the dominant culture.

Anarchist activists in America did find an audience among the hard-driven millhands, factory workers, and packinghouse employees in Chicago and other midwestern cities. American society during the Gilded Age was so stratified and intensely unequal that workers and farmers looked to radical solutions. A momentum of protest during the 1870s and 1880s allowed anarchist ideas to surface and contribute to a broad agenda of opposition. Its subsequent allocation to the realm of the excluded, however, buried anarchism under a mountain of distorted sensationalism. Both experiences—one of momentum, the other of exclusion—defined the German anarchist movement and its individual members in the period between 1880 and 1914. But like the society at large, anarchists engaged in a "search for order" of their own, which they found in the basic tenets of anarchism's social critique. These principles formed a bond that made the movement possible despite rampant ideological strife. Anarchists opposed all forms of authority, which during the turn of the century were identified as the state, church, and capitalist wage system. They saw the individual as an autonomous entity endowed with ethical and imaginative powers who could never be a servant to nor be served by anyone. Even democratic politics was representational and hence unacceptable. For anarchists, it was inconceivable that change could be achieved through the political process. Instead, they believed that a spirit of revolt simmered among the disaffected of the world and that it could be roused by spontaneous rebellion—physical or intellectual.

The Haymarket affair of 1886–87 is one of the most dramatic and defining moments in American labor history. The bombing and trial, in which several German anarchists were involved, took place in Chicago, but the reverberations reached all corners of the nation and beyond. It came at a time when a nationwide movement to reduce the workday to eight hours gained renewed momentum. Industrial centers like Chicago buzzed with radical activity by reformers, socialists, and anarchists. But there was no dialogue between labor and capital, only deep-seated apprehension and even hatred. Every strike or demonstration in Chicago was the scene of violence, and a bellicose atmosphere hung over a city known for its trigger-happy police force. The popular press did everything it could to discredit—indeed, to criminalize—the protests of the men and women who had literally built the nation. On 4 May 1886, the year

Frédéric-Auguste Bartholdi's Statue of Liberty was dedicated on New York's Bedloe's Island, a large meeting was called by anarchists—mostly Germans—at Chicago's Haymarket Square to protest the killing by police of several workers at a strike the day before. The meeting in Haymarket was peaceful, and the mayor, who attended for a short while, ordered the police not to intervene. At the end of the meeting, when many people had gone home, a large police force suddenly marched toward the crowd, insisting that the meeting be closed. At that moment, a bomb was thrown into the police ranks, killing one instantly. In the confusion, seventy people were injured, six of whom later died, most of them police officers. An unknown number of attendants and bystanders were also injured or killed. The bomb thrower has never been identified. In the days after, eight anarchists were arrested, six of whom had not even been present at the meeting. During the trial, no evidence was presented that connected any of the accused to the incident. In the midst of public hysteria, all eight were found guilty, and five received the death penalty (one of them committed suicide). The verdict stunned reformers and radicals alike. On 11 November 1887, Albert Parsons, August Spies, Adolf Fischer, and Georg Engel were hanged. They became anarchist martyrs, and 11 November became engraved in the anarchist collective memory.

Haymarket was a watershed, but it did not destroy the anarchist movement, although to some extent its wings were clipped. For anarchists, Haymarket ironically legitimized the notion that the United States is not fundamentally different from autocratic Europe, an idea that had always existed in the minds of German anarchists. It reinforced the anarchists' refusal to put faith in or take part in the established channels and institutions of public policy, whose legitimacy they openly denied. It is widely accepted that the Haymarket trial was a travesty of justice, but the fact remains that a bomb attack occurred at a meeting organized by anarchists. This was enough to confirm long-held suspicions among the general populace that anarchists plotted a violent overthrow and were not afraid to carry it out.

Haymarket also made clear that the anarchists' public campaign of peaceful propaganda had become a dangerous undertaking. There was another dimension to the movement, however. This book contends that the anarchists' opposition to the state—their civil disobedience—became the foundation for a self-sufficient culture of defiance. This culture existed physically in a space replete with its own signifiers, symbols, and rituals. There is much evidence to suggest that these anarchists formed a spatial countercommunity that is as relevant as, if not more relevant than, their public campaign.[8]

Consequently, this book explores how the movement "moved" by grounding it firmly in the geography of greater New York. I do not present an intellectual or philosophical treatise on revolutionary anarchism but rather a topography and history of the movement; the focus is as much on places and spaces as on ideas and ideals. Saloons, lecture halls, picnic groves, and to some extent the streets and squares constituted a radical space in which the movement lived and breathed. Social theorists such as Henri Lefebvre, Michel de Certeau, Edward Soja, and Robert E. Park have argued that social space is not merely the backdrop or stage for events to unfold independent of space.[9] Robert Park, one of the pioneer scholars of the urban condition, is of particular interest here because he penned much of his ideas (in 1916) only slightly after immigrant anarchists were fashioning their own spheres within the city. Park advanced an "ecology" of the city in which separate moral worlds coexisted along class and ethnic lines. This "mosaic of little worlds" had an influence on the emotional experience of city dwellers. Anarchists inhabited such a world, a moral space with little interpenetration from other worlds. Every individual, including the anarchist, "finds somewhere among the varied manifestations of city life the sort of environment in which he expands and feels at ease." Anarchists, in other words, had their own "moral climate."[10] With the German anarchist community in New York, we have an opportunity to corroborate much of Park's 1916 innovative interpretation of urban environments.

Segregated space is not only found or occupied but also created and conceptualized. To use Lefebvre's argument, anarchists did not simply occupy space; they consciously *produced* it by appropriating places for themselves and inscribing them with meaning that reflected their ideology and identity. Soja insists that "human geographies become filled with politics and ideology."[11] German anarchists derived much of their political identity from what some have called "geographies of resistance": back rooms of saloons or even elaborate picnics in secluded areas of the city's parks.[12] The spatiality of anarchism, its geopolitical realm, is therefore crucial to understanding the history of the movement because it adds a spatial dimension to an otherwise exclusively temporal examination.

Such "geographies of resistance" remain hollow if they are not placed within the larger spatial context of New York City. It is common knowledge that the American metropolis at the turn of the century functioned as the center for commerce, finance, media, and entertainment. But its physical layout—its stark grid of streets and avenues, parks, bridges, railroads, and port facilities—all hardwired New York as a supreme capitalist space with its own hegemonic values. Its human-made geography, at least on a visible level, served the orderly circulation of goods, services, and people. In the context of this dominant and dominating organization of urban space alternative geographies obtain significance. Even simply finding and appropriating alternative spaces constitutes resistance. "Resistance is less about particular acts," claims de Certeau, "than about the desire to find a place in a power-geography where space is denied, circumscribed, and/or totally administered."[13] However, for German immigrant anarchists resistance was not solely a desire for space but also represented particular acts of sedition and rebellion.

When German anarchists found a place within a "power-geography," they went on to produce a spatial community that they conceived as the embodiment of anarchist ideals. In other words, they not only *ascribed* an anarchist function to it, they also *inscribed* its philosophy in it. Activities such as backroom lectures, discussion evenings, singing rehearsals, mass celebrations, outdoor recreation, and other anarchist events *produced* and at the same time *signified* the radical space in contrast to the surrounding dominant space. This extra dimension of the anarchist movement has been largely ignored by historians, but it allows us to comprehend how and where anarchists existed and to evaluate them on their own turf. For example, Justus Schwab's beerhall on First Street was not only a convenient place to talk politics; it was imagined and visualized through decorations and portraits as a haven of anarchy itself. It was a terrain where the anarchist ideal could be lived presently, a place of defiance and a space of resistance and revolutionary consciousness—a miniature anarchist society.

The idea that an anarchist society need not be a utopian ideal for the future but a way of life in the here and now has been elaborated by anarchist thinkers such as Gustav Landauer, the New Left forerunner Paul Goodman, and the British anarchist writer Colin Ward, among others. Goodman spoke of "spheres of free action," and Ward wrote in his influential book *Anarchy in Action* that "an anarchist society, a society that again sees itself without authority, is always in existence, like a seed beneath the snow, buried under the weight of the state and its bureaucracies, capitalism and its waste, privilege and its injustices, nationalism and its suicidal loyalties, religious differences and their superstitious separatism."[14]

The spatial community of German anarchists in New York was interwoven in the capitalist geography of New York. If space, ideology, and identity form a matrix of a social movement, dynamics of power manifest themselves in myriad and subtle ways. Immigrant anarchists were a marginal group, and as political repression in the United States grew, they increasingly became a subordinate group. Their opinions, indictments, and threats were not always tolerated, and expressing them was potentially dangerous, especially after Haymarket. As the expression of shared opinions and attitudes of the anarchists became more sheltered, it became at times what the political scientist and anthropologist James C. Scott has termed a "hidden transcript," confined to the group and in a secure environment.[15] The anarchists depended on their own meeting places to express these opinions, to vent against the oppressor, to dream and organize. The saloon's role as "safe haven" was critical to the movement's integrity; it was a space in which resistance could be saved from utter erasure. This book attempts to present an ethnography of an immigrant anarchist movement, highlighting its ideological, spatial, and historical dimensions.

To get a better sense of what "anarchism" was understood to mean at the time, a short overview of the development of anarchist thought is in order. After all, it was their professed ideology that distinguished them from their compatriots as well as from mainstream society. Anarchism as a modern political philosophy dates only from the 1840s and was part of a growing radical sentiment within the lower and middle echelons of European society. The threat of popular revolt that had kept European rulers awake since the days of 1789 became reality with the uprisings of 1830 and 1848, when working people revolted against their autocratic governments. But it was the growing class divide between the haves and have-nots that fed continuous protest throughout the century.

The Frenchman Pierre-Joseph Proudhon, like so many of his contemporaries, was poised to find a solution for the "labor question," the seemingly inevitable subjugation of the producer (laborer) to the increasing power of the owner of the means of production (capital). Proudhon was the first to appropriate the term "anarchist," a term coined during the turmoil of the French Revolution, when it served to deride the ultra-left wing of revolutionaries. Proudhon proposed the establishment of producer and consumer cooperatives that would govern themselves in defiance of official centralized government. Relations within his new system would be based on principles of equitable cooperation and exchange—a theory of mutualism.

Karl Marx dismissed Proudhon's ideas as hopelessly utopian and instead advocated the scientific study of capitalism's historic—and presumably inevitable—march toward disaster. For Marx, it was unmistakable that the working class, if rightly educated and organized, would someday seize the means of production by establishing a dictatorship of the proletariat. As the titular head of the international workers' movement, Marx saw his plans jeopardized by an unusually vocal opposition of anti-authoritarian socialists who categorically rejected any notion of centralized government within the worker's movement. It was the son of a Russian landlord, Mikhail Bakunin, who would emerge as the leading figure among the anarchist federations by confronting Marx directly. Bakunin is credited for taking the anarchist philosophy to the streets. He believed that anarchism could be translated into a revolutionary praxis, a movement of disaffected people challenging and attacking forces of domination, power, and greed, not at a future date but now. Marx and his followers insisted on building a strong labor movement, consisting of political parties and trade unions, powerful enough to take over the state when the time was ripe. This state would then dissolve to inaugurate the age of emancipation. Anarchists rejected the proletarian state, fearing it would introduce yet another repressive system—a mere changing of the guards. Putting words into action, Bakunin and his followers set up small, autonomous groups working toward social revolution by distributing propaganda and occasionally instigating brief skirmishes. Bakunin envisioned a society in which private property would be abolished and production controlled collectively. Individuals would be rewarded in proportion to *labor* rendered. This collectivist anarchism became especially popular with industrial and agrarian workers in less-industrialized countries, but also with radicals in France, Belgium, Switzerland, and Germany.

The standoff between Marx and Bakunin came to a head in 1872, when the Russian was unceremoniously expelled from the International Workingmen's Association (IWA). For many, this event marked the "official" split between socialists and anarchists, never to be undone. The schism occurred at a time of widespread government repression in the wake of one of the century's largest urban insurrections: the Paris Commune of 1871. In a spectacular uprising, Parisian workers of all stripes, including anarchists, seized control of the city. The communards, as they were called, were subsequently crushed by the army with astounding brutality. The event shocked everyone but claimed a special place in the collective memory of the international radical movement.

The repression that followed effectively forced left-wing radicals underground, which had important repercussions for the attitude and tactics of a growing anarchist movement. Their status as outlaws confirmed for anarchists that emancipation by way of politics was futile. Even their own organizations had become impotent. With groups infiltrated, meetings watched, and comrades constantly shadowed by detectives, some anarchists began to take matters into their own hands. During the late 1870s, a strong anti-organization current swept the movement. It was at this time that "propaganda by deed," the elevation of individual action—violent or not—as the primary agent for revolutionary advancement, began to preoccupy a large part of the activists. Aided by this cult of free individual initiative, it was perhaps inevitable that swindlers, criminals, and agents provocateurs entered the ranks with alarming frequency. The few instances of revolutionary violence—some of them in Germany—have unfairly blackened the name of anarchism to this day.

Anarchism came relatively late to Germany partly because a well-organized socialist movement had taken root, making the few anarchists nearly invisible. German socialism during its formative years in the 1860s was divided between followers of Marx and followers of Ferdinand Lassalle. Delegates at a unity congress in 1875 put their differences aside and founded the German Social-Democratic party, a formidable national power. Germany seemed on its way to making socialists full-fledged partners in the running of national affairs of Europe's continental industrial powerhouse, but Chancellor Otto von Bismarck had no intention of transforming the newly unified Germany into a participatory democracy. It was Bismarck's sweeping suppression of socialism in 1878 that radicalized a sizable minority of socialists, who were forced to leave their country into exile. Ironically, political assassinations, presumably linked to anarchist cells, galvanized support for Bismarck's plan to punish all socialists. But the chancellor perhaps unwittingly achieved the opposite effect: suppression and the humiliation of political dissidents bred revenge. London, and later New York, became a haven for German exiles, intractable, beaten, their lives uprooted, and their minds resolutely embracing a crude anarchism; the rhetoric of revolutionary violence sounded like a good idea for reclaiming their beloved Germany and destroying autocracy for good. But the exiles' attack was not directed so much at Bismarck but at the quiescent socialist leadership, the parliamentarians, senior journalists, and officials who seemed unwilling to resist the new order while rank-and-filers risked their livelihood.

Hundreds of radicalized German socialists, now adopting the epithet "social revolutionary," journeyed to New York to begin a new life among their countryfolk, some of them kindred spirits. At the end of the 1870s, German American socialists—mostly long-term residents—were involved in a secession war of their own. The uprising of American workers in 1877 and its murderous suppression took socialists off-guard. They began to question the sincerity of American democracy when working people exercising their right to free speech were repeatedly met with gunfire. Marxists and other left socialists shifted their attention to trade unions as vehicles for change. American socialist leaders, bent on building a strong party, ignored them and mounted a new election campaign. But the radicals saw no point in elections and instead advocated stronger unions, and some called for arming workers in self-defense. Eventually, the dissidents left the party and set up their own clubs. They found soulmates in the radicals who had recently fled Germany, and both resolved to build what would become the first revolutionary anarchist movement in the United States.

How revolutionary the movement ought to be was still unclear, especially in a country celebrated for its civil liberties. Older residents among the anarchists naturally possessed a better understanding of the American system than newcomers and began to caution zealous neophytes against underground tactics in a relatively open society. It appears that political conditions in America tempered the allure of revolutionary terrorism, even though New York exiles of the early 1880s did not mince words in their press or on the pulpit. Most newcomers were utterly ignorant of American ways and conditions, and some clashed with the opinions of fellow comrades, leading to factional strife between older and newer German radicals. It seemed that longtime resident Germans had made their peace with having to leave their homeland, whereas recent exiles held a grudge and harbored feelings of revenge. (This duality of residents and exiles within the movement will be explored in chapter 2.) What brought all of them together was a profound aversion to hierarchical and electoral party politics. Bismarck's coup in Germany and political corruption in America had proven them right; political action within the system could (and should) never succeed. The willingness of orthodox socialists to compromise their platform or to accommodate an autocrat like Bismarck was particularly loathsome. Fortunately or unfortunately, antagonism between socialists and anarchists runs like a thread throughout our story. To a large extent, it became part of the anarchist identity.

In the United States, the anarchist label was not commonly used by revolutionary socialists until after the split with the state socialists around 1880. Before that, German dissident socialists called themselves social revolutionaries (Sozial-Revolutionären) to distinguish themselves from the reform-minded social-democrats (Sozial-Demokraten). Because "anarchist" had long been a term of derision, revolutionaries were at first apprehensive to adopt the label. During the 1880s, however, the term became more in vogue and even attained some status of *cool,* to use a modern term. Just as male homosexuals of the same period initially resented appellations such as *queer* and *fairy* but later made them their own, anarchists eventually embraced a culturally negative term.[16] They soon began hyphenating to further differentiate among themselves: individualist-anarchist, communist-anarchist, anarchist-syndicalist. This was not a frivolous exercise, however; it reflected different strands of anarchist thought.

In the mid-1880s and 1890s, communist-anarchism began to replace Bakunin's collectivist anarchism as the dominant philosophy in Europe and America. Communist-anarchists like Peter Kropotkin, Errico Malatesta, and Elisée Reclus criticized Bakunin for being too abstract and incoherent, formulating only vague notions of anti-authoritarian revolt. Bakunin's insistence that free workers be awarded according to their labor was seen as too cumbersome, requiring a central decision-making body. A communist-anarchist society, in contrast, would distribute the fruits of labor to all people according to need, a principle deemed more radical and just by its adherents than Bakunin's individualism. Kropotkin sought to eliminate all seeds of inequality and authority and invoked the principle of mutual aid. He underpinned his system with a scientific method and a social ethics steeped in optimism about human nature that was emblematic of his time. But many collectivist anarchists, young Johann Most among them, thought communist-anarchism too utopian, for it would inevitably create an army of idlers and parasites, since no clear incentive to work existed.

Nevertheless, communist-anarchism steadily gained influence among German-speaking anarchists, but certainly not all of them. The philosophical allegiance of a German revolutionary was to some extent forged by his or her geographic location. The vast majority of German Social-Democrats who became revolutionaries in the wake of Bismarck's policies adopted a hodgepodge of ideas pertaining to Bakuninist direct action. Others were directly influenced by communist-anarchism. This group tended to operate outside the Reich's borders in radical centers such as Geneva and Paris. They considered the collectivism of Bakunin an outmoded theory. German and Austrian communist-anarchists came to be known as "autonomists" and advocated a thoroughgoing decentralism not only for the future but also for how the movement operated in the present. In chapter 4, I will show how these ideological differences overlapped with personal rivalries, resulting in the fragmentation and insularity of the movement.

Anarchism meant different things to different people. The history of anarchism formed an important context, but the ways that individuals derived meaning from it was rarely a matter of doctrine. What this story reveals, among other things, is that anarchism is meaningless without human agency. Anarchist convictions, while based on commonly held principles, were colored by individual experience, age, and character. A newly arrived bachelor who had been forced into exile might have harbored a more vengeful attitude toward authority than a married saloon keeper who had lived in New York for years. Family responsibilities and job security could make a man—most activists were male—think twice before delivering a lecture on the arming of workers, especially during periods of heightened surveillance. It was not uncommon for younger comrades (some second-generation) around the turn of the century to resent the paternalism of the old guard. They joined rival groups and began to place more emphasis on intellectual and educational advancement in the movement, and many were more sensitive to gender equality than their fathers or mentors had been. Internal frictions, while testifying to ideological diversity within the movement, also reveal a dark side when high-minded people engage in visionary politics. Personal, ideological, and even ethnic divisions ruptured the German anarchist movement in America, a rift at times so passionately cultivated as to occasionally paralyze the movement, which lasted for thirty-four years, with its heyday in the mid-1880s.

It would appear that German anarchists in urban America came and went without leaving us much to remember them. Their marginal and criminalized status as an ideological minority in an overall pragmatic and acquisitive nation is partly to blame for a long period of inattention on the part of scholars. As it turns out, volumes of German American anarchist periodicals have been preserved, gathering dust in a handful of archives in Europe and the United States. This press not only features juicy editorials and news but also announcements and reviews of cultural and recreational events. These pages provide a window into the geography we have tried to reconstruct. It is often forgotten that this body of writing—fifteen periodicals in New York alone—also constitutes an American literature. Non-English speakers comprised a majority of the anarchist movement's membership, and they produced most of its written record. The fact that anarchists left us without stunning political victories, maverick third parties, or bold, innovative legislation can hardly be held against them. They simply did not set out to attempt those things. As this study shows, their influence and legacy is more elusive and subtle. The pioneer role of the Germans certainly influenced Russian Jewish anarchists, who relied heavily on the infrastructure laid out by their German precursors. German anarchists created a political bohemia in New York long before the days of Greenwich Village, a bohemia that was working-class, radical, and meaningful.

While it cannot be argued that German anarchists were directly responsible for New York's counterculture in the twentieth century, it nevertheless serves the historical record to know that they existed and that they had places all their own. Such a radical, independent milieu, untarnished by commercialism, is exactly what is attractive to young people today.

1 A Radical Geography: The "Social Space for a Dissident Subculture"

In the summer of 1892, the journalist John Gilmer Speed headed to the crowded streets of the Lower East Side in an attempt to meet some of the anarchists he had heard so much about. He reports that he obtained "the addresses of various places where anarchists publicly consort" from a socialist working in a downtown print shop. "In these first visits," Speed notes, "my first impression was confirmed, that I could learn nothing of the men and women belonging to the groups, and get only brief speech of them, by simply asking them to talk with me."[1] His frustration is not surprising. Unbeknownst to him, Speed did not only enter a common working-class barroom but an anarchist space in which he as a member of the mainstream press was seen as an intruder. To the anarchists, the space they occupied was as important as the theories they might have shared with Speed. Investigative journalists like Speed had become fashionable in the highly competitive world of the mainstream daily newspapers. Speed treated anarchists not as criminals but as lunatics. Like others, he was looking for a vicarious venture into the underworld of the great city, an "exploration of forbidden and menacing spaces," as Alan Trachtenberg phrased it.[2]

A social and cultural history of German anarchists in the greater New York area must take into account the geography of the movement, its physical connection to the urban landscape. This movement was not merely an intellectual phenomenon, or some elusive threat—the ghost of anarchy—in the minds of respectable citizens. It consisted of men, women, and children of exiled and immigrated families, of impetuous activists who were part of the citizenry of New York, as men like Speed realized. Locating individual German anarchists in New York is difficult, but locating their meeting places is not. Following Speed's example, we must first identify the various neighborhoods of anarchist activity in New York and New Jersey. In a second section, attention is directed to the nature and meaning of anarchist meeting places such as saloons and lecture halls.

Streets and Neighborhoods

The German anarchists anchored their movement in the seabed of urban America. Densely populated working-class neighborhoods in Manhattan, Brooklyn, and northern New Jersey industrial towns became the theater of action. These neighborhoods were long established and relatively isolated from the dominant culture. They were dotted with countless beerhalls (Bierhalle), bakeries, groceries, and labor halls. Along with other residents, anarchists hurried along busy streets to the workshop, factory, or corner saloon; they wandered the East Side avenues posting flyers for upcoming demonstrations; they whisked past pushcarts on their way to a large demonstration in Union Square, looking askance at mounted police headed in the same direction. These activists also gathered around the entrance of Thalia Theater on the Bowery to view a performance or perhaps to decorate the auditorium for a commemoration later that evening. They flocked to the doorways of Cooper Institute to get a glimpse of Johann Most, the popular anarchist speaker.

New York's metropolitan area was geographically unique compared to other radical centers. The main centers of activity, Manhattan, Hudson County, Newark, Paterson, Brooklyn, and Queens, were all separated by rivers and marshes, requiring ferries and public transportation (and thus money) to effectively sustain a network. Like thousands of other New Yorkers, immigrant anarchists took the elevated train up- or downtown and purchased ferry tickets to cross the Hudson or East Rivers. There was another peculiarity about New York: it had outgrown the rest of the region, even the country. New York was a world on its own, nearly as European as American in character. Lucy Robins Lang, who mingled with New York anarchists, once wrote that "many radicals were saying that in New York they were shut off from American life."[3] This perception that New York resembled an island calls to mind Michel de Certeau's image of New York being "cut out in between two oceans (the Atlantic and the American) by a frigid body of water."[4]

German anarchists did not settle randomly in the great metropolis. Almost without exception, these radicals were part of the larger German ethnic community, and it was ethnicity, not ideology, that determined where they lived and convened. There was no circumscribed anarchist neighborhood but rather clusters of anarchist meeting places within the larger German community. By 1880, German Americans lived in long-established, close-knit communities nourished by an unending flow of newcomers. From 1881 to 1910, some 2.3 million Germans came to the United States, or 13 percent of all foreign arrivals during that period. For the period from 1881 to 1900, Germans accounted for 22 percent of the total amount of immigrants, of which two million were German. Each year they made up around one-fourth of the total number of immigrants, sometimes even exceeding one-third.[5] In 1890, four out of five New Yorkers was either born abroad or of foreign parentage.[6]

Apart from immigrants from the German Reich, Austrians and German-speaking Swiss also made their way to America. Until the end of World War I, Austria was a double monarchy. The Austrian-Hungarian Empire was a vast polyglot Central European realm including modern-day Hungary, the Czech and Slovak Republics, Slovenia, Croatia, Bosnia, parts of Romania, and Galicia. German speakers within the monarchy lived in what is now Austria proper, Silesia (now in southern Poland), Bohemia, and Moravia (in the present-day Czech Republic). Most revolutionaries among these immigrants settled in New York after having been active within the labor movement in Vienna and the industrial towns of Bohemia and Silesia.

The thousands of German, Austrian, and Swiss immigrants who stayed in New York upon arrival found a home in crowded tenements

Table 1. German immigration to the United States, 1841–1920.

Decade	Number	% of total immigrants
1841–1850	434,626	25.4
1851–1860	951,667	36.6
1861–1870	787,468	34.0
1871–1880	718,182	25.5
1881–1890	1,452,970	27.7
1891–1900	505,152	13.7
1901–1910	341,498	3.9
1911–1920	143,945	2.5

Source: Dinnerstein and Reimers, *Ethnic Americans,* 206–8.

Table 2. Immigrants from Austria-Hungary and Switzerland to the U.S., and % of total, 1861–1910.

Decade	Austria-Hungary	%	Switzerland	%
1861–1870	7,800	0.3	23,286	1.0
1871–1880	72,969	2.6	28,293	1.0
1881–1890	353,719	6.7	81,988	1.6
1891–1900	592,707	16.0	31,179	0.8
1901–1910	2,145,266	24.0	34,922	0.4

Source: Dinnerstein and Reimers, *Ethnic Americans*, 206–8.

or boardinghouses. Some settled in surrounding towns such as Brooklyn or Newark, where housing was better. Such outlying towns were rapidly industrializing and becoming integrated into the marketplace of greater New York. Each neighborhood and town had a distinct character determined by its location, ethnic makeup, and industrial development. Regional differences among Germans in New York also colored the character of specific neighborhoods. In 1870, Bavarians and Prussians made up the majority of Germans entering New York (among those for whom such information is available).[7] A majority of New York Germans during the last quarter of the nineteenth century were working-class and religious—either Catholic, Protestant, or Jewish. The majority were also skilled artisans or merchants, with a few middle-class entrepreneurs as well. German men dominated nearly every trade, from cabinet making, brewing, and cigar making to tailoring and shoe making. Many German anarchists were among those tradesmen.

Only a small portion of the German immigrant community was socialist (in the broadest sense of the term). Socialists included those adhering to a popular Marxism, followers of Ferdinand Lassalle, and since 1880, a sizeable group carried the banner of social revolution and adopted the anarchist label. These radical Germans—socialists and anarchists—managed to become a vocal minority within the larger ethnic group. They scoffed at bourgeois and religious compatriots as much as they criticized America's political and economic elite. Radicals were particularly active in journalism, a fact not lost on leaders of mainstream German New York. One Catholic German editor noted that "among the German Catholics prevailed a sad feeling on account of the want of an organ to defend their cause and interests, especially because so many German radical papers attack and insult us daily."[8]

MANHATTAN

Manhattan was the focal point for anarchist activities in the greater New York area. It was home to the largest number of German anarchists, mainly concentrated in the Lower and Upper East Sides. In 1880, about 40 percent of New York's population (then consisting of Manhattan and the Bronx) was born abroad; a decade later, the foreign-born made up 42 percent. In 1880 and 1890, immigrants born in Germany comprised one-third of all foreign-born in the city and about 14 percent of the total city population. In other words, about one in seven New Yorkers in 1890 was born in Germany, and about the same ratio was born in the United States with one or both parents born in Germany.[9] Much changed after 1900. The share of Germans in overall immigration to the United States declined from about 14 percent in the 1890s to 4 percent in the following decade, when still over 340,000 Germans entered the country. At the same time, the visibility of the German-born population diminished as other ethnic groups—mostly southern and eastern Europeans—poured into the already overcrowded port city (consolidated into five boroughs in 1898). The 1900 census revealed that one out of ten New Yorkers was born in Germany. Ten years later, visibility shrunk to one in seventeen.[10]

Manhattan's Lower East Side was the heart of German New York. Since the 1850s, a distinct German neighborhood had emerged there, covering the Tenth, Eleventh, Thirteenth, and Seventeenth Wards. Germans referred to it as Kleindeutschland, or Little Germany. Bounded by Fourteenth Street on the north, Third Avenue and the Bowery on the west, Division Street on the south, and the East River on the east, it was one of the first distinct ethnic quarters in urban America. To pre–Civil War Americans, a foreign presence of such proportions was quite new. For the first time, native-born New Yorkers riding along First Avenue below Fourteenth Street found little opportunity to speak English. Hundreds of shops, beerhalls, groceries, and bakeries posted signs in German, while residents conversed in German dialects. "Life in Kleindeutschland is almost the same as in the Old Country," observed one resident, "there is not a single business which is not run by Germans."[11] Luc Sante, in his book on New York's subterranean culture, wrote that in the Lower East Side in the nineteenth century, "more people spoke the Saxon tongue than the Anglo-Saxon."[12]

Second Avenue, south of Fourteenth Street, was the main artery of the German and Austrian neighborhoods; the Austrian enclave on Second Avenue's lower stretch was known as Klein Wien, or Little Vienna. The southern part of the Lower East Side, beneath East Houston Street, contained several anarchist meeting places, although this soon became the nucleus of New York's Jewish quarter. The Bowery was the city's principal avenue for cheap entertainment and working-class nightlife, with a record twenty-nine saloons along seven city blocks. As the western boundary of German New York, it counted numerous German taprooms and beer gardens from which oompah music spilled out onto the busy thoroughfare.[13] The Bowery, with its popular elevated railway, was the plebeian counterpart to Broadway, connecting the Lower East Side to New York's up- and downtown districts. By 1875, German Americans constituted 64 percent of the total population of these four wards, an area of some four hundred city blocks.

But Little Germany was far from homogenous. Localism and regional loyalties played a significant role within the German community. After all, "Germany" only became a unified country in 1870, and even after this highly celebrated event, Germans clung to their local dialect, regional customs, religion, and music. Even so, they did share a common language, a love for beer and music, and a sense of ethnic pride.

By 1870, German socialism and later anarchism was deeply rooted in Kleindeutschland. Trade unions, workers' associations, mutual-aid societies, and a panoply of cultural and educational groups held meetings in the beerhalls and labor halls of the Lower East Side. Starting in the early 1880s, German anarchists formed their own organizations. Identifying key anarchist saloons has revealed distinct patterns of settlement throughout the New York City area. Clusters of such beerhalls, owned or frequented by anarchists or anarchist groups, were found on First, Fourth, Fifth, and Sixth Streets as well as Avenues A and B and First and Second Avenues. This was the center of German anarchist activity during the 1880s, located in the historic heart of Kleindeutschland.

Starting in the 1890s, German anarchists, like their non-anarchist compatriots, moved uptown. This move continued into the next century and reflected the general trend among Germans to settle in the outer enclaves of greater New York. Anarchist groups frequented a handful of meeting places along and near Second Avenue between the Lower East Side and Yorkville, such as Fritz Bachmann's Teutonia Hall on 404 First Avenue and Philipp Roos's beerhall on 508 Second Avenue.

Yorkville became the main residence for second-generation Germans in Manhattan. This Upper East Side immigrant neighborhood was bounded by Seventy-sixth and One-hundredth streets between Central Park and the East River. In the 1850s, Yorkville was already predominantly German. The Germans who moved there at the end of the century took advantage of cheap wooden housing and the convenience (and expense) of commuting downtown by horse car. Beginning in December 1878, the Third Avenue elevated railway operated between South Ferry and 129th Street.[14] Many Yorkville Germans, including anarchists, worked in nearby cigar factories or took the Ninety-second Street ferry to Long Island City to start the workday at Steinway's piano factory.[15] Housing conditions in Yorkville were far better than the tenements of the Lower East Side, although downtowners frequently used the area's vacant lots for disposing of garbage and manure, and riverside factories were an eyesore for Yorkville's residents. Cuban immigrants—mostly radical cigar workers who took rooms in local boardinghouses—arrived during the 1890s. By the early twentieth century, Hungarians, Czechs, Italians, and Jews had settled throughout Yorkville, although Eighty-sixth Street remained the center of a decidedly German community.

Anarchist meeting places in Yorkville were concentrated between Seventy-first and Eighty-third Streets. Several saloon keepers, many active in the movement, provided anarchists with places to hold meetings. George Moser, for example, owned Yorkville's Concordia Hall, which had opened its space to German anarchists since the 1880s. Names such as Germania or Concordia were common among German radicals and were not uniquely American. Socialist singing societies in Germany carried names like Concordia, alluding to the ideal of harmony.[16] Other than the drinking venues, German anarchists—sometimes in cooperation with other ethnic groups—launched libraries and reading rooms, an illustration of a more intellectual anarchist movement developing around 1900. Hans Koch, a well-known German anarchist publisher, had his residence in Yorkville in 1907.

A small circle of German anarchists made their home in East Harlem, a neighborhood further north on Manhattan's East Side. This remote corner became a destination for Italian immigrants who found Lower Manhattan overcrowded. By the 1890s, these Italians had moved up to Harlem, sharing the northern Manhattan lots with Irish and German newcomers. In 1890, German anarchists founded Group Harlem of the International Working People's Association (IWPA), with regular meetings at a local saloon on First Avenue.[17] German anarchists remained active in this part of Manhattan up to 1905.

A few anarchists lived in Manhattan's busy downtown area, buried in the bustle of the financial and commercial heart of the city. Group Downtown's clubhouse was located there on William Street. The editorial offices of *Freiheit,* the movement's most important paper, and the residence of its editor, Johann Most, were also located on William Street.

Hell's Kitchen on Manhattan's West Side was traditionally an Irish slum west of Eighth Avenue, comprising an area from Twenty-ninth Street up to Fifty-ninth Street. Religious, ethnic, and racial violence plagued the area during the last decades of the nineteenth century. Like the East Side, residences were planted amidst factories, railroad depots, and foul-smelling slaughterhouses. Apart from the Irish majority, many German working-class families lived there, including a number of socialists (the reformer Henry George found many supporters in this area). In August 1889, a handful of German anarchists organized the Westside Group (Gruppe der Westseite), with Charles Ehrhardt's beerhall on 405 West Thirty-fifth Street as its clubhouse. Several other meeting places were located on or near West Forty-first Street. Carl Wölky, one of the most active anarchist speakers and a close associate of Most, established his own saloon and boardinghouse in the area.[18]

BROOKLYN

Brooklyn was an independent city until 1898, when it was incorporated as one of the five boroughs of New York City. Like its rival across the East River, post–Civil War Brooklyn boomed. The number of factories skyrocketed from five hundred in 1865 to over five thousand in 1880, transforming Brooklyn into a modern industrial city.[19] Initially, most of the built-up area lined the waterfront, but soon new residential areas further east were brought into the city, forever altering western Long Island's once rural landscape. Greenpoint, Williamsburg, Bushwick, and Brooklyn Heights became distinct neighborhoods within the city of Brooklyn, which in 1870 ranked as America's third largest city after New York and Philadelphia.

Like other booming industrial centers, Brooklyn's municipal services failed to keep up with the pace of urban development. Housing was somewhat cheaper and tenements less crowded than in Manhattan, but streets and sanitation were below standard. "Brooklyn has many things to be ashamed of," reported one newspaper in 1885, "but the shame of her streets eclipses all."[20] Poor transportation was often viewed as the cause of Brooklyn's problems. Beginning in 1890, slow-moving horse cars were being replaced by swift (and often deadly) electric trolleys. Brooklyn's connection with Manhattan—entirely dependent on ferries—also became troublesome when the influx of goods from farms and breweries into Manhattan overwhelmed the infrastructure, making the trade too costly and cumbersome. During the 1860s, the first stones were laid in an ambitious project to span both cities with an enormous suspension bridge. Two decades later, on 24 May 1883, the gigantic Brooklyn Bridge ceremoniously opened to traffic.

As a major manufacturing center, Brooklyn housed and employed thousands of foreign-born laborers and craftspeople. By the end of the Civil War, 36 percent of the population was born abroad; most were Irish, with Germans following close behind.[21] In 1870, Brooklyn counted 36,769 Germans out of a total population of 376,099—nearly 10 percent (16 percent in New York).[22] By 1890, Germans exceeded the Irish with a nearly 12 percent.[23] Around this time, many second-generation Germans moved out of Little Germany into outlying neighborhoods such as Brooklyn's Williamsburg (Sixteenth Ward) and Bushwick (Eighteenth Ward) districts, both of which contained over 35 percent of the city's total German population.[24] Working and housing conditions were substantially better here than on the Lower East Side. In 1880, according to the census, 60 percent of German Americans in the Fifteenth and Sixteenth Wards were skilled workers or employed in retail. About one-third of families in those wards were born in Bavaria.[25] An 1885 housing report published in the *Brooklyn Daily Eagle* described the Sixteenth Ward as

> essentially a tenement house ward, but the houses are of a peculiar kind. They are neat frame buildings, painted white and with the conventional green shutters. These houses are almost invariably three stories in height and contain at the most six families, except in extraordinary cases. Usually the owner is a German of moderate means, who lives in the house himself, occupying part or whole of the first floor and looking after his property himself. Usually also the tenants are of the same nationality as the landlord. As a rule, they are cleanly and are respectable working people, who take pride in having bright, cheerful homes. The houses are much crowded in this ward, however, front and rear houses being found upon the same lot more frequently than in any other part of the city.[26]

Not surprisingly, most anarchist meeting places were located in the Williamsburg and Bushwick Districts. Like in Manhattan, anarchists sought the convenience of living and convening among their countrypeople. Several of their venues were clustered around Broadway and Throop Avenue, between the intersections of Union and Myrtle Avenues. Henry Winter Jr.'s Teutonia Hall on the corner of Harrison and Bartlett, for example, was a major rendezvous for German Americans. It featured concert- and barrooms and by the 1890s boasted a telephone connection.[27] Members of Group Brooklyn, the first anarchist club there, met every second and fourth Saturday of the month starting in 1883. Another meeting place was Edward King's saloon on the corner of Throop and Walton, a few blocks from Teutonia Hall. King was a Scottish-born labor activist who became more active in the growing anarchist movement.[28]

Bushwick lay further east and was connected to the Brooklyn waterfront by Myrtle Avenue. Like Williamsburg, it was heavily German during the 1890s. A string of breweries in the area accentuated its ethnic flavor. Between 1850 and 1880, eleven such operations extended along fourteen city blocks, an area referred to as "brewer's row."[29] Speedy public transportation only became available in 1888, when an elevated railway line to Manhattan was opened. German anarchists convened in several beerhalls between Myrtle and Flushing Avenues, both main thoroughfares. Anarchist groups did not always stick to one meeting place. Group Bushwick, for instance, met at four different Brooklyn locations in the course of its eight-year history, including Brooklyn's Labor Lyceum on Willoughby Avenue. Furthermore, William Merten and Max Metzkow, two important local activists, resided in Bushwick.

Anarchists were no different than other Brooklynites in their taste for outdoor gatherings. Parts of the city were underdeveloped or consisted of large green areas. Liberty Park, situated along Cooper Avenue in Ridgewood, was by far the most popular recreation area in Brooklyn. This thirty-five-acre park, owned by German immigrants, was once advertised to readers of *Freiheit* as the "largest park in Greater New York for forest excursions, picnics, national festivals etc." Its spacious dance pavilion, bowling alleys, rowboats, and playground became the setting for numerous German anarchist festivals, picnics, and dancing events.[30] Other than renting from a private party to stage their own events, anarchists also used public parks to escape the rough and tumble of city life and evoke a sense of anarchist harmony amid the chaos of the modern machine age.

QUEENS

In 1870, Queens was still an underdeveloped rural area intersected by waterways and tidal marshes stretching north of Brooklyn to the waters of the East River and Long Island Sound. The area lacked an urban nucleus and was one of the last boroughs of New York City to fully urbanize. Not surprisingly, the principal towns—Astoria and Long Island City—were located near the East River waterfront and were linked to midtown Manhattan by ferries. The most ambitious development in Queens after the Civil War took the form of company towns developed by industrialists lured by cheap and abundant land for their facilities. German businesspeople were among the most prominent of these manufacturers. Their company towns were as much an illustration of Germans' anti-assimilationist attitude as of entrepreneurship. Indeed, Germans in urban America preferred to live among themselves and as a whole were not receptive to the dominant Anglo-Saxon culture. Anarchists were no different, although they had other reasons for brushing aside mainstream American society.

The town of Astoria, located in the northwestern section of Queens, was the site of the German piano maker William Steinway's factory town. In 1870, he converted large tracts of Astoria's woods and meadowlands into a modern production facility, including docks, a foundry, sawmills, and later a full-fledged town. Steinway City, as it was called, reached to the shores of Bowery Bay and grew into an immigrant community dominated by Germans, who comprised 81 percent of the population in 1880.[31]

Steinway was not only committed to the preservation of German culture, he was also sympathetic to the needs of his workers. He constructed houses, baths, and parks. He even supported labor unions but stopped short of recognizing strikes as an acceptable tactic. For many workers, his approach was overly paternalistic; socialists found him typically bourgeois and condescending. Predictably, Steinway did not hold these social idealists in high regard. In fact, his move to Astoria was partly motivated by increased activities by German socialists and anarchists in Manhattan. "'There were two reasons we sought outside the city,'" Steinway explained. "'In the first place we wished to escape the anarchists and socialists [Germans] who even at that time were continually breeding discontent among our workmen and inciting them to strike.'" Steinway further believed that "'if we could withdraw our workingmen from contact with these people, and with the other temptations of city life in the tenement districts, they would be more content.'"[32] But the workers would not be cowed into docility; they simply brought their amusements to Queens. In 1870, to give one example, the German Cabinetmakers Association opened Schützen Park, a ninety-one-acre estate with shooting galleries and dancing halls in nearby Long Island City.[33]

Anarchists began organizing their own circles in this sparsely populated region in the 1880s. In August 1883, a handful of local anarchists formed Group Astoria with W. Kubisch as secretary, and in January 1884 a new group was organized in Woodside, just south of Astoria.[34] Most of their meeting places were located along the main artery, Flushing Avenue (now Astoria Boulevard). German anarchist families and groups were particularly attracted to the unspoiled woodlands and the seaside scenery of northern Queens. Not only local radicals but vacationers from Manhattan frequented the area's parks, shooting ranges, beer gardens, dance pavilions, and picnic areas. Spots along Bowery Bay and the North Beach development were especially popular. Jäger-Hütte, a hunting lodge in Bowery Bay Heights near Flushing Avenue, for example, was owned by Wenzel Führer, a Moravian-born anarchist and former cabinet maker.

College Point, northeast of Astoria, was another company town dominated by German immigrants. The Enterprise Rubber Works, a factory founded by Conrad Poppenhusen, was the main employer in the area with one thousand workers in 1880. Nearly every family member worked in the rubber factory. Most of the workers had moved from tenements in Manhattan and Brooklyn, transforming College Point into "Little Heidelberg." Intermarriage between persons from different regions in Germany was nearly nonexistent, strengthening the homogenous character of this community.[35] In short, 74 percent of all College Point residents in 1880 were either German-born or New York–born of German parents.[36]

The socialists and anarchists among them sought to organize the workers, who were often expected to work long hours and urged to abstain from habitual beer drinking. Anarchists may also have found Poppenhusen's self-styled position as community patron presumptuous and offensive. Despite generous support for the community—he donated one hundred thousand dollars to the local community and established a kindergarten—anarchists looked at such actions with suspicion, believing that they only served to appease and control the workers. In 1883, several anarchists founded Group College Point. It is unknown how many members joined, but such groups were typically small.

Maspeth was another industrial town located just east of Newtown Creek on the border of Queens and Brooklyn. Early on, factories and especially oil refineries appeared on the banks of Newtown Creek, a small waterway that crawled out to the East River. Fertilizer works and lumber yards soon intruded upon Maspeth's townscape as well. Its population rose dramatically from 1,449 in 1875 to 4,300 in 1898, but remained relatively small compared to Long Island City's thirty thousand inhabitants in 1890.[37] Group Maspeth started in 1890 and in time grew to thirty members—the largest German anarchist group in Queens. Most meeting places were located on or near Grand Street, a thoroughfare connecting Williamsburg with Flushing (anarchist meeting places could be found on main avenues as well as in side streets). Sometimes saloon keepers left the tenement district in Lower Manhattan for more spacious accommodations in Queens. Charles Judis, for example, had lived on First Avenue until 1891, when he moved to Maspeth to open his International Hall.

Long Island City was formed in 1869, when industrial Hunter's Point incorporated itself under a new name. The more affluent communities of Ravenswood and Astoria came under Long Island City's jurisdiction when a new county seat was installed. Population increased from a little over seventeen thousand in 1880 to over thirty thousand a decade later.[38] Despite the ambition to create an urban center, Long Island City remained a decentralized community with various settlements separated by wetlands. This did not prevent industrial development; like Williamsburg, Long Island City became an East Coast oil-refinery center. Bakeries and breweries were especially prominent among small businesses, employing a large number of Germans. In fact, it was from within the socialist Bakers' Union Local 84 that the first German anarchists emerged. During a meeting in October 1891, radical members disagreed with the call for participation in elections to better their miserable working conditions. The disagreement was a reflection of deep-seated rivalries between socialists and anarchists. The latter had no use for electoral politics and voted to leave the local and join the anarchist International. Eventually, fourteen dissidents formed Group Long Island City and established a meeting place at a Flushing Avenue saloon.[39]

THE BRONX

The Bronx, situated north of Manhattan across the Harlem River, attracted many first- and second-generation immigrants in their search for less-crowded living arrangements. Beginning in the 1850s, several breweries operated in the Bronx, supported by New Yorkers' growing appetite for German lager beer. These breweries took advantage of cheap land and in the process attracted workers from the more populated areas. The heart of the Bronx consisted of three villages—Kingsbridge, Morrisania, and West Farms—that in 1874 were annexed to New York City. The population of the three villages combined grew to more than thirty-six thousand in 1875.[40]

With a population of just over nine thousand in 1860, Morrisania and its surroundings remained rather rural, an "'almost purely country district, with hill and dale, upland and meadow,'" as the Census Office described it in 1880.[41] Not until 1886 did fast and efficient public transportation link Morrisania with Manhattan. In that year, an elevated service crossed the Harlem River and from 1891 was able to bring passengers from the Lower East Side to Morrisania riding along the Bronx's Third Avenue.

Morrisania became the scene of modest anarchist activity. Before radical groups were formed in the Bronx, German anarchists from Manhattan occasionally held picnics in the area's parks and forests, such as High Ground Park on 151st Street.[42] It did not take long before a Manhattan comrade founded a separate group after a lecture. In March 1890, Group Morrisania was formed at an organizing meeting at August Albinger's saloon-hotel at 3465 Third Avenue between 167th and 168th Streets, which would remain a regular assembly room for at least six years.[43]

STATEN ISLAND

Staten Island was the least populated of all the New York boroughs. Its early nineteenth-century economy was largely agricultural and maritime, although inevitably major manufacturing industries were also drawn to Staten Island for its vast tracts of undeveloped land. Population remained low, however. Some thirty-nine thousand people lived there in 1880; a decade later this number rose to a little under fifty-two thousand.[44] Communities of German workers lived on the island beginning in the 1850s, when the American Workers' League (Amerikanische Arbeiterbund) attempted to organize them into a political force. However, there is no evidence to suggest that any anarchist groups ever existed on the island. Still, like the Bronx and northern Queens, Staten Island was a popular destination for outdoor activities. German anarchists and their families boarded the Staten Island Ferry in Lower Manhattan to cross the Upper New York Bay, sailing past the Statue of Liberty on to the landing dock at New Brighton on the northern tip of the island. Here, too, German anarchists tended to rent from Germans. Anton Heil's Park in Fort Wadsworth was a popular resort, later taken over by Emil Manzel. The breweries on the island also provided recreation space for costumers and picnickers.

NEWARK

Newark was the largest city in northern New Jersey and a major industrial center increasingly drawn into New York City's regional network. The city was bounded by marshlands to the south, the Passaic River to the northeast, and small villages to the west. The Paterson-Newark Railroad connected Newark with Paterson, while the New Jersey Railroad brought passengers south to Elizabeth. One could take the same railroad across the Hackensack River to Jersey City and catch a ferry to Manhattan. The period from 1870 to 1890 was a time of rapid development, with the emergence of telephones, department-store chains, and a decent system of street railways. In 1880, Newark's population stood at 136,500. Between 1880 and 1890, the population rose by a third, and then by another 35 percent the next decade.[45]

Newark was above all an immigrant city. In 1890, no less than 67 percent of its inhabitants were born abroad or of foreign parentage.[46] Germans accounted for 15 percent of the city's residents in 1870, and by 1890 one-third was German-born or of German parentage, according to one census researcher.[47] Nearly all of them clustered along Springfield Avenue west of High Street (now Martin Luther King Jr. Boulevard) and stretching east away from downtown. "'The German quarter on the hill is one of the interesting features of the city,'" wrote Martha Lamb in 1876, "'a section nearly two miles square is a snug, compact, well-paved city within a city." She also observed that "the Germans who dwell here are chiefly employed in the factories and nearly all own their own houses.'"[48]

A German anarchist community emerged here in the early 1880s. Like in Manhattan and Brooklyn, anarchist meeting places were located in the heart of old German Newark. All the beerhalls and other venues frequented by local anarchists were on Springfield Avenue or its side streets, including Frank Bühler's Germania Hall, among others. Edward Willms's beerhall on 39 Mercer Street was one of the best-known anarchist meeting venues and served as headquarters for Group Newark as well as the Newark Educational and Defense Society (Newark Lehr-und-Wehr Verein). Willms had led a life of political activism before he turned to saloon keeping. His trajectory is not uncommon among other exiles and political immigrants, many of whom also entered the saloon business. Willms was born in the Ruhr region, the son of a communist who was active during the 1830 uprising. Willms quickly rose to the fore of the regional labor movement, and Ferdinand Lassalle himself secured him a position of secretary of the ADAV.[49] It is not known when he arrived in America, but he settled in Newark to become one of the most respected comrades. He was also a poet and wrote articles for *Freiheit*, usually under the pen name of Mephisto or Rebell.[50]

ELIZABETH CITY

In 1880, Elizabeth City (now simply Elizabeth) was a working-class, immigrant harbor town of twenty-eight thousand inhabitants; by 1900, its population had risen to fifty-two thousand.[51] Situated five miles south of Newark, the town consisted of downtown Elizabeth and Elizabethport, the dockside community overlooking Newark Bay. Starting in the 1870s, Elizabeth attracted many manufacturers, oil refineries, and shipbuilders, who took advantage of rail connections with the vast hinterland of Pennsylvania and the Great Lakes region. Industrial development transformed the city into an immigrant town, and by 1890, two-thirds of its residents were born abroad or of foreign parents.[52] German anarchists met in saloons located on or near Elizabeth Avenue, a broad street connecting the Elizabethport waterfront with the downtown area. Group Elizabeth, active since 1884, convened at Mauthe's beerhall at 605 Elizabeth Avenue.

HUDSON COUNTY

Stretched along the Hudson River and upper New York Bay, Hudson County is directly across from Lower Manhattan.[53] In the late nineteenth century it was linked to Manhattan by several ferry lines. Geographically, the area is characterized by a steep hill or palisade running north to south about a mile from the riverside. Jersey City Heights, Union Hill, and West Hoboken, towns where anarchists resided, were located on this hill.

Jersey City grew quickly during the mid-nineteenth century to become a major transportation center with railroads linking Pennsylvania's anthracite coal region to the seaport of New York. This attracted factories and an army of mostly immigrant workers. In 1860, the county was already 42 percent immigrant.[54] Germans did not initially dominate; in 1870 they represented less than 9 percent of the population.[55] During the 1880s, however, large numbers of German and Irish newcomers streamed into the city, making it the most populated in Hudson County: in 1870 Jersey City's population stood at 82,546. This number increased by 46 percent in 1880, and another 27 percent the next decade, to stand at 163,000 in 1890. Another forty-three thousand people were added in the following decade.[56] In 1890, 73 percent of its inhabitants were either foreign-born or native-born of foreign parents.[57] A majority of the anarchist meeting places were located not in Jersey City but in Jersey City Heights, such as Kerner's beerhall, headquarters of the Hudson County anarchist groups located on Summit Avenue.

Hoboken, just north of Jersey City, also experienced rapid growth and saw most of its buildings erected in the second half of the nineteenth century. Like Jersey City, Hoboken benefited from its proximity to New York and functioned as a major shipping terminal for transatlantic liners. This industry drew an exceptionally large number of German workers, and in a short time German became the city's second language. Just over twenty thousand people lived in Hoboken in 1870. Twenty years later its population had doubled, and by 1900, Hoboken counted a little under sixty thousand inhabitants; four out of five were foreign-born or of foreign parentage.[58] One source claims that in 1890 Hoboken was the most German city in America, after Milwaukee, with two-thirds of its population Teutonic.[59] A number of anarchist meeting places were located near the docks around Grand and First Streets, including Wagner's beerhall on Adams Street, the headquarters of Group Hoboken.

West Hoboken and Union Hill were two smaller industrial townships north of Hoboken situated on the hill overlooking the Hudson River and midtown Manhattan. German anarchists referred to it as "on the hill" (*auf dem Berge*) or "on onion hill" (*auf dem Zwiebel-Berge*), perhaps a word play on Union Hill. Incidentally, Johann Most briefly took up residence in nearby Jersey City Heights in 1884, where he once mused wittily about his new surroundings to a friend: "Where I live one has a view of the entire region. . . . From this height one could blow everything to smithereens with the help of a few dozen cannon or dynamite catapults."[60]

West Hoboken and Union Hill were heavily immigrant; a whopping 83 percent of the former town's 1900 population was foreign.[61] Several anarchist saloons could be found on Summit Avenue. An anarchist mainstay during the 1890s was Krause's saloon on Bergenline Avenue in Union Hill. The New Casino, the largest assembly hall "on the hill," frequented by anarchist groups, was located further north on Shippen Street in Union Hill. A small number of German anarchists also resided in the townships of Weehawken and Guttenberg, where they formed a separate group.[62]

PATERSON

The city of Paterson is located on the Passaic River, thirteen miles west of Manhattan. The Great Falls of the river provided cheap power for a booming industrial development focused mainly on the textile industry. Nicknamed Silk City at the turn of the century, Paterson contains some of the nation's oldest textile mills. It is no exaggeration that Paterson was one of New Jersey's most important industrial towns in the last quarter of the nineteenth century. Its population jumped by more than 50 percent twice in less than a generation. With more than thirty-three thousand inhabitants in 1870, Paterson grew to over 105,000 thirty years later, becoming New Jersey's third largest city.[63]

The textile industry, especially silk manufacturing, made Paterson into an immigrant working-class town. Apart from Hoboken, Paterson had the lowest percentage of native-born residents of any city in New Jersey in 1890. From 1890 until 1910, three out of four Patersonians was born abroad or of foreign parentage.[64] Like in Jersey City, Germans were initially a relatively small group among foreigners: less than 5 percent of residents in Paterson's 1870 census were German.[65] This number would increase during the next two decades.

Paterson counted several German anarchist groups that were active from 1881 until at least 1900. Philipp Hanse's beerhall on 8 Fair Street, not far from Broadway, was possibly the best-known venue for local anarchists. It was the headquarters of Group Paterson, a circle that grew to eighty members by 1892. Several other venues were located along Main and Market Streets. Communist-anarchists—who had by then formed their own clubs as distinct from the Mostians—convened at Beek's saloon at 963 Madison Avenue in the southern end of town. The city's scenic waterfalls must have been the perfect backdrop for a late summer outing. Indeed, in September 1890, local anarchists invited comrades from New York for a family picnic to the Great Falls accompanied by New York's premier anarchist singing society.[66]

Additionally, a few German anarchists lived in New Rochelle, ten miles north of the Bronx, and in Bound Brook, a small town near the upper Raritan River in New Jersey, thirty miles southwest of Lower Manhattan.[67]

Meeting Places: Bierhalle and Lecture Halls

> The cafés gave the Lower East Side a head, a body, a mind—and a brilliance that is brutally missing today.
>
> —Harry Roskolenko, *The Time That Was Then*

A casual observer, then or now, would hardly have noticed that anarchists were voracious socializers. Germans in particular, it seems, had an insatiable appetite for scheduled meetings, discussions, and lectures accompanied by a plentiful supply of beer. Most of these gatherings were held at the group level and attended by ten to a few hundred comrades. The weekly meeting or discussion gathering formed the cornerstone of this militant oppositional movement. It was also a hallmark of social as opposed to individualist anarchism, which shunned collective action and stayed away from involvement in the labor movement.[68] Using the insights of the social theorists Henri Lefebvre and Edward Soja, we can see that the anarchist saloon was not simply a "box" of unchanging space in which anarchists convened; they transformed it to suit their needs. By stepping through the saloon door, the German anarchist entered the realm of political activism. He or she was no longer simply an employee, a parent, or a Prussian but also a member of a revolutionary movement. His or her local group constituted the basic unit of this urban movement.

Nearly two hundred German beerhalls associated with the movement have been identified in the greater New York City area in addition to the large lecture halls rented for cross-ethnic celebrations or protest meetings. What did an anarchist café look like? What can it tell us about immigrant anarchism in America? What meaning did this type of meeting place exert? In an attempt to answer these questions, we must follow the German anarchist inside the beerhall, meet the proprietor, observe the decorations and amenities, order a lager beer, and proceed into the back room to join a discussion or lecture.

Anarchists could draw on a long history of symbiosis between political radicalism and drinking establishments. Since early modern times in Europe and America, taverns have served not only as places to eat and drink but also as venues for information exchange and at times for political discussion, preparation, and action. In Germany, the tavern (Wirthaus) acquired an important role in the fledgling labor movement during the mid-nineteenth century: It served as an informal gathering place for organized workers and craftspeople. Many working families were constantly on the move within a town or city, making the local beerhall a place of much-needed stability. The significance of working-class taverns in Imperial Germany becomes even more apparent if one considers the authoritarianism of the regime. Any liberationist movement was seen as a threat and was forced to operate outside the limelight. Harassment of liberals and radicals in Germany increased after the failed revolution of 1848 and continued under Bismarck's strict governance. Members of the German labor movement therefore went to great lengths to create safe havens to congregate and openly discuss their political agenda.

Finding suitable and safe places to convene was often a precarious affair. This quest for secure meeting spaces—also referred to as *Lokalfrage*—had a long history for radical organizations. Socialists in Germany were relatively successful in finding sympathetic proprietors who allowed them to use rooms rent-free, provided members drank during discussions. Some beerhalls became wholly associated with the socialist movement and functioned as clubhouses of trade-union locals, singing societies, or mutual-aid organizations. They were sites outside the realm of officialdom where "organized workers could mix beer drinking and lighthearted banter with more serious talk about family, work, and the labor movement," as the historian Vernon Lidtke put it.[69] The socialist Karl Kautsky also alluded to spatial boundaries and the friction of identities within the geopolitical realm when he characterized saloons in Germany as "'the only bulwark for political freedom for the proletarians.'"[70]

German anarchists in New York shared many traits with the larger immigrant culture, even though political radicalism drove a wedge between anarchists and mainstream German Americans. Customs of drinking and recreational habits unified all Germans and even transcended class boundaries. Even more so than in the home country, cultivating such habits in America furnished "a cultural and political means of asserting self and identity."[71] Cultural differences were indeed reflected in alcohol consumption. In 1904, beer consumption per capita in Germany was more than twice that in the United States, while wine consumption was more than triple.[72] The association of alcohol with political radicalism, however, provided the respectable classes with a powerful stereotype of the socialist drunkard, an image shared by conservatives on both sides of the Atlantic.

Shunning outsider opinions, German immigrants regarded leisure and family activities as indispensable for a balanced life in a time when skilled labor was devalued in the service of mechanization. German working-class saloons and beer gardens in New York were an extension of domestic life. The entire family—men, women, and children—took part in social activities in saloons, beer gardens, and parks. There simply wasn't much to compel them to spend their free time at home. Housing conditions were so poor, especially due to the lack of fresh air and sunlight, that it hampered the pleasures of domestic and private life. Working life was no more inviting, with its long hours and harsh conditions. The saloon or beer garden became the prime forum for family and collegial socializing. German drinking establishments were well lit, serving familiar lager beer instead of ales or whiskey common in Irish American saloons, and many offered free lunches featuring Vienna sausage, sauerkraut, and potato salad supplemented by bread, soup, and beans. Bottom-fermented lager beer was not only less alcoholic but much easier to preserve. It was one of many contributions German immigrants made to drinking habits in America. They also refined brewing techniques and cooling and preservation methods that allowed beer to be stored in portable kegs that could be tapped.

The "poor man's club" functioned as community center, a "'clearinghouse for the common intelligence,'" as one contemporary termed it.[73] They were centers for information, friendship, and pleasure, as was true for all urban saloons. Madelyn Powers has argued that urban working-class saloons were not all havens of lewd behavior, nor were they simply retreats from reality for beaten workers.[74] They were an integral part of the urban social fabric and occupied an important place in the workers' daily struggle for bread and meaning.

American saloons were an all-male terrain. Women were allowed to enter only through the "ladies' entrance" located on the side of the building toward the rear. This way, women did not intrude upon male customers in the barroom but could still access the back room to attend family gatherings or find their partners. Men, women, and children frequently attended German beer gardens and numerous social events, although the anarchists did not necessarily value such extravaganzas, which they deemed bourgeois and parochial; they preferred their own workingmen's saloons. Indeed, the beerhalls frequented by anarchists saw few women enter, let alone participate. Let this observation be a first hint at how male-dominated this movement was.

The architecture of a working-class saloon was unremarkable, but certain features made it congenial to small-scale club life. The typical layout was long and narrow. Greif's beerhall, one of Chicago's best-known German radical hangouts, for example, was about sixty feet long. As one entered from the street into the barroom, a counter—usually without stools—was situated on the left or right side. Chairs and tables were scattered about with a stove in the middle. The hardwood floor was covered with sand or sawdust to help absorb spilled liquor. Nearly all saloons had a back room, a separate enclosed space used for meetings or celebrations. They were rent-free because the proprietor could rely on compensation through the group's formal commitment to consume a substantial amount of beer for the duration of the meeting.

But to see beerhalls as nothing more than places to buy a drink obscures their deeper meaning and function. Beerhalls mirrored the anarchist sensibility. Political parties and elections were anathema to the anarchist movement. In the absence of such forums, less formal activities in saloon back rooms, lecture halls, and at picnics assumed a more central role. Three key characteristics explain why urban anarchists conceived of their community the way they did: The array of anarchist beerhalls in New York served as a decentralized network in which the nodes of decision making were multiple. Anarchist saloons were inherently oppositional to orthodox socialist culture as well as to mainstream culture. And they advanced the tradition of the bohemian-artisan in a bid to reclaim the vanishing world of the independent craft tradition.

Decentralization is a cornerstone of an anarchist analysis of power and domination. Anarchism warns against the concentration of power and advances a philosophy of organization, summed up in what E. F. Schumacher has called "small is beautiful."[75] Small groups of producers and consumers were seen as more effective and possessing greater integrity than an impersonal central authority, which invariably invites corruption and abuse. Also, the individual is restored to his or her rightful place as an autonomous entity endowed with rational and imaginative powers. "Each man is a law to himself," as one Austrian anarchist explained, "and when he sees his duty he does it."[76] Anarchist organization therefore prides itself on being small, personal, and just—a triumph of quality over quantity. The historian Russell Jacoby has argued that meaningful alternative communities can exist in the smallest places. "The aerial view of society should not forget that in the lives of intellectuals—the lives of all individuals—it just takes several friends to make the difference; and these friends can meet in a coffeehouse in St. Louis or a bookstore in Seattle. Bohemia can be this small, this vital."[77] The beerhall, with its back room and other amenities, promoted this kind of vitality. To the anarchists, the saloons constituted a radical space, a chance to practice anarchism as much as to advocate it.

The anarchists' opposition to the dominant culture added a second essential layer of meaning to the beerhall. Mainstream society saw anarchists as a tiny but dangerous minority of foreign malcontents; this perception in turn made the anarchists more insular, defiant, and assertive. The radical saloon was thus seen as an island of anarchism itself. An element of safety and familiarity attracted anarchists to these places. Group meetings, discussions, and lectures unfolded in the privacy of the back room under the protection of the proprietor. The majority of meetings, which were not secret, proceeded without police harassment in a place of free expression where anarchism was lived, discussed, and praised in ways perhaps less advisable in more public venues.

The German anarchists' opposition to temperance and antisaloon movements heightened their sense of estrangement from mainstream America. Puritanical middle-class reformers targeted the production and consumption of alcohol as much as they maligned an entire immigrant working-class culture. Attempts to regulate the liquor business in New York date from colonial times. The 1840s and 1850s saw a renewed effort to ban alcohol altogether. After the Civil War, attention shifted to regulation and temperance rather than outright prohibition (which nevertheless occurred in the 1920s). The Sunday closing laws were possibly the most hated restrictions imposed on beer-drinking immigrants, especially Germans, Bohemians, and Scandinavians. Still, enforcement was weak and violations commonplace. German anarchists, along with others, defied such measures on a regular basis. Noncompliant saloon keepers were fined and saw their name and address in the local newspaper. One of those was Henry Winter, the owner of Teutonia Hall in Brooklyn, a popular venue for German anarchists, whose name appeared in the paper in 1877 and again in 1882.[78] Temperance activists also called on the police to force hall owners not to allow alcohol during meetings. For instance, in the runup to the 1887 Commune Festival, a major event on the anarchist calendar, John Stimmel, the proprietor of Germania Assembly Rooms, was warned by the New York police not to serve alcohol before midnight.[79] Moreover, anarchists and socialists were a special case in the eyes of moralists who viewed the combination of alcohol and revolution as a particularly odious threat to the country—a fear summarized in a 1902 religious exposé by Hugh Vaughan Crozier, *The Saloon and Anarchy, the Two Worst Things in the World, versus the United States of America.*

A third layer of meaning of beerhall culture was its artisan and bohemian character. Among working people, artisans had always been the first to appropriate notions of class-consciousness and trade solidarity precisely because they saw mechanization and methods of mass production as a direct threat to their livelihood. German artisans were receptive to philosophies advocating decentralism and the restoration of a society of small and independent producers. Radical saloons in New York restored a modicum of artisan solidarity and camaraderie amidst the frenzy of America's unabashed center of capitalism. Anarchist artisans prized the craft-work ethic, but they also valued leisure and sought to protect it within their overall productive lives. This was, of course, in direct opposition to the ethos of the new efficient economy trumpeted by middle-class reformers. The saloon offered an amenable setting for leisure and informal education. Jacoby reminds us that "thinking and dreaming require unregulated time."[80] Saloons were unregulated spaces, without a time clock, without the discipline of the shop floor, and without the pressure of the unequal power relationship between worker and owner. "Intellectuals perpetually lingering over coffee and drink," writes Jacoby, "threaten solid citizens by the effort—or the appearance—of escaping the bondage of money and drudgery."[81] Intellectual and artistic pursuit was without question an integral part of the life of a German anarchist, especially after 1900. Beerhalls and later reading rooms combined activism and recreation. Anarchist venues also attracted native-born outcasts who ventured south of Fourteenth Street to explore early signs of what would become Lower Manhattan's famous bohemian district.

If beerhalls associated with the German anarchist movement had much in common with other urban saloons on the outside, there were differences inside. Interiors were usually decorated with symbols and representations from the labor movement and radical tradition. These inscriptions of meaning and memory onto the ordinary space of a saloon distinguished it from other taprooms. The walls at Greif's saloon were covered "with pictures of Lassalle, Marx, Bebel, and Liebknecht" and "a bust of Louis Lingg . . . on a pedestal" (Lingg was the Haymarket defendant who committed suicide in his jail cell). Not only were saloons altered physically or decoratively but occupants also frequently expanded their initial function—that of drinking establishments—to include uses that further conceptualized their space as alternative and oppositional. Anarchist groups and radical unions chose saloons as a storage room for their paraphernalia and even bookkeeping. Various unions kept "'minutes, flags, and other insignias'" in large cupboards.[82]

Decorating and arranging German beerhalls into anarchist spaces transformed these meeting places into club headquarters, clearinghouses, and repositories of anarchist history and memory. Our intrepid reporter John Speed once visited Zum groben Michel (Tough Mike's), a meeting place of autonomist anarchists located on East Fifth Street. His eyewitness account is worth quoting in full. Consistent with other saloons, he describes the place as "a narrow, dark, and dingy bar-room," with the name printed in white letters on the window. But the sights and sounds—indeed, the entire atmosphere—transcended the ordinariness of most workingmen's saloons.

> This is the basement under a tenement house, and there are two rooms. The bar is on one side of the front room. In front of it is a large table at which men were drinking beer and on which was a zither and a man thumping out the "Marseillaise." . . . Beyond the table was a reading desk, upon which were files of anarchistic papers, and above them portraits of the anarchists that have been executed for their crimes. . . . Just beyond the bar, the table, and the reading stand was a pool table stretching nearly across the room, and leaving scant space at either hand for the handling of a cue. Several men stood about this table with cues in their hands, but they ceased playing when I entered. . . . Beyond the pool table was a smaller room, and in the center of this was a table at which half a dozen men sat drinking beer out of those large glasses known on the Bowery, I believe, as schooners. And still beyond, at a smaller table, and next to a window that looked out into a small dark court yard, sat a young woman [Emma Goldman] who, had she not seemed so entirely at home, would have appeared out of place in such surroundings. She was reading a book, with a glass of beer by the side of it on the table.[83]

Speed's last observation of an alternative anarchist space is a case in point. He was perhaps especially surprised to see a single woman sipping beer in a working-class saloon, but Goldman did feel at home, and so did the pool players and musicians who had made it their stomping ground—an alternative space. Even ordinary apartments of radicals could be transformed. "Small and narrow, with its diminutive table and solitary chair," wrote Alexander Berkman of his shared Suffolk Street room, "the cage-like bedroom would be transfigured into the sanctified chamber of fate."[84]

An even more detailed glimpse into the anarchist haunts of New York was penned by Comyns Ray, who in 1887 decided to pay a visit to the editorial office of *Freiheit,* a popular paper edited by Johann Most.

The ground floor of 167 William Street was a lager-beer saloon, while the offices were located upstairs. Ray reported matter-of-factly that upon "[e]ntering the hallway you will notice, as soon as your eyes are able to penetrate the darkness, a large red banner on the wall bearing the inscription, 'Vive la Commune.'" Alluding to the notoriety of the editor, he resumed: "A cast-iron letter-box, marked 'John Most,' attracts one's attention for a moment, and then we ascend two flights of narrow, creaky stairs, and step into a large, dilapidated room, extending over the entire top floor of the building." Ray was not fascinated by the office's function as a production facility for an anarchist paper but rather the way its occupants chose to decorate it. "'The walls of the room are almost totally covered with pictures, portraits, newspaper headings, etc. In crazy-quilt fashion is arranged Lieske, Shakspere [*sic*], Hoedel, Rousseau, Karl Marx, Feurbach [*sic*], Stuart Mill, Thomas Paine, Richard Wagner, Marat, Hans Sachs, St. Simon, LaSalle, Proudhon, Anton Kammerer, Stallmacher [*sic*], the Irish patriots, Brady, Kelly, Curley, Tynan, Wilson, Gallagher, and Normann, a life-size portrait of Louise Michel, an excellent photograph of prince Krapotkine [*sic*], pictures from Puck, Punch, Fleigende Blatter [*sic*], sketches from George Eber's "Egypt"—a queer collection indeed.'"[85] Again, an ordinary place is transformed into a countercultural space adorned with its own heroes as a reaction to their presumed neglect in mainstream society. Figures who had been condemned as terrorists or criminals, such as Anton Kammerer and Hermann Stellmacher, were here restored as freedom fighters, perhaps to shock an outsider like Ray. Furthermore, as if to warn the uninitiated, this anarchist space announced its true identity to visitors in the hallway by celebrating the highly controversial Paris Commune on a banner.

Few contemporary descriptions of New York anarchist saloons exist. The ones that survive were all recorded by investigative non-anarchists, suggesting that anarchists had created an aura of mystery and secrecy in the eyes of outsiders. The police and reporters knew that radical saloons were a hotbed of political activism and a stage for incendiary speechmaking. Louis Rott, an undercover police detective (who was German), attended—and infiltrated—a meeting at Frederic Krämer's beerhall on the night of 12 November 1887—a day after the Haymarket anarchists were hanged. Krämer's had been the headquarters of a German anarchist rifle club and the anarchist machinists' union. Rott successfully mingled with the crowd, men shaken by the events in Chicago of which they tried to make sense. "We went into the beer saloon, which is in front of the hall, at about 7:30 o'clock. It was full of men, and all were drinking beer. I sat down at a table and ordered some beer, and got to talking with several of the men there. We talked about the hanging of the Anarchists in Chicago." Rott was well aware that the subversive activities about to unfold would not take place in the barroom but in the back room. "After a few minutes I went back into the hall in the rear. It is about 30 or 40 feet long and is the width of the building. It was crowded. I should say that there were about 100 men there. I stood up in the hall, a little to the left of the door, and about 20 feet away from the table [at] which the Chairman sat. After I had stood there for about five minutes [Johann] Most came in through the beer saloon and entered the hall. The crowd cheered him wildly."[86]

Saloon meeting rooms were sometimes located above the barroom, but most often they could be found in the rear, as in Krämer's place. These rooms were referred to as halls (Halle) and featured tables and chairs or rows of chairs with one table in front. The backroom meeting was an organized event, scheduled in advance, with a political as well as a social dimension. On the one hand, it was an opportunity to come together, to strengthen bonds of camaraderie accompanied by the disinhibiting effect of alcohol. On the other hand, an anarchist group meeting was a political endeavor. By endowing their meetings—widely seen by the public as conspiratorial—with regularity and their own methods of democratic process, anarchists legitimized their movement in the eyes of the participants and neophytes. Idealism was made practicable; it proved that they meant business. Meetings provided a secure forum, a social space in which the anarchists' agenda, frustrations, dreams, and plans could be spelled out in relative safety.

German anarchist groups engaged in two types of backroom meetings. One was the business meeting, in which internal group affairs were discussed; these gatherings were usually closed to outsiders. The second type was the open discussion forum featuring a speaker and open to anyone interested. Each anarchist group had its regular meeting place arranged through mutual agreement with the owner, who frequently belonged to the movement. This arrangement was maintained for years. August Schlag's saloon, for instance, became the official labor information bureau for all radical German furniture workers, offering patrons access to a nationwide directory of furniture manufacturers as well as to a catalog of all the trade journals.[87] Many other groups, however, were periodically forced to look for another space due to the owner's bankruptcy or police surveillance.

A typical backroom meeting started with the election of several functionaries for that particular session, such as a chairperson and recording secretary. Another functionary was the beer collector (Bierkollektor), a function more common with larger organizations that illustrates the centrality of beer to German social life. Since meetings were held behind closed doors, the beer collector arranged for the orderly and efficient consumption of beer during the meeting. Dues were collected from the members before the start of formalities and handed over to the proprietor. Small groups fulfilled their end of the bargain by having each member drop a dime or two for a common drink fund. This not only ensured payment for the use of the room but also affirmed the mutual trust between the group and the saloon keeper. The meeting could then proceed undisturbed while the owner—in the role of sergeant at arms—dutifully guarded the entrance to the back room while at the same time supplying the ordered beer.

Anarchist meetings were as much about education as political activism. "'[The saloon] is the principal place in which ideas underlying the labor movement originate, or at any rate become consciously held,'" the bohemian Hutchins Hapgood wrote.[88] Similarly, M. E. Ravage, a Romanian immigrant bartender in Manhattan, found a barroom "'as good a start toward a well-rounded education as you could desire.'"[89] Discussion evenings and lectures addressed topics ranging from German history and philosophy to atheism, marriage, and Darwinism. The writer James Gibbons Huneker, who praised the Lower East Side's multicultural atmosphere, recalled a visit to an anarchist meeting. "Well I remember the night, years ago, when finding ourselves in Tompkins Square we went across to Justus Schwab's and joined an anarchist meeting in full swing." Huneker immediately recognized the discrepancy between society's view of anarchists as criminals and what went on at this meeting. "There were no bombs, though there was plenty of beer. A more amiable and better-informed man than Schwab never trod carpet slippers. The discussions in German and English betrayed a culture not easily duplicated on the West Side—wherever that mysterious territory really is. Before Nietzsche's and Stirner's names were pronounced in our lecture-rooms they were familiarly quoted at Schwab's."[90]

Justus Schwab's saloon on 50 First Street (on the corner of First Avenue) was unlike any other immigrant saloon on the East Side. Since the mid-1870s, Schwab's place was known as a haven of international radicalism. Located in the basement of a five-story brick building, the saloon itself measured eight feet wide and thirty feet deep.[91] "The rear room of his little place on First Street was a Mecca for French Communards, Spanish and Italian refugees, Russian politicals, and German socialists and anarchists who had escaped the iron heel of Bismarck," remembered Emma Goldman.[92] Like other radical spaces, this one was ornamented to evoke a cultured and revolutionary tradition. One newspaper reporter noticed a bust of Shakespeare and several frames depicting scenes of the French Revolution.[93] This international and decidedly proletarian atmosphere made Schwab's one of the first urban left-wing bohemian spaces in New York, decades before the emergence of Greenwich Village. The American writers Ambrose Bierce, James Huneker, and Sadakichi Hartmann, as well as the labor leader John Swinton, were attracted to its cosmopolitan ambience. An intoxicating mixture of humor, art, and politics was daily fare for anyone entering this East Side beer cave (Bierhöhle, a pun on *Bierhalle*). Schwab once advertised his establishment as "Pechvogel's Hauptquartier," evoking the image of the loser, the antihero, the bohemian outcast ridiculed by mainstream society. To the poets he promised that his international beerhall was "home and workshop to all rhymesters who wish to thrash their Pegasus."[94] The facetious appropriation of negative images—the beer cave and outcast—directed at marginal subcultures by mainstream society has been a long-standing tactic and reminds one of similar practices in the gay liberation movement and 1970s punk culture.

Music was also a central aspect of the ambience of Schwab's saloon. Schwab himself was a member of the Internationale Arbeiter-Liedertafel (International Workers' Choral Society), New York's best-known anarchist singing society. He was also an occasional performer of comical pieces.[95] Huneker remembered that by request he "played The Marseillaise and The International Hymn on an old piano—smoke-stained, with rattling keys and a cracked tone—which stood at the rear upon a platform. All was peace and a flow of soul."[96] Schwab valued political debate and activism but also insisted on the necessity for humor and pleasure; his corner café was simply "the gathering-place for all joyful and freedom-loving spirits."[97]

In the spirit of a radical subculture, Schwab's saloon was more than a taproom or artists' den. It was a veritable infoshop, a term popularized by the contemporary anarchist movement denoting a radical community space combined with the functions of a library. Stacks of anarchist and socialist newspapers abounded, in addition to a small library of no less than six hundred volumes.[98] Emma Goldman made ample use of Schwab's generous lending policy to educate herself in Western liberal thought, poetry, and spiritualist authors. "Walt Whitman, Emerson, Thoreau, Hawthorne, Spencer, John Stuart Mill, and many other English and American authors I learned to know and love through the friendship of Justus," she wrote.[99] Libraries inside saloons and inns associated with the labor movement had been common in Germany, with book collections ranging from one cabinet to several bookcases.[100] German anarchist saloons in New York and other cities played a crucial role in the exchange of literature in the form of books, periodicals, and pamphlets as well as theater handbills and political flyers. The presence of such wide-ranging literature added an intellectual dimension to the saloon experience, creating an alternative and informal "space of freedom" (Raum der Freiheit), as Bruno Reinsdorf termed it.[101] On the outside, these saloons appeared ordinary, blending in with the surrounding street or neighborhood. But inside there was a palpable atmosphere of resistance to the dominant culture.

There was not a consensus on the role of beerhalls even within the German anarchist movement, however. Sometimes German anarchists criticized the movement's reliance on beerhalls, charging that their fellow comrades wasted too much time on recreational activities instead of on pure propaganda efforts: the mission to export anarchism to New York's working classes was hampered by excessive socializing. Bruno Reinsdorf, an anarchist close to Johann Most, thought saloon-based clubs and groups a liability. "Should we support comrades who are saloon keepers?" he wondered. He went on to question the integrity of proprietors who let anarchist groups meet in their establishment. "Let us not forget that most of them become 'comrades' only after they can have a group on the premises. If this group leaves the premises, so does the comradeship of the proprietor."[102] Some saw the cost of drinking as detrimental to the movement. Too much money was wasted on beer, Reinsdorf charged, even detecting a grain of truth in the arguments of antisaloon leaguers. Instead of a beerhall he proposed a different type of meeting place without beer or wine, but remained vague as to where such a space might be found. "Most of the time," he continued, "debates deteriorate into something personal instead of something human due to the influence of alcoholic drinks."[103]

Other militants criticized what they perceived as a petty club mentality, often referred to as Vereinsmeierei or Vereinsspielerei. Clubbing undermined activism, they charged, and was one of the causes of a dwindling revolutionary spirit among German anarchists. Additionally, it tended to promote rivalry and infighting. One radical group even went so far as to call an end to all recreational associations and instead proposed a strong federative network of agitation groups.[104]

Despite these misgivings, cultural, educational, and trade associations as well as picnics were as much a part of the anarchists' sense of self as were political propaganda circles. Differences in opinion among anarchists reveal a tension, perhaps inherent to a lively subculture, between a militant, doctrinaire zeal, on the one hand, and a more inclusive, playful activism, on the other hand. Proponents of the latter viewed picnics, theater, and other pastimes as the embodiment of an anarchist lifestyle here and now. Most anarchists seem to have valued both approaches.

German anarchists frequently held mass meetings in large lecture halls attended by hundreds, often thousands of people. The purpose was to reach a broader mass of sympathetic people and to address the entire movement. Halls were rented and used for special occasions such as protest meetings, celebrations, or commemorations with an audience consisting of many nationalities. The most popular halls for German anarchists were Cooper Union, Germania Assembly Rooms, Clarendon Hall, and the New Irving Hall, though this is by no means a comprehensive list. Numerous local halls in Brooklyn, Paterson, Newark, Hoboken, and other places were rented for special happenings as well. Turner halls, where socialist gymnastic associations met, were also used, as were well-known Bowery theaters such as the Thalia and Windsor. These commercial halls were as much an anarchist space as the more intimate saloons, and though more subject to public intrusion, they were effectively transformed into an alternative sphere in which radical politics thrived.

Cooper Union, located at the convergence of Third and Fourth Avenue near East Sixth Street, was one of Manhattan's best-known lecture halls. Conceived by the American industrialist and philanthropist Peter Cooper, the six-story brownstone opened its Great Hall in 1859. Cooper envisioned a venue where all progressive opinions could be voiced, a forum for the people, a space where democracy could come to life. Cooper Institute, as it was also known, housed several discussion rooms, but the Great Hall was one of the most commodious in the country. It was located below street level to conserve space, optimize temperature, and reduce street noise. The low-ceilinged space could seat 2,500 people in ornate iron chairs with cushioned seats. In 1884, major renovations expanded the auditorium to an area of 125 by eighty-two feet. The stage was relocated, and seats were arranged in amphitheater style, allowing a larger audience and better acoustics.[105]

Anarchists and socialists rented Cooper Union throughout the 1880s and 1890s. For many anarchist groups, rent was a hefty expense. Small groups such as anarchist trade unions and singing societies organized conventions jointly to share the burden. An organizing committee was formed for each event to oversee preliminary tasks such as procuring the venue, inviting music groups, printing and distributing announcements and handbills, and, last but not least, arranging decorations. In

January 1893, the organizing committee of New York Group I decided not to rent Cooper Union because rent had increased from $75 to $150. Instead, arrangements were made with the owner of Thalia Theatre on the Bowery.[106] After 1903, when Congress enacted anti-anarchist legislation, Cooper Union was no longer available to anarchists, and in September 1905 management refused to allow socialists to meet as well.[107]

Germania Assembly Rooms on 291–93 Bowery was another popular German meeting place. This building contained saloons, bowling alleys, and assembly rooms. It started out under the name Steuben House in the 1850s, and by the next decade it served as a meeting place for German trade unions and other labor organizations. During the last quarter of the century, Germania Assembly Rooms became an East Side community center, hosting meetings and balls. In 1885, for example, Circolo Filo-Drammatico Italo-Americano, an Italian American theater group, performed in the Germania Assembly Rooms.[108]

The protest meeting featuring one or more scheduled speakers was a typical occasion. German anarchists organized such gatherings to denounce or express support for recent events. Speeches were usually conducted in German, but many times English, Italian, and Yiddish speakers were also booked. In this way, anarchists accentuated the multiethnic and international character of their movement. One of the largest protest meetings occurred following the guilty verdict and death sentence for the Haymarket defendants on 20 August 1887. Socialists and anarchists gathered at Cooper Union on 19 September 1887 to express their disgust with America's legal system. Johann Most, Sergius E. Schevitsch, a prominent Russian socialist, and Emilie Baudisch, an anarchist immigrant from Austria, made speeches in German and English.[109] In January 1899, some 3,500 New York anarchists and sympathizers of various ethnicities gathered at Cooper Union to protest the International Anti-Anarchist Conference held in Rome a month earlier. It was reported that a large number of Americans attended this meeting and that the Germans initially doubted more than a dozen souls would show up.[110]

German anarchists also organized annual celebrations such as Christmas, New Year's Eve, and the anniversary of an organization's founding. They successfully turned these common holidays into events all their own in an effort to enjoy them in an anarchist spirit. Despite their anticlericalism, German anarchists held a Christmas Eve party (Weihnachts-Feier) for the entire family. Presents were collected beforehand and handed out through a raffle. It is unclear if all German anarchist groups held Christmas celebrations; only a few announcements have been found, in stark contrast to the wealth of ads for other events. The popular New Year's Eve celebration (Sylvesterfest) was an elaborate family feast. Halls were decorated with flags and banners of the participating organizations, thereby conceptualizing the space to mark the anarchist occupation of it. The first part of the celebration featured speeches and musical interludes. Speakers looked back at events and accomplishments of the ending year and vowed to continue propaganda efforts in the next. This was followed by a raffle. Sometimes comrades were requested to drop off presents weeks in advance at a number of anarchist saloons so that all trophies could be displayed at the start of festivities.[111] A dance party followed the countdown to the New Year. It was a time to celebrate the good things in life, but politics was never absent; it resided in their unity, in their provocative presence in a subverted public space. Festivals to celebrate the founding anniversary of an organization (Stiftungsfeste) were also popular occasions to meet in one of the large halls. All these celebrations were family-oriented, combining political solidarity with social and ethnic conviviality.

Large halls were also used to stage commemorations of historical and revolutionary events. These gatherings were much more political in nature and served a propaganda purpose. Even so, women and sometimes children attended these events. The most common tribute was undoubtedly the anniversary of the Paris Commune. German anarchist groups, sometimes in cooperation with other ethnicities, held the much-anticipated Commune Festival annually. With some two thousand tickets in circulation at fifteen cents per family, these festivals could be a lucrative way to raise money for the movement. On such occasions, auditoria were richly decorated with banners, while the front of the stage was decked with portraits and busts of well-known anarchists such as Louise Michel and the Haymarket victims, together with red and black flags. Each of the participating groups brought their own flags and insignias to be placed alongside the anarchist martyrs. A large banner reading "Vive la Commune!" graced the proscenium arch. That these images should appear on a stage is no accident. An element of performance was always at play within the anarchist movement. Anarchist figures were heroes, star actors whose life and fate were continuously reenacted. They also served as exemplars of the anarchist ideal, and in that capacity their portraits sanctified the space that living anarchists were occupying—a symbol of inviolability for a beleaguered oppositional community.

An anarchist Commune Festival in New York consisted of an elaborate program of music, singing, declamations, drinking, and dancing. Since the events of 1871 in Paris were reviled by respectable society, a Commune Festival was truly a subversive statement, something the anarchists exploited by marking it with excessive imagery. Festivities commenced at eight in the evening. Typically, a speech by the chairperson was followed by several orations on the significance of revolutionary events in Paris, Berlin, and Vienna. These lectures were interspersed with tableaux vivants and vocal and instrumental music performed by the best anarchist musical societies. This "official program" lasted until midnight, at which time most youngsters stormed the dance floor for the annual ball in a different hall of the building. The Germania Assembly Rooms, for example, witnessed a migration of people to the dance hall after the midnight chime, while others swarmed to the bar.[112] When chairs were cleared and the first beers consumed, the Sunderdorf music ensemble—one of the best-known German anarchist bands—struck the first chord of the Marseillaise. A thousand voices burst out the words of this universal tune of the revolutionary tradition. After that, the ball could last until the early morning hours. Alfred Kolb, a German worker and traveler, once attended a Commune Festival in Chicago organized by the anarchist paper *Chicagoer Arbeiter-Zeitung:*

> If you know Berlin, you know how many giant halls are necessary to comprehend the crowd on such days. Chicago contents itself with a suburban theater. It was well attended. Men, women, children; nearly all Germans. Many in broad-brimmed Hecker hats[113] that are otherwise rarely worn in Chicago. On stage and from the galleries a few red and black [anarchist] flags as well as some signs and insignias. Below, tables and chairs, beer and tobacco smoke. No police. The performance started at eight. Song recitals, tableaux vivants, ball. In addition there is of course a formal address; in German. I've had to listen to many in my life, never to a worse one. . . . After the performance there was a ball. At the table I found myself in company with a carousing railwayman bragging about Johann Most, and who gave me a few issues of *Freiheit.* His pretty daughters taught me how to dance American waltzes.[114]

The anniversary of the execution of the Haymarket defendants on 11 November 1887 was undoubtedly the most important commemorative event for German American anarchists. The unfairness of the trial and the call for blood throughout the country had stunned the anarchist movement. The day of execution is inscribed in the anarchist collective memory up to this day. What's more, three of the hanged were Germans. The funeral that followed was the largest ever seen in Chicago. November 11th acquired a powerful meaning not dissimilar to the May Days of 1871, when the Paris Commune was suppressed with the summary execution of tens of thousands. One London anarchist paper characterized Haymarket as an event "which every worker, every lover of liberty, ought to engrave in fiery letters on his heart."[115] Thousands of anarchists, socialists, and sympathizers gathered every year at large halls in New York and other cities to pay tribute to their fallen comrades, to collect money for the surviving families, and to proclaim their undiminished strength and resilience in the face of murderous repression. It was a memorial to mourn the dead but also to embolden the living. These meetings were solemn gatherings, however, though speeches contained anger and rage. No dance party followed. When Emma Goldman filed out of Cooper Union after attending her first November 11th commemoration, she was deeply affected. "I could not speak," she recalled, "we walked on in silence."[116]

Mass meetings such as protests, celebrations, and commemorations always had to consider the possibility of police harassment. Political meetings were obviously more prone to surveillance than social events. Plainclothes detectives were invariably present at the larger meeting halls, and stenographers occasionally accompanied officers to record potentially inflammatory speeches. The presence of uniformed police officers during any type of Cooper Union event was not unusual, however; it ensured that the proceedings were orderly. A minimum of 150 officers were on duty in Cooper Union at any given time for Haymarket anniversary meetings, but undercover agents and reporters also descended as soon as the anarchists announced a meeting.[117] During times of repression, police approached hall owners to prevent anarchists from meeting. One such meeting in New Jersey, at which Lucy Parsons, the spouse of one of the Haymarket defendants, was to speak, had to be rescheduled twice.[118]

Despite police intrusion, political meetings such as Haymarket memorials or protest meetings had the advantage of displaying solidarity to the outside world, a show of force that was not possible in the back rooms of saloons. Anarchists knew that detectives and especially reporters invariably mingled with the crowd. The spectacle of two thousand activists and sympathizers carrying flags and banners filling Cooper Union to the tunes of the workers' music bands was sure to intimidate any outsider. The magnificent harmony resounding from all those people singing the Marseillaise accompanied by Sunderdorf's ensemble must have been truly impressive.

For a marginal and mostly reviled subculture as the anarchists were, a well-attended mass meeting, complete with insignias, flags, and music, was a particularly forceful form of resistance, a display of collective power in which the individual enjoyed anonymity and was thereby encouraged in his or her expression of undesirable opinions. Protesting in unison with others can be a thrilling experience. "The collective exhilaration of finally declaring oneself in the face of power," writes James Scott, "will compound the drama of the moment."[119] But safety lay not only in the group dynamic but also in the space the attendees occupied. The lecture hall, like the saloon, was transformed—even if only for an evening—into a place of rebellion, a secular place of worship, a giant pulpit for the religion of revolution, a massive courtroom in which the case for justice was pleaded with the power of a thousand lawyers.

It is important not to view anarchist meeting places as mere hideouts or places where activists sought to escape political involvement. Once decorated and inaugurated, saloons and lecture halls constituted an alternative space where anarchism could be lived and expressed; they were anarchism. It gave the members of an oppositional movement a chance to voice "offstage parody, dreams of violent revenge, [and] millennial visions of a world turned upside down," as Scott writes.[120] This fits exactly the speech Most gave at Krämer's that prompted his arrest. Even so, on most occasions beerhall gatherings were safe havens for anarchists to release their critique and mockery of the established order, especially during times of heightened repression. Indeed, outsiders—especially journalists—sometimes compromised the safety of the saloon. When John Speed walked into Zum groben Michel, all activities ceased.

During calmer times, between episodes of labor unrest, public dissent was tolerated under certain conditions. As a result, the anarchists' public voice was often as inflammatory as their in-house discussions, even though punishment, such as arrest and imprisonment, followed in a number of cases. It should not be forgotten that it was above all the Haymarket affair that sharpened the lines between public and private politics precisely because public assertions of rebellion had suddenly become a "mortal risk."[121]

2 *From Heimat to Exile*

A revolutionary anarchist movement in America, one that was consciously separate from the socialist movement from which it sprang, emerged during the first years of the 1880s. German and Austrian immigrants took the first steps, even though Swiss, Bohemians, and Scandinavians also participated in it. Most were artisans who knew America only as a foreign culture, and the majority of them were profoundly unfamiliar with American politics and customs. An exploration of the political background in Germany and New York can explain how so many exile and immigrant socialists came to be anarchists. Once the dissident socialists recognized their affinity with anarchism, they took steps to organize themselves in a foreign city, first defining themselves as social-revolutionaries and later as anarchists. Two important conventions—one in London and one in Chicago—of the nascent revolutionary movement had a profound impact on the shaping of the German American anarchist movement, especially on radical circles of New York and New Jersey.

Social-Democrats and Social Revolutionaries

German American socialists—immigrants who had lived in America for years or even decades—initiated the movement. Germans by 1880 were one of the largest ethnic groups in the United States; 14 percent of New York's total population in 1880 was German.[1] The German socialists in America, comprising only a fraction of ethnic Germans, regarded America as their home for nearly half a century, and new kindred spirits arrived every year, most of them through the port of New York. The newcomers during the late 1870s and 1880s constituted a new wave of people driven from their homeland by repression and despair, and some were to join the anarchist movement. The socialist party in America was modeled on the German party, and it developed similar divisions among its members. A comprehensive study of the German anarchist movement in New York must therefore examine the political and perhaps mental geography of German radicals on both sides of the Atlantic prior to 1880.

The making of anarchists in Germany unfolded differently than in other European countries. Germany's peculiar political situation—the relationship between socialist politics and anarchist sentiments—helps explain the political and experiential background of the radical German immigrant.

Anarchism as an ideology and certainly as a movement came relatively late to Germany. The French socialist Pierre-Joseph Proudhon had seriously challenged the teachings of Karl Marx, but it was Mikhail Bakunin who dominated the nascent anarchist movement in Europe during the 1870s. The Russian gathered a substantial following but eventually found himself expelled from the International Workingmen's Association in 1872. The social revolutionaries then set up a new International at St. Imier in Switzerland, with delegates from Italy, Spain, and the Jura. They adopted Bakunin's program of autonomous groups devoted to the struggle against capitalism.

The German delegates in the IWA strongly supported Marx and remained unswayed by Bakunin's influence. Beginning in the 1860s, the socialist movement in Germany had followed a dual course of Marxist socialism (Eisenachers) and the state socialism of Ferdinand Lassalle (Lassalleans). The Eisenachers stressed trade unionism, whereas the Lassalleans insisted on capturing political power for the German proletariat. The Gotha Congress of May 1875 reconciled the two factions and transformed German social democracy into a political force to be reckoned with. Shortly after Gotha, the Socialist Workers' party of Germany (Sozialistische Arbeiterpartei Deutschlands; SAPD) was formed. The Gotha program called for the abolition of the wage system, a single progressive tax, and the abolition of child, Sunday, and unhealthy women's labor. It recognized a class society and the mission for the working class. But the program retained much of Lassallean socialism. It called for the establishment of "socialistic productive associations" instead of nationalizing all means of production, as the Eisenachers would have liked. In fact, Marx himself criticized the program. Only in 1891, with the Erfurt program, did Marxian socialism become fully embedded in German social democracy.

This consolidation of Germany's socialist ranks effectively prevented anarchism from gaining a foothold. The only attempt to disseminate anarchist propaganda into Germany was made by a handful of radicals connected to the Jura Federation in Switzerland, a group close to Bakunin. The leading figures included the French Communard Paul Brousse and the Germans Emil-August Werner and Erich Otto Rinke, among others. In 1876, they launched a paper called *Arbeiterzeitung* to spread anarchism among German workers, but the venture ran aground the next year. August Reinsdorf, another leading anarchist figure, undertook propaganda tours, but in the end his efforts also proved futile.

Ironically, it was the policies of Chancellor Otto von Bismarck that facilitated the adoption of anarchist ideas by many socialists. Germany at this time was an authoritarian monarchy effectively ruled by Bismarck, a Prussian realpolitiker with a knack for diplomacy. Almost singlehandedly, Bismarck secured military victories over the Austrians and the French and, on top of that, in 1871 unified the German-speaking principalities into a robust realm under Prussian tutelage. Despite an ingrained regionalism among the Germans, they were swept up in a wave of patriotism and a sense of destiny that proved prophetic forty years later. Bavarians, Hessians, Rhinelanders, and Swabians all rejoiced at Germany's inevitable, though belated, ascent as a great power in Europe.

Bismarck, a Machiavellian maneuverer, was never committed to participatory democracy, an ideal that had spurred the liberal bourgeoisie into action during the 1840s but then failed miserably. Bismarck was pragmatic enough to allow the Reichstag, the lower house of the German Parliament, to have a say in national affairs, but in reality, the assembly was weak and often a plaything in the hands of the chancellor. By allowing the SAPD to send deputies, Bismarck was able to rein in the increasingly militant voice of the socialists by channeling their demands into parliamentary action and thus thwarting the movement. As a result, many socialists grew frustrated with the Reichstag even as they clung to what power they could wield in Berlin.

By this time, the grassroots socialist movement in Germany was quite vibrant and consisted of an extensive network of local workers' associations, trade unions, and mutual-benefit organizations that empowered and gave meaning to the lives of members and supporters. Cultural activities such as theater and picnics as well as periodicals and pamphlets further enriched this movement.

The event that rocked the unity of the Social-Democrats in Germany was the passage of the Antisocialist Law (Sozialistengesetz) by the Reichstag on 19 October 1878.[2] Two assassination attempts on the kaiser in

May and June of 1878 effectively persuaded the majority of the deputies that socialism was terrorism, even though the assassins acted on their own. Bismarck, by exploiting these fears, embarked on a campaign to eliminate socialism once and for all. The Antisocialist Law prohibited any public expression of socialism, made illegal any publication, meeting, or workers' gathering, and stipulated strict sentences for violators, including exile from Germany. It created a hysteria of red-baiting not dissimilar to the American red scare of 1919–20, as Max Nomad has suggested.[3] The only socialist voices permitted were the handful of deputies in the Reichstag, who suddenly found themselves isolated from their constituencies. Wilhelm Liebknecht and August Bebel, two guiding forces within the SAPD, immediately denounced the new legislation but refrained from underground resistance. At the same time, the party refused to surrender its independence, which would have allowed Bismarck to dictate the terms under which Germany's wage earners would be represented. The party leaders consequently opted for caution and patience.

Not all socialists shared this strategy of the leaders in Berlin. Ordinary workers and artisans were infuriated by the suppression of their recreational and educational organizations, which were so central to their day-to-day lives. Many party members and militants called for continued agitation, including the advocacy of violence to counter the arrogance of the chancellor. Bismarck's policies pushed some militants into a corner, where they had to choose between obedience or outright illegal acts of resistance. Doctrines of spontaneous revolutionary acts and conspiratorial tactics, both major ingredients of Bakunin's textbook, suddenly became an inspiration to a number of activists. At the same time, the strategy of the leaders was to avoid causing a stir, "'to give the Reaction no possibility of using Social Democracy as a Red Terror.'"[4] They realized that the specter of the Paris Commune of 1871 still haunted respectable society.

Johann Joseph Most and Wilhelm Hasselmann, both Reichstag deputies at one point, became the most outspoken critics of the Social-Democratic leadership. It is important to stress that both men did not sympathize with anarchism until after 1881. Still, with growing intensity they lashed out at what they saw as cowardice veiled in reformist politics of the party instead of a head-on fight against Bismarck's despotism. The dissident socialists found themselves carried away by a powerful current of Bakuninist and Blanquist ideas, a radicalism that defined its methods outside the political realm.[5] "Anarchism recruited followers by default, not by an intrinsic attraction to its theory," according to the historian Vernon Lidtke.[6]

The dissident socialists, who adopted the name of social revolutionaries, adhered to two key ideological tenets: antiparliamentarism and internationalism. The German political system had frustrated socialist deputies for years, but the nationwide suppression of socialism starting in 1878 exposed the utter futility of official politics. Most emerged as one of the fiercest critics of the socialist leaders and of electoral politics. He had gone to London to edit the dissident paper *Freiheit,* the main organ of anti-establishment socialists. In London, Most gradually escalated his verbal assault on the party and went so far as to advocate the founding of small cells that would engage in conspiratorial activities, precisely the type of thing the party elders feared all along. Furthermore, when the socialist leaders approved Bismarck's military spending bill on the grounds of not wishing to appear unpatriotic, the social revolutionaries immediately accused them of militarism and betrayal of solidarity with the international workers' movement. According to Karl Schneidt, a radical socialist and insider, there was also opposition inside the circle of delegates between moderates and the left wing. Schneidt observed that the social revolutionaries, already removed from the party, gave full support to the left wing in order to discredit the leadership.[7]

For the purpose of this study, one of the most important provisions of the Antisocialist Law was the punishment of expulsion, a violation of the basic freedom of movement. "Persons who constitute a danger to the public safety or other," read paragraph 28, "can be refused residence in the district or town," causing hundreds of socialists to leave their country.[8] This definition was sufficiently vague to suit the regional and municipal authorities, rendering the enforcement of the policy arbitrary and despotic. Some were expelled from multiple districts or towns in the course of a year until they were forced to board steamers to England or America. The journalist Jens Christensen, for example, was expelled from Berlin in July 1886 but arrested elsewhere and imprisoned for three months. In November he was given forty-eight hours to leave Zwickau. In July of the next year he was given thirty hours to leave Bromberg, then only two hours to leave Koburg, and twenty-four hours to bid farewell to the Weimar District altogether. In the end, he made his way to New York.[9] Johann Friedrich Gardthausen, a basket maker from Holstein, married with one child, endured two house searches in twenty-four hours in August 1881. During one house search, the police read family letters dating from 1874, to which Gardthausen loudly protested. Eventually, he was exiled from Hamburg and immigrated to New York.[10]

Between 1878 and 1890, the year of repeal, some eight hundred individuals were exiled under paragraph 28 of the law, according to a study by

Heinzpeter Thümmler. Of all those, 18 percent immigrated to the United States.[11] Many were married, and some had children. A great number of them experienced imprisonment and humiliation by the police. More than 70 percent of exiled émigrés were adults under the age of thirty-six, and 61 percent were between the ages of twenty-six and thirty-five. Evidently, a much greater number packed their bags voluntarily or simply saw no other choice than to leave and join the swelling exile communities outside Germany. A percentage of these exiles would become anarchists in the New World.

The sudden and sweeping suppression of an entire subculture of German working men and women from 1878 until 1890 radicalized many socialists who knew little about anarchist theory. Bismarck's policies had thus unwittingly presented anarchism (in a primitive form) as an attractive alternative to Social-Democracy, whose leaders insisted on appeasing the regime. The subsequent anarchist movement resembled more a kneejerk reaction to state authority stemming from humiliation and expatriation than a conscious intellectual development within the German Left. The result was a rather isolated community of radicals suffering from intellectual incoherence and homelessness. The historian Ulrich Linse has rightly characterized this early anarchist movement as operating in between utopia and reality—utopia because anarchists held fast to the belief that a majority of German workers rejected the state, which was not the case.[12] In fact, workers were rather conservative in their protests and committed to what Vernon Lidtke has termed a "group discipline."[13] Anarchists also insisted that revolution in Bismarck's Germany was imminent, a vision wholly unrealistic according to Social-Democratic leaders. Still, if the Social-Democrats opted for political hibernation between 1878 and 1890, one could argue that the anarchists were the only left-wing oppositional alternative in the face of a growing German nationalism.

The expatriate community of dissidents, a topic deserving of more scholarly attention, is not unique to the German situation. Nonconformists in ancient Greece and Rome clustered in overseas settlements, and in the seventeenth century the liberal Dutch republic became a haven for expelled Sephardic Jews from the Iberian Peninsula. Perhaps the best example is the congregation of Russian exiles in Switzerland during the 1860s. Typically, the host country acted as a home base for propaganda against autocracy and injustice at home. A key tool for this approach was the organization of an efficient smuggling operation. In our case, the German exiles congregated in neighboring countries like Switzerland, Belgium, England, and eventually the United States.

London was by far the most important community of exiled German socialists in Europe. Since the revolutionary upsurge of the 1830s, Britain's capital had a tradition of harboring several enclaves of political refugees. French, German, and other workers organized clubs to sustain their communities and to circumvent the early closing hours of English pubs. The most noteworthy of these clubs was located on Marshall Street in Soho; from 1850 on, it was commonly referred to as the Communist Workers' Educational Society (Communistischer Arbeiter-Bildungs-Verein; CABV). Inevitably, quarrels among the workers led to the formation of other clubs, and in the summer of 1877, a Social-Democratic Club was founded with the goal of streamlining cooperation between German and English radicals. Johann Christoph Neve, a dedicated socialist who would come to play an important role in the anarchist movement, became one of the most active members. Frank Kitz, an English radical of German parents, described Neve as "'tender-hearted and generous'" and praised him as "'the life and soul of the German movement in London.'"[14] One year later, the clubs merged, and a new renovated clubhouse opened on 6 Rose Street. According to Franz Josef Ehrhart, another leading figure, the German section of the Rose Street Club counted 255 members in October 1878.[15] This was the month the Antisocialist Law took effect in Germany, and great efforts were made to accommodate the stream of German refugees.

As the number of exiles and emigrants from Germany grew, a peculiar atmosphere of anger and hope permeated the London expats. Karl Schneidt has pointed to the distinction between exile (Verbannung) and emigration (Auswanderung) among the newly arrived.[16] Exiles embraced the cause of propaganda in the hope of returning to a free Germany. Emigrants also engaged in propaganda, but they resolved to find a better life elsewhere. "Who goes into exile is the idealist," wrote Schneidt. "Who emigrates, the realist."[17] For all newcomers, the clubs provided much-needed assistance such as English lessons, and they even ran libraries to satisfy the comrades' intellectual appetite. Club life was especially beneficial to women, who found themselves uprooted alongside their husbands. Many women in exile familiarized themselves with pertinent political issues and started organizing political and recreational events.[18] But for many, London was only a way station to the United States, a temporary residence, a place to take a breath before embarking on the long transatlantic voyage. Always anxious for news from home, the radical German emigrant, whether in Geneva, London, or New York, never dislodged completely from his or her ethnic background. This often created isolation from the larger foreign society, a condition that was also present among the New York anarchists.

To continue the flow of propaganda from abroad, German radicals realized that they needed a paper that could be produced unhindered and then smuggled into Germany. As early as the summer of 1878, months before the Antisocialist Law passed, German exiles in London made plans to launch a paper to combat the growing repression at home. Wilhelm Liebknecht made the first attempt to publish a socialist newspaper abroad (in London), but his plan was quickly aborted for unknown reasons. Carl Hirsch, a senior journalist and party member, succeeded when his journal *Laterne* appeared in Brussels in the autumn of 1878.

It was Johann Most, the man who would play a crucial role in the American movement, who took charge of the most important radical German exile paper, *Freiheit.* After serving as a deputy, Most now scorned parliamentarians. From 1868, the year he entered the labor movement, until 1878, he spent a total of five years behind bars, which gave him a reputation and a following. In December 1878, he was exiled from Germany, and at the end of the month he arrived in London, intending to travel on to Liverpool and embark for America. Friends convinced him to take up the editorship of the newly founded *Freiheit.* On 25 December he accepted, and the first issue appeared on 4 January 1879. The Social-Democrats at last had a paper to resume agitation in German-speaking Europe. As a result, *Freiheit* became, in the words of the historian Max Nettlau, "'the most eagerly hunted counterband [*sic*] in Germany and Austria.'"[19] An elaborate and inventive system was devised to smuggle the sheets over the border. But one thing bothered the party leadership: *Freiheit,* welcomed by most rank-and-file members, had been launched without party approval.

Ideologically, *Freiheit* started as a straightforward Social-Democratic organ adhering to the principles set out at the Gotha Unity Congress of 1875. By the end of 1879, the staff and friends around Johann Most began to change the tone of their agitation. Antiparliament sentiments flared up among the radical socialists, and calls for revolutionary action further alienated them from the leadership. Most had never been intellectually stable and tended to borrow ideas from various sources. His political convictions were, as he admitted, mostly shaped by friends such as the Austrian socialist Andreas Scheu, the Belgian Victor Dave, and Johann Neve. Most's ideas and opinions veered in the direction of Bakuninism. In the end, the party leadership saw no other solution than to expel Most and Hasselmann from the SAPD in August 1880 during a secret congress in Wyden Castle in Switzerland. In reaction to this, *Freiheit* simply published Bakunin's *Revolutionary Principles* on 2 September. A month later, Most stated, "'We have not become Anarchists. But it is true that we regard them as honest social revolutionaries.'"[20]

Most ventured from Social-Democratic deputy to dissident socialist, and by late 1880 he considered himself a social revolutionary. "'The social revolution must consist,'" he wrote in November of that year, "'in nothing but the most absolute destruction of all existing instruments of "order."'"[21] Personally he felt uprooted, estranged from friends in Germany and Switzerland, discredited by the leadership, and sometimes pushed by comrades in London. At the same time that Most was calling for the "absolute destruction" of the present order, Wilhelm Hasselmann, who briefly wrote for *Freiheit,* left the claustrophobic atmosphere of the London clubs and arrived in New York City on 15 September 1880.

Two and a half million Germans immigrated to the United States between 1851 and 1880.[22] Only a tiny fraction of them, perhaps a few thousand, were socialist. Nonetheless, the Germans dominated the socialist movement in the United States. The movement's history roughly paralleled the development of socialism in Germany, except in the case of Bismarck's assault on everything socialist during the years 1878–90.

After Bakunin was expelled from the International in 1872, Marx feared that anarchist influence over the workers would only grow and decided to move headquarters from London to New York. The New York sections, almost entirely German, had been prominent in the American movement, and their leadership was affirmed by the move. In 1873, a severe economic depression hit the country and proved to be much harsher than any previous economic downturn. Unemployment rose dramatically, while thousands of American workers suffered hunger, homelessness, and despair on a daily basis. This depression lasted until 1879 and took socialists by surprise. Action of some sort was clearly needed, but on this issue of how to turn the tide in favor of the worker ideological fault lines began to rip through the ranks. As in Germany, the Marxists (or Internationalists) favored trade-union action over elections; they called for street protests, strikes, and even riots. But Lassalleans, who stressed the importance of winning political power, called for the use of the ballot and vowed to stick to democratic methods. Since Lassallean socialism was successful in Germany, German American followers had reason to hope for success.

As the depression raged on, so did the internal strife within the ranks of American socialism. Eventually, the Lassalleans left the International and founded their own Social-Democratic Workingmen's Party of America. News of the Gotha Congress in 1875 forced socialists of all stripes to rethink their strategy by putting aside their differences. A year later, the International, only a few sections strong, dissolved itself, and its members approached the Lassalleans in the hope of establishing a new organization modeled on the Gotha principles. The result was the formation of the Workingmen's Party of the United States at the Unity Congress in Philadelphia in July 1876. Its platform was in many ways a victory for the Internationalists.

The differences between the factions—"trade union" and "political," as they were now called—did not disappear. A few favorable results during elections in 1877 gave more credence to the possibility of a political solution. Even in Chicago, the hotbed of trade unionism, the election fever struck, even though the stipulations of the congress prohibited sections from participating in local elections before success was deemed realistic. At the convention in Newark in December 1877, the political faction clearly asserted its dominance; the German-language weekly *Vorbote* was the only voice to remain trade unionist. In Newark the delegates agreed to change the name of the party to the Socialist Labor party (SLP; or Sozialistische Arbeiter-Partei). They adopted the Gotha program and affirmed the role for the SLP in managing political campaigns.

Another issue of contention, especially in Chicago, was the formation of socialist military organizations such as the Lehr-und-Wehr Verein, or defense and educational society. Since the violence of the 1870s—especially during the strikes in the summer of 1877, when hundreds of workers had been shot by militia and national guardsmen—some socialists set out to organize armed defense units. On 13 June 1878, the SLP's National Executive Committee immediately denounced such groups. The question of self-defense and arming (Bewaffnungsfrage) remained a thorny issue in Chicago, where the SLP sections comprised some 870 members.[23]

The return of prosperity in the fall of 1879 ended the successes at the polls for the socialists, but it did not dramatically weaken the position of the political faction within the SLP.[24] Members of the trade-union faction became more radical, however, suggesting that electoral politics should be abandoned altogether. It was at this time that *Freiheit* in London intensified its critique of parliamentary politics. Disgruntled German exiles and immigrants fortified the position of the trade-union faction.

From 26 December 1879 until 1 January 1880, the SLP held its national convention in Allegheny City, just north of Pittsburgh. According to the labor historian John Commons, twenty-five delegates participated, although the National Executive Committee gave no membership figures in the report. Commons and August Sartorius von Waltershausen agree that the party was in bad shape and had lost many members. According to Waltershausen, by the next summer the SLP counted only 1,500 dues-paying members.[25] The delegates at Allegheny City reiterated their opposition to military organizations, after Moritz A. Bachmann, a longtime New York socialist and journalist, together with some Chicago members expressed their view in favor of self-defense.[26] The convention then moved on to what it considered the primary issue: the presidential election of 1880. To the dismay of the radical wing, the debate focused on cooperation with other progressive causes such as the Greenback movement, a largely middle-class amalgam of farmers and reformers. The SLP leadership, aware of the decline in membership, proposed sending delegates to the Greenback party conference in Washington in January 1880. Socialist delegates from New York, including Bachmann, opposed nominating candidates on a joint platform. Ultimately, forty-four socialists, including Albert R. Parsons (who would later became a prominent anarchist) and even Bachmann, attended the Greenback conference of 756 delegates and adopted an uninspired platform with no specifically socialist ingredients.[27] The trade unionists, who stayed behind the scenes during the Greenback negotiations, adamantly opposed such compromise.

When election results proved disappointing, the trade-union faction felt vindicated and formulated an eloquent case against any political action. Moreover, Frank Stauber, the only socialist council member reelected, was excluded from office through political manipulation by the Democrats. "'The unseating of Stauber,'" one socialist remembered, "'did more, perhaps, than all the other things combined to destroy the faith of the Socialists in Chicago in the efficiency of the ballot.'"[28] Paul Grottkau, the editor of the *Chicagoer Arbeiter-Zeitung,* and Peter Petersen, the editor of the Danish-Norwegian paper *Den Nye Tid,* took the lead in an aggressive polemic against the Greenback compromise.

By mid-1880, the SLP was sharply divided into a radical and a moderate wing. The radicals strongly opposed any electoral involvement and criticized the party leadership for disregarding local autonomy and for their tendency toward centralism. Many radicals advocated trade-union action, but others embraced revolutionary methods to bring about a complete reversal of the status quo. The recent political dealings, especially the Stauber case, pushed the militants to instigate what Paul Avrich has called "a secessionist movement."[29] The party referendum in August, which endorsed the Greenback candidate, unleashed serious antagonism; New York, of course, voted against. Undoubtedly, the revolutionaries caught wind of the speech delivered by Wilhelm Hasselmann in the Reichstag on 4 May, where he sympathized with the Russian nihilists, and in August, Hasselmann and Most were expelled from the party. In a parallel move, ten SLP members were expelled in October for their relentless criticism of what they saw as the authoritarianism of the National Executive Committee. The most prominent heretics were Grottkau and Petersen, as well as Oscar Neebe and August Spies, two later defendants in the Haymarket affair. As early as July, New York Section 1 requested that its secretary "contact other sections in different states to prevent another congress, with the purpose of deposing the party officials and to revise the constitution in a strictly legal and constitutional manner."[30] After this failed, they simply left the party and founded their own club. At this time, the majority of SLP members, including dissidents, were still overwhelmingly German-speaking—about 80 percent between 1878 and 1881.[31]

The development of a "secessionist movement" within the Socialist Labor party obscures an important nuance among dissidents of the Chicago and New York sections. Chicago had always been a center of trade unionism, and the anticompromise sympathizers (many of them revolutionaries) allied themselves with the trade unionists. In New York, however, the trade unionists had already left the party as early as 1877. Therefore, New York became the scene of an internal battle between moderates, gathered around the *New Yorker Volkszeitung*, and revolutionaries, reinforced by the constant influx of German exiles. New York revolutionaries held bitter memories of the 1877 police violence and the Stauber affair, but they also frowned upon trade unions, which they regarded as another form of hierarchy. Unlike Chicago and other midwestern cities, New York radicalism was infused with a pure revolutionary spirit that laid the groundwork for the emergence of an uncompromising anarchism, whereas in Chicago, trade unionism developed into a type of anarchosyndicalism, with Parsons and Spies at the helm.

German anarchists emerged out of similiar circumstances in Germany and the United States. The SAPD and the SLP had both been born out of a unifying congress of Marxists and Lassalleans. Both parties invested energy in the campaign for political power, and both harbored dissidents who were looking for more radical methods. On both sides of the Atlantic, these dissidents were dissatisfied with the increasing autocracy of the party leadership. German socialism, however, was utterly suppressed in 1878, creating a severe crisis of faith in German democratic politics for many socialists. But the German American dissidents experienced a similar disillusionment after legal elections in 1879 and 1880. The merger of German and German American radical dissenters in the

New York metropolis proved a powerful mixture of revolutionary fervor, a veritable sturm-und-drang atmosphere.

To a considerable degree, this small group of German radicals in New York was detached from American culture. Karl Kautsky once described this radical minority as "that part of German immigrants who lost an appreciation for German conditions, without gaining an appreciation for American conditions, and therefore living in an imagined world with no solid ground to stand on."[32] This minority, however, was not homeless or amorphous. Once the rift with the socialists was visible, the social revolutionaries were free to build a movement of their own. Autonomous club life was only one way in which these radicals "imagined" their world.

Hasselmann, Schwab, and the Social-Revolutionary Club

"It would be much better to drop the mask," Hasselmann once said, "and to proceed at once with violent revolution, without which we cannot go on. . . . [I]f it would fail, which in the present circumstances is to be foreseen, nothing would be lost, for blood is a particular juice that will at least indissolubly cement the party together."[33] This statement was made inside party ranks in December 1879, at the same time that the SLP was holding its convention in Allegheny City.

In May 1880, the German Reichstag convened to renew the Anti-socialist Law for the third time. Hasselmann, now thirty-six years old, decided to go public with his views. In a speech he stated that the law was proof that cooperation with the government and the ruling classes was no longer possible. He concluded with the following remarks: "'Like we see how in Russia the anarchists are working, like we see how the French workers have sacrificed themselves, so, gentlemen, will the German workers do also. The idea that the time of parliamentary chatter is over and the time for deeds begins has thoroughly penetrated the conscience of the people.'"[34]

This speech infuriated the socialist delegates. The references to the Russian nihilists and the Paris Commune were particularly troublesome; the leadership had always stressed the distinctive societal conditions in Germany. Wilhelm Liebknecht publicly wondered how much Hasselmann had been paid by Bismarck. But Hasselmann was no agent provocateur; he was simply embittered about the prospect of socialism in Germany.

Friedrich Gotthard Eduard Wilhelm Hasselmann was born on 25 September 1844 in Bremen to Friedrich Hasselmann, a linen seller, and twenty-five-year-old Christina Meyerkort. Shortly after birth, his father left for America, never to return. From this time on, Hasselmann's childhood was marked by a dependence on the goodwill of others. After his mother died, he was placed with a wealthy uncle, who treated him as an inferior relative. According to the historian Franz Mehring, Hasselmann's bitter childhood experience contributed to his often hostile taciturnity later in his life.[35] As a student he showed an interest in mathematics and science. From 1860 to 1863 he attended the Polytechnic School in Hannover, after which he enrolled at the University of Göttingen in 1864. It was at this time that Hasselmann first attended a political meeting and began reading the French revolutionary Auguste Blanqui, who instilled in him a long-lasting "hatred of the propertied classes."[36] He continued his education at the University of Berlin and later became a chemist.

Hasselmann's formative years as a socialist were spent in the General German Workers' Association (Allgemeine Deutsche Arbeiter-Verein; ADAV), founded in 1863 in Leipzig by Ferdinand Lassalle. Its goal was to embrace the interests of the workers and fight for a classless society through legal means such as universal suffrage. In 1866, Hasselmann met J. B. von Schweitzer, the president of the ADAV, who was immediately impressed by the student's talents. When Hasselmann left the university, Schweitzer hired him as a member of the editorial office of the *Social-Demokrat,* the unofficial organ of the association.

Hasselmann became a devout Lassallean, revering the founder of the ADAV to the point of idolatry; he even compared Lassalle to Jesus Christ. His position at the *Social-Demokrat* allowed him to dominate the political dialogue among the ADAV's membership. Some socialist leaders resented Hasselmann's attitude but had to concede that he had become the virtual leader of the ADAV, an impressive feat for a twenty-five-year-old graduate. But Hasselmann's ideological outlook was still in a formative stage. Contrary to most Lassalleans, he supported trade unions. He also applauded the war against Napoleon III in 1870, although he later criticized Bismarck's foreign policy. Hasselmann's hesitant sympathy for the Paris Commune in the spring of 1871, however, reflected the overall "sterile position," as Günther Bers called it, of the Lassalleans toward the revolutionary events in France.[37]

Observers agree that Hasselmann displayed an excessive desire to increase his prestige within the socialist movement. Karl Schneidt, a friend, explained Hasselmann's hunger for power as a way to retaliate against the wrongdoers of his boyhood. In March 1871, he unsuccessfully ran for office in the first legislative elections. As editor, he resisted the sharing of power, causing more resentment among other socialists. But Hasselmann had many qualities useful to the movement. He was able to convey difficult economic theories in popular language. Eduard Bernstein recalled that Hasselmann was well versed in the "art of rousing the passions." "'Hasselmann knew like no other,'" Hugo Friedländer wrote, "'how to stir the masses, to fanaticize them.'"[38] This quality he shared with Johann Most.

In the years leading up to the 1875 congress at Gotha, Hasselmann began a particularly vicious polemic against the Eisenachers and the International Workingmen's Association. At one point he used anti-Semitic diatribes, and to some his unrestrained war of words revealed the character of a troubled introvert. Bernstein described him as "'embittered and distrustful'" and an "'unscrupulous polemicist.'" Mehring observed in Hasselmann a "'lack of self-esteem.'" Some Eisenachers retaliated by suggesting that Hasselmann was a police spy because he had never been arrested, an unfounded assertion according to his biographer, Günther Bers.[39]

In 1873–74, Hasselmann was elected to the Reichstag as a deputy from the Barmen-Ebersfeld District. Addressing the chamber, he called for a militant class war and referred to the Paris Commune. His in-depth knowledge of social and political issues earned him respect. On the issue of equality for women he opposed immediate establishment of suffrage for women, arguing that women had not yet attained the proper education. The view that gender equality was an issue for a future date was also held by many older anarchist activists in America during the last quarter of the nineteenth century.

A year after Gotha, Hasselmann was offered a position in the editorial office of *Vorwärts* (Forward), the new party organ, but he refused to work alongside Liebknecht and left for Barmen-Ebersfeld to launch his own paper, *Rothe Fahne* (Red flag). This paper was nothing more than a propaganda sheet, and it became obvious that Hasselmann was following an independent course. He lost in the next elections, despite a busy lecture tour in the industrial Ruhr region. In June 1878, the entire editorial staff of the *Bergische Volksstimme* (Bergische people's voice), another paper he published, was arrested and jailed. His campaign for the next elections brought success, but he did not stick to a hard-line socialist agenda and instead addressed issues with broader support: he defended postal employees, rallied against profiteering and monopoly, and embraced the patriotic issue of raising war pensions for invalids.[40]

By 1878, Hasselmann had distanced himself from orthodox Lassalleanism. During debates on the Antisocialist Law he publicly expressed doubts about the benefits of Germany's political system. "'I myself have known for a long time,'" he once told the deputies, "'that it will come to that, just as the followers of Blanqui in France and the friends of Bakunin in France and Russia have said: there is no hope in the old police state.'"[41] The passage of the Antisocialist Law in October seemed to support Hasselmann's analysis. Despite the suppression of socialist literature, Hasselmann traveled to Berlin to launch his "apolitical" paper *Glück auf! Familienblatt für das deutsche Volk* (Good luck! Family paper for the German people). Again, the party leadership accused him of disloyalty and irresponsibility, a charge that was also hurled against Johann Most. Hasselmann was expelled from Berlin on 29 November 1878 under paragraph 28; he moved to Hamburg, where he again started several publications.[42]

Hasselmann's Reichstag speech sealed his fate in the socialist movement in Germany. A history of mutual suspicion between the stubborn Hasselmann and the leadership came to a public explosion; he was labeled the "Berliner Marat" and a loudmouth (Maulheld). As could be expected, Most's *Freiheit* eagerly reported the affair, and the thirty-six-year-old Hasselmann became a ready contributor to Most's paper when his "Ein offenes Wort an das deutsche Proleteriat" (An open word to the German proleteriat) was published in the 31 July 1880 issue. At this point Hasselmann was not an anarchist—his Lassallean background (diametrically opposed to anarchism) remained with him—but he now gave more thought to direct action. He was influenced by Blanqui's idea of decentralized group action, although he was opposed to the Frenchman's conspiratorial schemes. Both Most and Hasselmann were expelled from the SAPD on 22 August 1880.

Wilhelm Hasselmann was a journalist, and he could not bear the financial burden when socialist publications were outlawed. He contemplated leaving Germany, but the decision to emigrate was forced upon him when he realized he had inadvertently used a police spy to carry messages to the offices of *Freiheit.* Hasselmann traveled with his colleague Schneidt to Belgium, and by the end of August 1880 he joined Most in London. Since their expulsion, Hasselmann had been seeking closer contact with Most. Schneidt tells us that before 1880 their relationship was reserved, but now both were united against the "Führerclique," while adopting a more internationalist outlook.[43] During a speech in Hampstead's Atheneum Club, Hasselmann clarified that Germany's unification was built "'on streams of blood and on heaps of corpses.'"[44] He further denounced the militaristic culture and called post-1878 Germany a "'naked police state.'"[45] It is clear that many of the radical anti-Bismarck exiles foresaw the dangers of growing chauvinism and nationalism. Hasselmann adopted many of Most's revolutionary ideas, shared subscription lists, and actively promoted *Freiheit.* But despite an ideological brotherliness between Most and Hasselmann, they were also two stubborn personalities perhaps competing for fame among radical Germans, and personal rivalries may have cut short Hasselmann's stay in England. He stopped writing for *Freiheit* and boarded a steamer for New York.

Before discussing Hasselmann's role in the nascent anarchist movement in New York City, it is important to assess his character. Who was Hasselmann the emigrant? "Hasselmann is someone with a closed character," Schneidt observed, "[a character] not easily judged."[46] He was intelligent and distrustful; he would never freely disclose information about himself or trust a colleague unconditionally. This made him inaccessible to friends and restless in intimate relationships. He was a tall, big-boned man who put on a rather hostile and cold mien. Friedländer remembered him as slim and unkempt, with blonde hair and a disheveled beard. His clothes were too raggedy for a Sunday meeting—as Friedländer joked, he would stand out too much among the workers. He was often ridiculed and dismissed by party members, an experience that reminded him of his childhood. Mehring even wrote that after years of socialist involvement, Hasselmann turned into one of the "'saddest caricatures of our public lives.'"[47] Nevertheless, Hasselmann was a skilled editor and a judicious journalist. He was also an efficient orator who, according to Schneidt, was a master in adapting a lecture to his audience.

By the time he left Germany, his following was small and unorganized. Schneidt attributes this to the fact that Hasselmann was extremely unreliable and often thoughtless in his relations with others. He rarely made it to a meeting on time and left letters and requests from friends unanswered. The result was frustration among scores of supporters who eventually abandoned him.

Hasselmann was single when exiled from Berlin in November 1878.[48] During his life in Germany there is no mention of a partner; he was known to his comrades as an "inveterate bachelor."[49] During his stay in Hamburg, just before leaving for Belgium, Hasselmann met and married Friederike Rohde, a worker born in Mecklenburg who had won the heart of this dark and gloomy man. Schneidt describes Rohde as a hard-working, economical woman raised under simple circumstances and gifted with a "common sense and a healthy mother's wit."[50] Again, such a stereotypical and patriarchal attitude toward women was not uncommon among German socialist and anarchist men. Rohde would eventually join her husband in New York; they had two children.

Wilhelm Hasselmann arrived in New York City on 15 September 1880, aboard the steamer *Saint-Laurent.* His move to America certainly did not go unnoticed. Indeed, socialist leaders in Germany found it necessary to cable the SLP warning them of Hasselmann's voyage, but the SLP refrained from openly obstructing his activities in New York. There must have been some correspondence prior to his departure between social revolutionaries on both sides of the Atlantic as well. According to the *New Yorker Volkszeitung,* the SLP's main organ in the city, Hasselmann was sent to America by comrades in London to assess the local labor situation.[51] This is confirmed by Schneidt, who attests that Hasselmann had made a deal with Most to send regular reports from "over there" (von Drüben) for publication in *Freiheit,* an indication that they were still on friendly terms.[52] In New York, Hasselmann met with many German comrades he had known since the days of the ADAV.

Three days after his arrival, Hasselmann delivered a speech on the "present-day social and political revolts in Germany" at Germania Assembly Rooms, a popular venue with German New Yorkers located in the Bowery.[53] He described the situation in Germany under the Antisocialist Law and opposed any use of the ballot. According to the *New Yorker Volkszeitung,* which could be biased, he also advocated the establishment of a secret organization.[54] At the end, he reiterated his reasons for leaving Germany, especially the Neumann affair, after which the German police threatened to arrest him for treason.

His main contact in New York was Justus Schwab, a radical saloon keeper on the Lower East Side. Schwab's saloon on First Street had become a distribution point for *Freiheit,* and he would remain a pivotal figure in the New York anarchist movement until his death in 1900. His personality, and certainly his saloon, anchored the anarchists to Manhattan's social geography. The Lower East Side became the center of immigrant radicalism, and during the 1880s, its population was still largely German and Irish. Schwab was born in 1847 in Frankfurt-am-Main in Hesse. His father was a forty-eighter and served four years in prison for rioting against Prussian forces attempting to bring the rest of Germany under control.[55] The *New York Times,* though not reliable when it comes to radicals, reported that his father owned a tavern. The paper also wrote that the younger Schwab stood heroically in front of a Prussian cannon.[56] A friend of Schwab who knew him "intimately for more than ten years" asserted that he had inherited a small fortune from his father, whom the writer described as "a late well-to-do citizen in Frankfort-on-the-Main."[57] Unsympathetic writers, such as the reporter John Speed, used Schwab's financial boon against him, charging that he made his fortune off the anarchists while preaching the doctrine of communal property.[58] Schwab learned the masonry trade and possibly engaged in the labor movement during the late 1860s.

Schwab immigrated to New York in May 1869, as he told a *New York Times* reporter.[59] He possibly lost his job during the depression of 1873 and joined the German section of the Workingmen's Association, headquartered in New York. When unemployment in the city reached alarming levels, workers demanded public assistance from city authorities, but to no avail. A Committee of Safety was organized to pressure the government. Schwab strongly believed the government should be run by and for the workers, but no sign of public aid was in sight. When a large meeting in Tompkins Square in January 1874 was violently dispersed, Schwab and some other German socialists resisted and were clubbed by police officers. When all was cleared, Schwab marched back onto the square holding a red flag and chanting the Marseillaise; he was promptly arrested and accused of inciting to riot and "waving a red flag."[60]

After Tompkins Square, Schwab married Louisa, an Iowa-born housekeeper of German parents, and by 1880 they had a two-year-old son, Justus Jr., and a one-month-old daughter, Louisa.[61] According to a *New York Times* report twenty years later, the couple had two sons and two daughters; one son worked as a machinist, the other in a bank.[62] It was at this time that Schwab opened his saloon on 50 First Street, which became a magnet for all international radicals. Like so many Germans, Schwab became a target of the growing temperance movement and crusade against saloons. In June 1876, he was arrested for selling lager beer on Sunday; he was released after a hearing.[63] During the great strike of 1877, Schwab became chairperson of the Committee of Arrangements and attended a peaceful meeting in Tompkins Square. In April of that year, Schwab was again arraigned in court for disorderly conduct, this time at a large meeting in Chickering Hall; he was later released.[64]

Schwab was an imposing man, broad-shouldered with curly blonde hair. A friend once described him as a "viking," a figure too large for his cozy little tavern. Another guest remembered Schwab's "stentorian" voice with the power to make the glasses tremble.[65] Schneidt describes him as a muscular fellow with an enormous appetite, a sense of humor, and a popular joviality befitting a southern German.[66] Emma Goldman, deeply affected by Schwab's death, called him a "champion of freedom, sponsor of labour's cause, pleader for joy in life." Goldman further remembered Schwab's "surpassing capacity for friendship, a veritable genius for responding generously and beautifully."[67] The Marxist intellectual Daniel De Leon once facetiously called him "that lager-beer anarchist" and "clown of the labor movement." [68] Schwab's standing among the East Side radicals cannot be overstated: his charismatic personality seemed to provide much-needed humor to an otherwise overly serious band of revolutionaries. "Justus Schwab attained a great deal of prominence among this class of revolutionists," wrote an 1883 *New York Times* reporter. "He has the appearance of a merry, contented Dutchman, but he declared war upon all non-Socialistic society with such vehemence that when he rose in meeting to speak the auditors remarked to each other: 'Now we'll see gore flow like water.'"[69] But above all, Schwab was known and loved for his good-humored humanity amid so much drudgery and anxiety in New York's working-class slums. "If you see Schwab," wrote a close friend, "as I often enjoyed the pleasure of seeing him, amidst his family, with his refined and honest wife, a good and brave woman, and his well-bred, nice children, you would greet in him the *man,* the brother, regardless of differences of opinion."[70]

In 1879, Schwab was a prominent member of the New York section of the SLP, but in January 1880, he and Moritz Bachmann became strong opponents of the party's cooperation with the Greenback party. Schwab was as much infuriated by the party hierarchy as by the reformist strategy of the SLP, and early on he subscribed to Most's *Freiheit.* As early as July 1880, Schwab insisted on revising the SLP constitution to curb executive power, an idea that was quickly brushed aside by the leadership.[71] The conflict came to a head in August, when the SLP voted in favor of the compromise platform with the Greenback party. At the meeting of the National Executive Committee on 17 August 1880, Schwab, who presided, insisted that "the party members cannot, in accordance with their principles nor with the Constitution of the Party, vote for candidates for President or Vice-President presented by whatever party. The function of President represents the principle of individual authority to the highest degree; a social democracy has no need for it." Voicing an argument for decentralization, he offered that "the functions of government may be fulfilled by members of departments who constitute an executive council allowed to elect their own president at every session."[72]

Schwab argued for the empowerment of the base and a thorough decentralization of executive power. His objections and propositions, echoing Bakunin's charges against Marx, threatened the socialist leadership, who in turn castigated him for no other reason than, as Schwab himself concluded, "disregarding the dictates of the would-be authorities of the party."[73] He, along with forty others, was shown the door.[74] Soon, a circle of left-wing socialists formed outside the SLP, and by October 1880, this group (with Schwab at the helm) called itself "social revolutionary" and decided to meet regularly at Schwab's saloon. The members embraced a crude negative anarchism in the sense that they opposed any hierarchy, and they vowed to fight against the established order by decentralized agitation; any formal organization, including trade unions, were frowned upon. There was little room for constructive analysis of domination in society. In many ways, the social revolutionaries focused on Germany, and the first project they launched involved setting up a fund for continued propaganda by pamphlets in Germany.[75]

Hasselmann, who endorsed the group, had been on a lecture tour and was experiencing what many less-prominent German exiles in America would face: an utter ignorance of American ways. Hasselmann's speeches and analyses seemed overwrought or even misplaced, and according to Waltershausen, his tour was a "lamentable fiasco."[76] Long-time German Americans often ridiculed newcomers, or greenhorns who seemed to think that Bismarck and his henchmen had followed them to the United States (this was not such an outlandish idea, since German secret agents did operate in New York and other cities, sending reports back to Berlin).

On 15 November 1880, the social-revolutionary circle, on Hasselmann's initiative, was formally constituted as the Social-Revolutionary Club (Sozial-Revolutionäre Klub). This is the first instance of an anarchistic organization in the United States founded and located separately from mainstream as well as orthodox socialist culture. Not surprisingly, they chose to be a "club" rather than a party or society, thereby highlighting a commitment to nonhierarchical and voluntary organization. On the night of 15 November, some fifty people convened in a saloon on Eldridge Street, not far from Schwab's. They came to listen to Hasselmann and discuss bylaws for their new organization.[77] Hasselmann insisted that the club's goal was to help overthrow the existing order. He stressed the individual's responsibility to style him- or herself as an independent revolutionist unafraid to use force. There were to be no leaders, a principle he illustrated by citing personalities from the Paris Commune who, according to Hasselmann, merely guided an already revolutionized populace. The club began its existence with twenty-seven members (the other attendants had left after the speech).

Throughout the 1880s, the Social-Revolutionary Club maintained a weekly schedule of meetings.[78] Typically, these meetings consisted of discussion sessions or lectures by members. They also organized large gatherings to celebrate the anniversary of the Paris Commune in March, for example, often in cooperation with French communards in New York. Their emphasis on self-defense and methods of force and terror was perhaps their most distinguishing characteristic, although no crime was ever committed by the group. When, on 13 March 1881, revolutionaries assassinated Czar Alexander II of Russia, the club immediately expressed its "sympathy with the deed of the Russian Nihilists" during a large meeting.[79] A pamphlet in German and English was circulated and published in *Freiheit* (the *New Yorker Volkszeitung* refused to print it).[80]

Defecting SLP members and newcomers from Germany gradually increased the club's membership. An event that received wide attention was the arrival of the steamer *Silesia,* carrying socialist exiles from Germany, only two weeks after the founding of the club. Thirty-four socialists (out of 957 passengers), twenty-four men and ten women and children, all wearing red flannels tied to their buttonholes, were welcomed by Schwab. A large red flag was unfurled from the deck of the ship. "A poorer looking lot than the 34 never passed through the [Castle] Garden," reported the *New York Times.*[81] Several days later, an audience of over two thousand socialists and social revolutionaries filled Germania Assembly Rooms to welcome their brothers and sisters.[82] Several of the passengers, such as Karl Broda, Karl Maaß, Hermann Wabnitz, Wilhelm Ernst Schweppendiek, and especially Carl Wölky, would play a role in the German anarchist movement.[83] Most were in their thirties when they arrived in New York; they were skilled workers, many married with children. Wölky, for instance, was born in 1849 in Heilsberg, East Prussia. He became a shoemaker and helped smuggle *Freiheit* through Hamburg, for which he was arrested and sentenced to two years in prison in 1879. He was exiled first from Berlin and then from Hamburg. Thirty-one and married, he arrived in New York and joined New York Gruppe I, making a name for himself as a prolific lecturer.[84] According to Waltershausen, the club had grown to sixty members by early December, undoubtedly a result of recent arrivals. By June 1883 it counted close to one hundred, including many Austrians.[85]

The Social-Revolutionary Club was undergoing a period of ideological formation between 1880 and 1881. Its principles, discussed during the founding meeting, were nearly identical to the Gotha program of 1875. In fact, during a speech in Philadelphia, Hasselmann stated that he had not abandoned social democracy and that his position was the same as fifteen years ago. The only difference was his willingness to support violent revolution to achieve what he called the Workers' Republic.[86] The Jewish socialist Abraham Cahan, who arrived in New York in June 1882, described Hasselmann as "'almost an anarchist.'"[87] The club veered toward anarchism more in its rhetoric of methods than in its critique of domination or the state as such: "'The violent revolution and the destruction of all exploiters and tyrants remains for the working class the only way to liberation from the yoke of wage slavery.'"[88] Socialists (that is, SLP members) were still welcome at club meetings, but on 18 November, a group of party members left after hearing leading club members deliver bold speeches about insurrection.[89] At the end of the month, the club still frequently employed the ambiguous term "revolutionary Social-Democracy."[90] Finally, on 30 January 1881, the Socialist Labor party forced its members to choose between the party or the club or face expulsion.[91]

The social revolutionaries were kept informed by Johann Most's London-based *Freiheit,* a paper that made no secret about its approval of extralegal tactics to further the revolution. After the assassination of Czar Alexander II, Most had published an article entitled "Endlich!" (At last!) and was sentenced to prison, which further increased his fame. In November 1881, the members of the club voted to adopt the principles of *Freiheit* and to affiliate with the International Working People's Association, the anarchist international resurrected at a London congress.[92]

Wilhelm Hasselmann had been instrumental in the founding of the club, but he never seems to have transcended a crude insurrectionary anarchist creed laced with Lassallean and Blanquist ingredients. He continued to give lectures at club meetings until 1887. His final lecture for the club appears to have been on 14 May at their headquarters in a beerhall on East Fourth Street, when he spoke about "clericalism and bigotry in America."[93] Hasselmann's popularity, while great in 1880–81, declined after the arrival of the impetuous Johann Most. He also founded a Natural Science Society (Naturwissenschaftliches Verein) in January 1885, in which he offered chemistry classes, but which was allegedly used to test explosives. Between one hundred and 120 comrades became members of this society, but this number fell back to thirty after four months of experimenting, according to Most, who derided the whole affair.[94]

In January 1886, Hasselmann returned to his old profession of editor and launched *Amerikanische Arbeiter-Zeitung* as an alternative to Most's *Freiheit.* Again, he advocated social revolution and the founding of free socialist workers' associations. After six months, he was forced to fold his paper due to mounting debts. The fortunes of the Hasselmann family took a turn for the worse when sometime before May 1885, one of their children died. Hasselmann's wife worked long hours for small wages, while he was unable to find employment. Reportedly, he studied chemistry in the hope of inventing a new technique for applying explosives to aid the cause.[95] In 1888, we find him running a saloon on Suffolk Street, a vocation not uncommon among German immigrants. Patrons described the saloon as intolerably dirty and run-down, an indication that his venture was short-lived. The few descriptions of his later life are unreliable, but it seems safe to say that Hasselmann, burdened by debt and despair, withdrew from the movement and led a secluded life in New York. He became a U.S. citizen, and sometime in February 1907 he moved from one Brooklyn tenement to another. It is perhaps telling that at the time of his move he did not notify *Freiheit* of his change of address. "You must have [moved], old man, but where are you hiding now?" a notice read in *Freiheit*.[96] He lived in the Williamsburg District of Brooklyn until his death on 25 February 1916.[97]

Apart from the Social Revolutionary Club, New York anarchists could also be found in the radical wing of the SLP's New York section. There it was again Justus Schwab who was perceived as the troublemaker. Unsympathetic party members accused the club, which welcomed radical SLP members, of being a clique of cutthroats and called them greenhorns who didn't realize that violent tactics would not be allowed in the United States. Finally, in January 1881, the split in the New York section was complete when the radical wing of social revolutionaries met separately and existed alongside their fellow comrades at the Social-Revolutionary Club.

Eighteen-eighty was a year of mutiny among German socialists. In Germany and the United States, political idealism had been struck a blow. In America it was the memory of striking workers shot dead by government soldiers in 1877 and the flawed elections of 1879 and 1880. In Germany, sweeping legislation had silenced any critique of the status quo. For some it was time to join the anarchist movement in Europe, and time also to consider extrapolitical means to achieve an ideal. But where to go from here? Some evaluation of the events of 1880 was needed as well as a meeting to unite all mutineers and forge a new movement that would not bow for any ruler but rather would aspire to a philosophy of freedom and resistance. Could anarchist ideas be transformed from something negative and reactive into a constructive approach to change society for the better?

The London and Chicago Conventions of 1881

The German social-revolutionary movement that sprang up after 1879, concentrated mainly in London and the United States, cannot accurately be called anarchist until several years later. However, as the would-be anarchists broke with social democracy, they found themselves drifting toward the European anarchist movement at a time when direction and inspiration were needed. What were the ideological contours of the anarchists during the 1870s? Mikhail Bakunin was the person most responsible for drumbeating anarchism as a revolutionary movement. His ideas and activities, while sometimes incoherent, inspired numerous radicals, mostly from southern European countries such as Spain and Italy. Bakunin's insurrectionism together with the idea of conspiratorial group action to foment social revolution coalesced into the idea of "propaganda by deed," a phrase first formulated by his Italian disciples in 1876, the year Bakunin died.

Propaganda by deed emerged in the context of agrarian social protest in southern Europe, especially Italy, where armed insurrection against the establishment was deemed a more effective method to find the support of the rural masses than dispersing leaflets and magazines. This early definition clearly focused on popular revolt and was infused with Bakuninist rhetoric. The London convention twisted the notion of propaganda by deed to mean individual acts of terror against the representatives of state and capital, and members pointed to the benefits of chemistry and technology to further the cause. This was a new—and, to many, morally questionable—idea that seemed to substitute a cult of the rogue personality for collective action against oppression. Dynamite terrorism has no basis in any anarchist theory or tradition; its appeal sprang directly from the spectacular assassination of Czar Alexander II, which received much attention in the radical press. Additionally, support for anarchism among the masses never materialized, as a string of failed revolutionary moments during the 1870s made clear. Frustration pushed anarchism further into isolation and secrecy. Anarchists witnessed the embrace of reformist social democracy by millions of European workers with alarm and anger, especially when seasoned anarchists like Andrea Costa and Paul Brousse recanted their revolutionary beliefs and adopted parliamentary methods instead. Furthermore, government repression and infiltration of insurrectionaries in Europe drove anarchists into the realm of illegality. Repression was followed by assassinations, setting in motion a cycle of violence resulting in complete isolation from the working class (in whose name radicals often advocated or committed such *attentats*). It is not surprising that revolutionary terrorism did not simply appear attractive to some anarchists but seemed like the only method left. In short, as one historian puts it, "[P]olitical terrorism constituted a desperate attempt on the part of the anarchist movement to escape the isolation which parliamentary socialism had sidetracked it into."[98]

The disintegration of the International in 1872 after the expulsion of the Bakuninists also contributed to a more splintered revolutionary strategy fought with illegal means. National sections of anarchists, once part of the International, disappeared, and small groups of zealous and often frustrated individuals emerged. Especially in Germany and Austria, where there was no anarchist movement to speak of, social revolutionaries employed fragmented, underground methods. Efficient distribution of anarchist literature in those countries was paralyzed, which fueled the demand for still more explosive forms of propaganda. "'Political terrorism, and not anarchism,'" wrote Nettlau, "'had come to replace social democracy, anarchism having been relegated to a goal in the far distance.'"[99] The anarchist historian Rudolf Rocker also pointed to the lack of anarchist literature available to German radicals, who turned to anarchism merely as an expression of deep antagonism toward parliamentary politics.[100] Propaganda by deed, whether insurrection or assassination, became the method of choice for many European anarchists because it allowed them to continue their fight against autocracy without diluting principles.

Not surprisingly, a call for a new convention of anarchists to resurrect the International in the spring of 1881 met with some hesitance. Southern European anarchists denied that the International had ever disappeared, while others simply didn't think such a body was necessary. Nonetheless, an international social-revolutionary congress was held from 14 to 19 July 1881 in the back room of the Fitzroy Arms in London. A total of forty-five delegates convened, consisting of anarchists, social revolutionaries, and Blanquists. The goal of the meeting was to unite all revolutionaries (as opposed to parliamentarians) in a new International and to devise a plan of action that would integrate the principles of unity and autonomy, an issue that remains with anarchists to this day. Among the leading anarchists who attended were Peter Kropotkin, Errico Malatesta, Johann Neve, Emile Gautier, and Louise Michel. Johann Most had been arrested in March after publishing an article celebrating the killing of the czar; his trusted friend Johann Neve attended instead. All delegates were designated by a number to ensure their safety.

Five groups from the United States, nearly all from the East Coast, participated. The New York section of the SLP, still headed by Schwab, did not send a delegate but was represented by Neve. This section had split off from the socialist section in January 1881 but at first remained hesitant to adopt a revolutionary stance. Schwab and his colleagues soon aligned themselves with the Mostians and authorized Neve to speak for them. But Neve grew impatient at the congress; "'too much talk and too little serious work,'" he complained.[101] The result was that he became inactive, although he was elected to an international committee to coordinate cross-border relations between the groups, a venture with little success. The French anarchist Gustave Brocher, one of the principal organizators of the convention, agreed to speak for the members of Icarie, a libertarian commune in Adams County, Iowa. Carl Seelig, a cabinet maker and founding member of the Social-Revolutionary Club in New York, represented two German social-revolutionary groups, one from New York and another from Philadelphia. Incidentally, Brocher deemed Seelig not very "developed" but thought he possessed "strong revolutionary convictions."[102] Interestingly, Seelig's mandate prohibited him from membership in any committee. The Boston Revolutionists, the fifth American group, sent Marie P. Le Compte to London as their representative.[103]

Discussions were heated and emotions ran high. All delegates were committed to an anti-authoritarian philosophy, but opinions differed on specific issues such as type of organization, the extent of autonomy, goals, and methods. Kropotkin was especially dismayed at the overall preoccupation with indiscriminate violence among nearly all delegates. The Russian held that deeds should always be linked to an idea, and violence can never be indiscriminate. Someone remembered that in the "overheated atmosphere," Kropotkin battled against the entire congress and through his eloquence succeeded in toning down the rhetoric of terrorism.[104] Still, proposals such as the self-study of chemistry and technology received widespread support.

The delegates of the American groups were no less caught up in these debates. Seelig adamantly defended the principle of autonomy but warned that America could not yet become anarchist. For this reason, he urged his colleagues to consider a resolution stating that each country had the right to determine what degree of autonomy was appropriate, which raised the issue of how much power the International could wield in setting up groups. Only the German delegates were willing to vote for Seelig's proposal, whereas Le Compte, who favored individual autonomy, called for a compromise.

During the discussion on the means of agitation, it became clear in certain proposals that a majority was ready to dismiss propaganda through the printed or spoken word and favored deeds—violent if necessary. Seelig defended the usefulness of a press and proposed an underground paper, but he withdrew this idea at the end of the congress (Le Compte favored underground multilanguage pamphlets). But the written word was of secondary importance, and many delegates supported Edward Nathan-Ganz, an illustrious anarchist from Boston who called for lessons in chemistry and its practical applications. Even though Seelig dismissed Nathan-Ganz's proposal, he was not entirely opposed to violence. He still regarded "'any strike at property and (political) persons'" as revolutionary.[105] And when Kropotkin insisted on including the word "morality" in the declaration (to prohibit indiscriminate violence), Seelig voted against it. "Morality should not be understood under the terms of the bourgeoisie," he once declared rather cryptically. "Morality should be understood as, since contemporary society is founded on immorality, the distancing from this immorality by any means which leads to morality."[106] Despite some mending by Kropotkin, the language of revolutionary terrorism prevailed.

The difficulty of reconciling unity, efficiency, and autonomy was again demonstrated with the issue of establishing an Information Bureau. Most delegates regarded a central bureau as a potential seed of centralized authority. Seelig was skeptical about the necessity of such a bureau, even though it would be stripped of any executive powers, and he remained unconvinced of the benefits of establishing one. In America, he argued, radical organizations operated openly to recruit members, alluding to the fact that the flow of information proceeded relatively unobstructed there. Kropotkin, however, insisted on the need for a clearinghouse to relieve the burden on periodicals that devoted several pages to letters and announcements. Brocher and Seelig then proposed to set up a bureau in each country. In the end it was decided to stick with one office located in London, to which Seelig, in name of the New York Social-Revolutionary Club, committed a quarterly contribution of four dollars.[107]

The international social-revolutionary congress of London reinstated the International Working People's Association (Internationale Arbeiter-Association; IAA), also referred to as the Black International, along federalist principles. No central agency was set up apart from an Information Bureau, which had no decision-making power. The idea of propaganda by deed was codified in the final text, a sign perhaps that Kropotkin's influence still had to yield to Bakuninist and Blanquist tenets. To the governments of the world, who received their information from exaggerated reports, the congress caused sensation and fear. In reality, the fragile anarchist movement was a tiny amalgam of loosely connected groups. As Max Nomad wrote, terroristic agitation gave anarchism a reputation "that made it appear much more dangerous to the existing system than it ever was in reality."[108]

What was the effect of these resolutions on the movement in the United States, specifically in New York? Seelig undoubtedly discussed the proceedings of the congress with his comrades in New York. As the representative of two German groups at the congress, Seelig expressed unease about the establishment of a European-based Information Bureau and his advocacy of autonomy for American anarchists. This suggests that a consensus could be found among some German American anarchists for the need to organize an American congress. After all, the London resolutions were vague, and the emphasis on group autonomy throughout the documents seemed to justify the building of an independent movement in the United States. Seelig was well aware of the different political circumstances in the United States—its relatively open democratic system and freedoms of the press and assembly.

By the summer of 1881, the German anarchists of New York were divided between two groups: the Social-Revolutionary Club and the seceded New York section 1, both affiliated with the IWPA. Both had gained new members, although totals probably did not exceed two hundred each. Still, the modest growth of the radical element was noticed. "'Several hints coming from that region,'" a German diplomatic envoy in Washington wrote in April 1881, "'lead me to suspect that New York threatens to become a headquarters of Anarchists.'"[109] The same diplomat worried that these New Yorkers were already discussing the idea of a congress to be held in New York. As it turned out, it was the Chicago radicals, mainly through the initiative of Paul Grottkau, who took this idea and made it possible. Grottkau envisioned the founding of a social revolutionary party, a plan the groups in New York could agree with.

Nineteen delegates gathered in Turner Hall on Chicago's North Side from 21 to 24 October 1881 to establish a revolutionary party in America. No less than ten came from the host city. Like in London, all delegates agreed that social revolution was the only road to liberation for the working class. The idea of propaganda by deed was from the beginning strongest among the New York social revolutionaries, many of them recent arrivals from Europe. Grottkau, who knew the country well, thought it impossible to achieve anything with such methods.[110] The Chicago social revolutionaries expressed strong support for self-defense and issued several pamphlets in association with the Lehr-und-Wehr Verein, a radical rifle club, to popularize it. As one paper had it: "Use the last bit of freedom that remains, build organizations, let everyone hold a good rifle, and the feeling of courage and independence will grow." It should be noted that there was an important difference in the vision of the rifle clubs and that of insurrectionists. The posture of the Lehr-und-Wehr Verein was mainly defensive, whereas advocates of propaganda by deed envisioned an offensive or direct-action strategy, a distinction that was not lost on the delegates. The convention was thus a gathering of anticompromise socialists, social revolutionaries, and anarchists. The SLP quickly ridiculed the congress, calling it "'a baker's dozen of Chicago malcontents and six delegates from outside cities.'"[111]

The foremost result of the congress was undoubtedly the adoption of a program that clearly reflected the dominance of the Chicago delegation and the creation of the Revolutionary Socialist Party (Revolutionäre socialistische Partei; RSP). The Chicago and midwestern groups, operating in America's heartland, sought to fashion an American activism opposing elections and the reformism of the SLP but embracing unionism as a means to revolutionize the workers. This approach differed from that of groups in New York and other East Coast cities with their eyes on the Old World, advocating direct action and uncompromising class war.

A regional difference between midwestern and East Coast anarchists was noted at the time. "It remains to be seen," pondered *The Labor Review* in October 1881, "how the Eastern revolutionists who ridicule trade unions as well as 'politics' will agree with the Chicago malcontents who advocate trades unions first and politics next, and in their published call profess to be opposed to dynamite schemes."[112] The Chicago program, drafted on 24 October, did not mention violent insurrection or political assassination but instead called on labor organizations to educate the masses through pamphlets, lectures, and workers' lyceums. In London, the tone of terrorism was too pervasive, and Chicagoans proceeded to amend the text. It was resolved that the delegates "'ratify the action of the Congress of the International Working People's Association, recently held in London,'" but stated that they had organized themselves "'in the United States in conformity with the conditions and circumstances surrounding us.'"[113] This addendum clearly sought to temper the idea of propaganda by deed, even though the delegates supported the Russian revolutionaries in their battle against the czar by any means necessary. But closer to home, the right of workers to defend themselves against assaults as well as a principled opposition to political compromise—the old points of contention with the SLP—were firmly codified in the Chicago document.

Even though the Chicago congress occupied itself with fleshing out an American social-revolutionary movement, it portrayed itself as an event within an international radical movement. In two resolutions, the delegates vowed their sympathy with and support for the Russian nihilists and the people of Ireland oppressed by the British government and English landlordism. Another resolution denounced the British authorities for jailing Johann Most, who by this time had served his seventh month in prison. Furthermore, three official party organs were chosen: Benjamin Tucker's *Liberty,* launched the previous August; the Danish-Norwegian *Den Nye Tid* (New times); and the German-language *Vorbote* (Herald). At the end of the congress, some three hundred men, women and children attended a reception to finalize a convention hailed for its harmonious proceedings. There was singing accompanied by musical societies and the recitation of poems by Justus Schwab.

Not much happened in the months after the congress. The Information Bureau, for instance, did not materialize until April 1883, and new groups formed slowly.[114] But the congress was not a failure. It acted as an American forum where radical socialists could lay out their visions and concerns, and it affirmed and clarified principles of class-consciousness and autonomy. Group life became the nucleus of the movement, the center of activity. When multiple groups existed in a city, a central committee—devoid of executive power—was set up to coordinate activities. Groups should at least have ten members who each paid a ten-cent monthly contribution, of which one-tenth went to the Information Bureau, which also received voluntary contributions. Expenditures exceeding twenty dollars were allowed only when all groups agreed. Schwab, as representative of the New York radicals, expressed doubts about the necessity of such a bureau. It is possible that Schwab resented the dominance of the Chicago crowd and may have wished for a New York bureau. Geographically as well as ideologically, New York was positioned somewhere between London and Chicago, waiting perhaps to affirm its own version of anarchism at a later congress. To judge the Chicago convention as ineffective or lacking in central coordination is to ignore the core concerns of the anarchist: individual autonomy, a critique of domination, and a secular, humanist vision for society. The mainstream and socialist press often equated the leaderless anarchist movement with a headless or irrational beast. If an anarchist leader such as Johann Most did emerge, the movement experienced intense unease and even strife. Anarchists valued autonomy and were suspicious of leadership.

Little information exists about the formation of groups in the wake of the Chicago congress. Some groups simply reconstituted themselves in accordance with the principles laid out in Chicago. (This was probably the case with the groups in the New Jersey industrial belt.) It is certain that by mid-December 1881, the New York section of the SLP reconstituted itself as Group I of the IWPA, which would become the main circle of German American anarchists in New York for nearly fifteen years. By April 1882, a German government agent reported the activities of New York Group I and the Social-Revolutionary Club.[115] Issues of arms and self-defense were the topic of the day, according to the same agent.

By 1882, the New York anarchist scene consisted of two groups in Manhattan, under the quiet leadership of Justus Schwab, and several smaller groups in New Jersey. The New York anarchists and social revolutionaries adhered to a different type of radicalism than the midwestern groups, dominated by Chicago. The historian Ronald Creagh has rightly pointed to the peculiar radical heritage New York harbored for decades. As an Atlantic gateway, it served as a dumping ground for European radicals, mainly from France, Germany, and Russia. New York had also been the headquarters of the International Workingmen's Association, a Marxist foothold in the lion's den of capitalism. The city was, among other things, the "cosmopolitan metropolis of the avengers."[116] Anarchist refugees translated their experience of European oppression into continued individual agitation in America. Unfailing support for the Russian revolutionaries (some of whom were arriving in New York) and the Irish nationalist rebels illustrates this reverence for the selfless rogue. As Ulrich Linse observes, the "insurrectional phase" of anarchism could be seen as "an ideological manifestation of what Eric Hobsbawm has described as the tradition of social brigandage and banditry."[117]

For these reasons, it would be a stretch to characterize the 1882 New York anarchist scene as an effective social movement. There was no coherent philosophy or convincing analysis of power or economic relations. It is doubtful that a strong commitment existed on the part of these anarchists to organize and educate workers. The nature of New York's labor force may have something to do with it. Unlike Chicago or a typical midwestern milltown, New York had no mines, railroad depots, or large-scale manufacturing. Smaller firms, especially clothing factories relying on individualized homework and subcontracting, drove its economy. Manhattan's workforce toiled in breweries, cigar factories, bakeries, slaughterhouses, and woodworking shops. But this is not the whole story: New York anarchists engaged in club life rather than collective labor agitation, as was the case in Chicago. "Each organization," Creagh wrote, "jealously defended its right of existence, and unscrupulously badgered its competitors."[118] From the beginning, New Yorkers shunned discussions of trade unionism, and participation in the labor movement was minimal.

The majority of the New York anarchists were German, but French, Bohemian, and Russian congregations of radicals stayed in close contact with them. The situation in autocratic Russia, especially the pogroms against Jews and the plight of the Russian radicals in their fight for democracy, was quite popular with many ordinary Americans. Political assassination, of course, appealed only to uncompromising anarchists. The Russian colony in New York took shape in 1882 and was largely made up of young intellectuals who frequented the various radical saloons and restaurants of New York's Lower East Side, especially Schwab's. Their ideas were a mixture of positivist and anarchist currents. The summer of 1882 saw the first instances of labor activism by Russian Jewish immigrants in the New York City area. Russian intellectuals founded the Propaganda Association for the Dissemination of Socialist Ideas among the Immigrant Jews (Propaganda Verein, in German), an association with little connection to the workers.[119] This circle immediately approached the German socialists, including members of the Social-Revolutionary Club, and held meetings together. Several outspoken Russian radicals eventually joined the socialist ranks, but many others tended to embrace a Bakuninist philosophy and felt out of place among German or Russian Marxists. "The Germans were inclined to be professorial," one historian wrote, "the Russians to be dashing and sentimental."[120] The nostalgia of revolutionary heroism shared by many Russians found a welcome ear with German anarchists. The Russians also refused to polarize socialism and anarchism, as the German Marxists were prone to do. Ideological camaraderie in the radical circles of New York thus crossed ethnic boundaries with Russian exiles, reinforcing the myth of the heroic revolutionist. Still, the Germans, united by language and other cultural traits, mostly networked and socialized among themselves.

There was an irony in the fact that the German anarchists constituted an insular ethnic entity and at the same time proudly portrayed their adherence to international anarchism as expounded by the congresses of London and Chicago. During these early years, a tension emerged between the ideal of internationalism and the reality of Americanism, a tension that would later pose problems of identity and relevance. New York anarchists, while isolated in a Manhattan ghetto, styled themselves as internationalists, and it is perhaps not insignificant that their most popular paper (*Freiheit*) was—for the time being—produced in London. Midwestern anarchists mainly subscribed to homegrown papers such as *Vorbote* and *Chicagoer Arbeiter-Zeitung*.

Chicago during the early 1880s was clearly the center of radicalism in the United States, with a sizeable anarchist movement asserting itself in the cause of labor. But New York would soon rival that prominence with a visit of Germany's most notorious—and to many, controversial—sons. In the eyes of many German radicals at home and abroad, Johann Most was an icon of revolutionary politics, and his activities in Britain were closely watched. He spent most of 1882 in jail, leaving the running of *Freiheit* to associates; he was finally released in October. Possibly through the initiative of Schwab, the New York Social-Revolutionary Club decided to invite Most for an extensive lecture tour throughout the United States. The club formed a committee to draft a letter outlining the main reasons for the invitation: strengthening the bonds between social revolutionaries on both sides of the Atlantic, revitalizing dormant anarchist groups in America, and providing Most with a much-needed diversion after months of imprisonment. The letter subsequently appeared in *Freiheit* on 21 October 1882; they expected Most's arrival in the first half of November.

Meanwhile, the *Freiheit* office in London received letters from continental groups urging Most to stay in England and resume the clandestine distribution of the paper into German-speaking Europe. *Freiheit* was the only German-language anarchist organ available to Germans and Austrians, and nearly all deemed it the backbone of anarchist propaganda for Germany. However, Most realized that financial support for such an undertaking was dwindling. Many of his best activists (such as Johann Neve) left for the continent, and the British government was less tolerant of the radical community in the heart of its capital. To make matters worse, the repressive climate made it impossible to find a printer willing to produce the paper. Before he set off to Liverpool, Most had contacted Schwab, requesting him to continue *Freiheit* in New York until his arrival.[121]

Most boarded the steamer *Wisconsin* in Liverpool on 2 December 1882. A week later, the first New York issue of *Freiheit* appeared, with an apologetic explanation for its removal to the New World. To many German activists, this meant the end of the propaganda movement in and around Germany. Interestingly, Schwab, who acted as interim editor, was confronted by opposition among members of the Social-Revolutionary Club, who also insisted that *Freiheit* should remain in Europe. It is possible that by moving his paper abroad, Most sought to escape opponents in London, and one is reminded of Marx's decision to move the headquarters of the International to New York.

3 *Johann Most and the Pittsburgh Congress*

Anarchists have always struggled with the difficulty of reconciling a well-organized, anti-authoritarian movement with the fundamental principle of individual autonomy. In other words, how can individualism and community coexist? All anarchist theorists and practitioners have wrestled with this conundrum, including the German anarchists in New York. The German intellectual tradition has produced two opposite poles of this social-philosophical spectrum: Max Stirner articulated the most extreme form of individualism, while Georg Hegel, and to some extent Marx, expressed the historical dimension (and mission) of the collective consciousness. Johann Most arrived at anarchism with substantial Marxist baggage, while many other Germans and Austrians had been educated by Bakunin, Kropotkin, and later Landauer. The following pages present Most as an exponent of organizational anarchism and mark his numerous contributions to the founding of a revolutionary anarchist movement in America.

Johann Most was a major figure in American anarchism, and he became the public voice for German revolutionary anarchism in the Atlantic world during the last two decades of the nineteenth century. Most convinced his fellow radicals that an organized revolutionary movement was not only possible but necessary. A stubborn, defiant firebrand, Most had no trouble attracting the attention of the press and the police. He was ridiculed, maligned, and jailed numerous times, but Most had grown a thick skin and managed to return every time to his editor's desk ready to roll off the next edition of his beloved paper. As an orator and editor, he took charge of a propaganda drive that revived a sleepy collection of social revolutionaries in a handful of industrial centers. He energized the German anarchists in the United States and made headlines in the process. When he arrived in New York, the center of journalism and popular culture, the mainstream press treated him initially as a curiosity and eventually as a villain. Nearly every story about him was distorted or sensational and sometimes downright false.[1] Every mass meeting on the Lower East Side drew an army of reporters and a few cartoonists as well. Beyond the publicity and caricatures lay a restless soul committed to his beliefs. He became one of many architects of an anarchist movement in America and was praised by those close to him for his intellect and integrity. His life's journey began in Bavaria, took him across central Europe to London, and eventually led to the New World, much of which he saw by train during lecture tours. He lived twenty-three years in the United States, mostly in Manhattan.

Due to media attention, Most's persona has been overblown. Too often his fame has obscured other aspects of the German anarchist movement. In the historiography of American radicalism, Johann Most and the Haymarket affair usually serve as a summary of German American anarchism. Most was certainly a key figure in New York's anarchist milieu, but closer inquiry reveals diverse opinions, personalities, and neighborhoods. Much of that diversity can be seen as a reaction, in one way or another, to Most's standing as leading revolutionary. He maintained this position through his control of *Freiheit,* New York's largest-circulating anarchist paper. Still, his personal history and his character, frustrations, and visions are important to understand the German anarchist movement in New York.

Throughout much of his adult life, Most was a lone wanderer who felt bitterness toward society and intense hatred for the privileged classes. This disaffection was rooted in his childhood. He was born outside marriage on 5 February 1846 in the Bavarian town of Augsburg because his father could not afford a marriage license at the time. His father was a lower clerk who dreamed of becoming an actor. His mother was a well-educated, freethinking governess who refused to let the religious conservatism of Bavaria enter the household. Only in school was Most exposed to the rigors of a traditional Catholic education, and it clearly was a difficult time for him. At age twelve, he was expelled for organizing a strike against a particularly strict teacher. The same year, the death of his beloved mother and a sister left lifelong scars. His father remarried, but Most never tolerated the rule of his sometimes cruel stepmother, whom he characterized as "'bigoted, coarse, [and] greedy.'"[2] Nearly all who knew Most or wrote about his early life attributed much significance to the boy's physical condition. He suffered a painful inflammation of the jaw, and after consulting several quacks, an operation in March 1859 saved his life but left his face markedly disfigured. This disfigurement was the cause of a string of humiliating and traumatic experiences in his young adulthood—though Most himself mentioned the ordeal only cursorily.[3]

Most first encountered unfair labor conditions when he was placed with a bookbinder as an apprentice. "'[The master] compelled me to work from fourteen to sixteen hours a day,'" he remembered, "'for which my father had to pay 100 florins.'"[4] At the end of an apprenticeship, it was customary for a novice to embark on an itinerant search for employment. From the beginning, Most had trouble finding work. Eventually he learned that no master wanted customers greeted by Most with his deformed face. For a time he turned toward acting, perhaps influenced by his father. When that also fell through, he contemplated suicide. The constant rejections drained his powers and fed a growing hatred of privilege. Over the course of twenty years, Most increasingly came to view the world with anger and distrust. It was a long enough period for the bitterness to take root in his personality. "'From my earliest youth,'" Most once wrote, "'I had the best opportunity for studying the whole social question from a practical and painful side.'"[5]

Johann Most never became a full-time bookbinder or a professional actor, although he did occasionally appear on stage as an actor during and after the 1890s. Most instead found his vocation as an orator and editor in the labor movement in Austria, Germany, and the United States. He discovered his calling in 1867 in western Switzerland, where he attended a labor festival organized by the local branch of the International Workingmen's Association, which he soon joined. The speakers gripped him immediately. Their ideas addressed questions he had pondered for some time. He never missed such gatherings and soon became a familiar face. When Most was given opportunities to address an audience himself, his eloquence and humorous renditions delighted the workers, and his speeches grew in popularity. His eloquence even helped to increase membership of the local branches.

Activities in neighboring Austria propelled him into the limelight of the labor movement, a turn of events that he could scarcely have dreamed of five years earlier. It was in Austria that Most, now a Marxist of sorts, built a following among workers drawn to his theatrical and satirical pieces. He became a master of tirade, invective, and caustic tongue-lashings against the bourgeoisie. His speeches were straightforward and popular, but not vulgar; his delivery was intense and gesticulant. Attending a speech by Most was not only an intellectual but a visceral experience. "The giant of the revolution rages and roars," remembered Israel Kopeloff. "His fiery words almost bring froth to his lips . . . his sharp phrases have the impact upon us of the bombs and the dynamite of which he so often speaks. . . . The audience was as if in an hypnotic spell the entire time. . . . I was certain that it was but for Most to give the word, and the audience would rush to build barricades and begin the revolution."[6] From the moment he mounted a platform, Most's bitter sarcasm and his love for histrionics transformed him into an effective—and to some, dangerous—propagandist, a talent he would later make use of in America. After a large demonstration in 1869, Most was arrested and sentenced to prison. But, as Max Nomad observed, "Most left the prison with a greatly enhanced ego."[7] He was deemed the ringleader by the authorities, who recognized his "'unusual intelligence and determined character.'"[8]

When the Paris Commune broke out in the spring of 1871, the authorities expelled Most from Austria. The "impudent foreigner," as the newspapers called him, returned to his native Germany and joined the labor movement there. Most's family life became affected by his rise in notoriety. While working in Chemnitz in 1872, he met Clara Hänsch, daughter of a local constable, and shortly thereafter they became engaged. Most, by this time a popular speaker, spent much of 1873 once more in jail for insulting the emperor and his army; he was released at the end of that year. His reputation secured him a seat in the Reichstag as early as January 1874. In that month, Johann Most and Clara Hänsch finally married.[9] During Most's other prison terms, Hänsch lived in Chemnitz, where rumors of her alleged adultery spread, contaminating their relationship.[10] Their first son, born in September, died a few weeks later. In December 1879, they settled in London but separated in 1880. Clara Hänsch died two years later, the year Most decided to travel to America.

Most's election to the Reichstag epitomized the determination and popularity of a man of humble origins and a troubled youth. This experience proved a letdown, and it represents an important step in his political development. He was rarely allowed to speak, despite numerous requests to take the stand. The ceremonious sessions of grand eloquence, echoed in the ornate auditorium, all seemed pompous and frustrating. The silencing by his distinguished colleagues forced him to develop a public persona outside the realm of official politics. His irreverence and theatricality were better suited for informal gatherings of working-class soulmates than for the stuffiness of the house floor. As Rocker noted, Most was a man of the public and of publicity.[11] He decided to return to the labor halls and beer gardens to address working people directly. During a speech at a rally in 1874, he praised the Commune but disapproved of individual acts of violence. He assailed the church during a series of lectures in 1877–78 in the Ruhr region. Yet, on most occasions Most's oratory was an embarrassment to the party elders, perhaps precisely because he enjoyed a wide and growing audience of supporters. Karl Marx at first welcomed Most's brash posturing but later attributed this to his "bottomless personal vanity."[12] One German American socialist wrote in a letter that Most's motive for his propaganda activities was "high-flown ambition."[13] Nevertheless, this gift for public speaking proved a central element of his role in the American anarchist movement.

Johann Most also excelled as an editor. The pamphlets and labor papers he edited were widely circulated in Europe and America. Although chiefly known for his editorship of *Freiheit,* Most began writing and editing as early as 1870, during his imprisonment in Austria. He first took to proletarian poetry, composing *Die Arbeitsmänner* (Workingmen), a ballad that became a classic for generations of German workers. He also edited a small prison paper. In Germany, he made his first foray into socialist journalism: between July 1871 and October 1873, he was editor of the *Chemnitzer Freie Presse,* and from 1876 until 1878, he co-edited the *Berliner Freie Presse* (each of these positions was interrupted by imprisonment). August Sartorius von Waltershausen noted Most's talent for critical journalism and his ready wit. In 1879, Most was asked to edit *Freiheit,* a new propaganda paper launched—without party approval—by Germans in London. This paper, which he would eventually control, became the forum through which Most developed his own often incendiary style of writing.

From the time he entered the German socialist movement in 1871, Most had to choose between conflicting persuasions in the muddied realm of political idealism. In the midst of factional discord between Marxists and Lassalleans, Most sided with the Marxists, though it should be emphasized that he was a moderate and often acted as a mediator, ready to compromise on some issues. As the editor of *Freiheit,* Most was immediately swept up in the factionalism of London's radical milieu, a clash of personalities and disagreement over issues of underground propaganda that would eventually split the movement.

Most's involvement in the labor movement was not solely a quest to strengthen his personal charisma, as some colleagues later charged. His sense of outrage in the face of injustice was deeply felt, and the plight of Swiss, Austrian, and German workers resonated with him. As an autodidact, Most constantly explored new ideas in politics, economics, and historical analyses that might remedy the woes of the world. Before 1882, when he first set foot in Manhattan, several sources had made a lasting impact on his thinking, and we see a continued evolution of his opinions throughout the 1890s. First in 1866, as a young man of twenty, Most began reading classics, historical works, and books on natural science. Some have suggested that his intensive study may have been a way to compensate for his physical malformation.[14] Most's intellectual maturation was also undoubtedly nurtured by his travels throughout much of Central Europe, including northern Italy, from 1863 to 1868. Hermann Gruelich, a socialist bookbinder in Zürich, was probably the first person to act as tutor to the young Most. He described him as a "'shy, young man, thin, beardless, with a crooked face.'"[15] Most further explored Marxism during the early 1870s and aligned himself with the Eisenachers. It was the first time he leaned towards a more militant stance. Waltershausen simply stated that Most chose the "side of Radicalism."[16]

Most undertook much of his learning and writing behind bars. From 1868 until 1878, he spent more than five years in prison, which he called his "'universities.'"[17] He read Marx's *Das Kapital* while in Chemnitz and Zwickau jails, and in 1874 he managed to publish *Kapital und Arbeit* (Capital and labor), the first popularization of Marx's magnum opus. He also studied the work of Eugen Dühring, a blind professor in Berlin whose anti-authoritarian, collectivist socialism captured the minds of many young Social-Democrats, many of whom were searching for a coherent philosophy. At the time, Dühring nearly eclipsed Marx and Engels in popularity. In reaction, they both set out to destroy the professor's influence. As a supporter of Dühring, this angered Most. Dühring sought to reconcile individualism with a socialism that was antistatist, or "anticratic," as he termed it. He advocated principles of free association in which decentralized productive groups were made up of autonomous individuals who held, but did not exclusively own, the means of production. His "free socialism" played a significant role in Most's philosophical journey toward anarchism, although Dühring's antistatism did not initially impress him.

If Most was a devoted card-carrying Social-Democrat until 1879, he was nonetheless perceived as a maverick, a self-taught rebel with a biting tongue and pen. No less than two months after his election to the Reichstag, Most published a sketch called *Parlamentarische Guckkastenbilder* (Parliamentary peepshows), an early glimpse of his growing antiparliamentarism. He never felt comfortable with rules of etiquette or hierarchy. This disdain for erudition and officialdom was more a character trait than a philosophical principle.

Most's expulsion under the Antisocialist Law in December 1878 turned him not only against the German state but also against the party leaders who seemed unwilling to resist Bismarck's policies. Compared to Germany, "free" Britain seemed a welcome change for Most. Yet, numerous undercover agents had infiltrated the London radical community, and Most was unprepared for the watchfulness demanded of the comrades. His friends repeatedly warned Most to be more vigilant because he acted careless at times and seemed too eager to trust strangers.

When Most arrived in London, he became an employee of the Communist club (CABV), and as the editor of *Freiheit* he gradually took a more revolutionary stance. During his stay—from December 1878 until December 1882—he continued to be influenced by members of the radical émigré circle. Karl Schneidt, for one, believed that the ideas of others in London had a great impact on Most. "Johann Most understands it very well," Schneidt wrote, "to make the ideas of others his own, he can then fully accustom himself to them to the point of regarding them as his own intellectual property."[18] Most was still a Social-Democrat, but the revolutionary fervor brewing in London brought him in contact with more extreme thinkers, such as anarchists. According to Ronald Creagh, Most had already met the anarchist August Reinsdorf and discussed issues of revolutionary violence.[19] Perhaps as a result of that meeting, Most became convinced of the soundness of propaganda by deed. This was a radical change from his previous attitude. In June 1878, only months before his move to London, Most had denounced Max Hödel's attempt on the life of the kaiser as an act of insanity. Most even produced a lecture in May on "assassinations and social democracy" that stressed the peaceful intentions of social democracy. In London, apart from propaganda by deed, Most was also deeply impressed by Russian revolutionary exiles and their unwavering dedication to the cause.

In addition to Schneidt and Reinsdorf, Andreas Scheu, Edouard Vaillant, and especially Victor Dave made the greatest impact on Most's intellectual development. Scheu was a key figure in the Austrian labor movement who had been imprisoned in Vienna with Most in 1870. Vaillant was a leader of the Blanquist movement in France and a Commune veteran. According to Becker, Scheu and Vaillant conspired to force Most to adopt purely revolutionary rhetoric in *Freiheit*.[20]

Victor Dave, a Belgian intellectual, was Johann Most's closest friend and mentor in London. He was born in 1845 in Jambes near Namur, Belgium, and went on to study at the Universities of Liège and Brussels. Early on, he developed a skill for journalism and mastered five languages, which he put to use by translating German authors such as Bernstein,

Lassalle, and Karl Kautsky. First influenced by Proudhon's writings, Dave from 1865 to 1873 was involved in the Belgian socialist movement and served as a journalist for the First International. In 1868 he traveled to Switzerland, where he met Mikhail Bakunin, who soon became his mentor. Schneidt remembered Dave as a trusted gentleman-friend one day and an agitator and schemer ready to crush a rival the next.[21] Dave took the side of Bakunin during the 1872 Congress of the International at The Hague. In Paris during the years 1878–79, he associated with a small circle of German revolutionaries, where he met Most for the first time; they quickly became friends. With his beard and steel-rimmed spectacles, Victor Dave had the appearance of a respectable middle-class erudite, but he nevertheless believed firmly in an anarchist community built on the ruins of the existing order. For Dave, the end justified the means, whether it was corruption, assassination, expropriation, or conspiracy. Violence in the form of armed resistance was simply unavoidable. The friendship between Most and Dave was symbiotic: Dave increased the flow of anarchist propaganda into Germany through Most's *Freiheit,* while Most expanded his reputation as editor at a time when the fight with the orthodox Social-Democrats and their organ, *Sozialdemokrat,* was in full swing. It was an animosity that grew more grim and personal. Socialists spread rumors that Most was insane and walked the streets with a dagger, obsessed with imitating the French radical Jean Paul Marat. Most's reaction was frequently hotheaded. Schneidt contended that the increasing nastiness of attacks on Most compelled him to expand the limits of permissible language of his rebuttals in the pages of *Freiheit.*[22] At the same time, socialist leaders were increasingly prepared to take more drastic measures to deal with party radicals such as Most.

Most was officially expelled from the SAPD in August 1880, during a secret party congress in Switzerland. He may not have been a tactful politician, but he held many ideas in common with his excommunicators and certainly did not wish to leave the party. The labor movement had brought immeasurable meaning to his life after years spent lost and floundering. His talents were widely recognized, and his party membership card proved that he was part of a larger movement and ideal. Though the expulsion affected him deeply, in the end it merely hastened his commitment to anarchism. A few months before the secret congress he met Reinsdorf again in Switzerland, an encounter that deepened his commitment to an anarchist perspective.

Johann Most now assumed a place at the helm of London's anarchist movement. Smuggling *Freiheit* into Germany (with remarkable success) was the primary task, aside from the formation of cells across Germany consisting of no more than six people to help distribute the paper. It is clear that Blanqui's theory of secret organization played a significant role in Most's and many of his friends' intellectual development.

By the time Most moved to America in December 1882, his radical philosophy consisted of a mixture of Marxist-Blanquist and Bakuninist ideas. Marx and Blanqui advocated the violent seizure of power and the establishment of a revolutionary dictatorship, but the latter opted for a secret organization as opposed to a political party. Bakunin agreed with secret agitation but did not approve of any form of temporary government staffed by an advance guard, even if proletarian. He sought to instigate a spontaneous rebellion rather than to lead a planned revolution. In light of Bismarck's policies, however, many Marxists and Lassalleans came to adopt Blanquist ideas. Most also retained Blanquist notions despite Victor Dave's influence. After Blanqui's death, for instance, Most produced a commemorative, black-rimmed issue of *Freiheit.* Even so, Most was perhaps more strongly pulled toward the mind of Bakunin. The 1881 London Congress, which Most was unable to attend, though he was aware of the proceedings, clearly favored Bakunin's legacy of spontaneous rebellion and protest in part because social revolutionaries realized they were too weak to topple the existing order. By 1883 Most considered himself something of a collectivist anarchist. "The anarchism that was then in my mind," he wrote in 1903, "was, theoretically speaking, of an extremely mediocre vintage."[23] The historian Heiner Becker has suggested that Most's entourage in London radicalized quicker than he did and that his duties as editor compelled him to include anarchistic material for which he seemed at times slightly apologetic. For example, when in 1881 *Freiheit* published Bakunin's *Revolutionary Principles,* Most was quick to assure his readers that "'we have not become Anarchists. But it is true that we regard them as honest social revolutionaries who stand closest to us.'"[24] This reveals how derogatory a term "anarchist" still was, clearly inferior to the use of "social revolutionary." Most's hesitance in identifying with anarchism seems to have disappeared as soon as he arrived in the United States. His conversion to anarchism may have occurred in his London prison cell, or perhaps during his ocean voyage to the New World. He may have presumed that an openly anarchist stance would do less harm in an open society such as the United States with a large German population and liberal laws concerning freedom of assembly and the press. His knowledge of America, however, was minimal; Justus Schwab was his most reliable guide.

On the cold winter morning of 18 December 1882 in New York City, a handful of Germans wearing red ribbons and carrying a red flag arrived at Pier 38 on the Hudson River at the end of King Street in Manhattan. The steamer *Wisconsin* from Liverpool had docked there around eight o'clock to allow the first passengers to disembark. One of them, a bearded man of middle stature, was greeted heartily. Johann Most had entered a new country of which he knew little. His arrival in the American metropolis came at the end of an eventful but dreary year spent mostly in a London jail. It was also the year his estranged wife Clara Hänsch passed away, and a time when the London movement struggled to maintain a sense of community. Prospects for the continuance of *Freiheit* seemed dim at best. But Most intended to return to Europe once he judged the situation safe. "As soon as I can," he answered Victor Dave as late as August 1884, when asked when he would come back. "Since *Freiheit* is so dear to me, and since its publication in Europe still cannot be made possible yet, I will have to remain here for awhile."[25] The cardinal importance of periodicals for the anarchist movement, something Most understood all too well, would one day become a source of bitter rivalries and tension.

The Germans who greeted Most that morning were all members of the Social-Revolutionary Club, which had invited him for an American lecture tour. Several social-revolutionary groups already existed across the eastern and midwestern United States. In New York, Justus Schwab had laid the groundwork for the network of anarchists, with his saloon acting as a key meeting place. This early infrastructure enabled Most to establish relations among German American radicals and expand the community in New York and elsewhere.[26] The most influential radical projects in the United States at the time consisted of the *New Yorker Volkszeitung,* a sometime independent-minded socialist paper in New York, and the Chicago groups centered around *Vorbote* and *Chicagoer Arbeiterzeitung,* where Paul Grottkau was a leading figure. Grottkau quickly realized that the arrival of Most could undermine his own leadership position.

The New York revolutionaries organized a large meeting in Cooper Institute to welcome Most on the day of his arrival. No fewer than five thousand people crammed into the great hall to hear the famed orator. Only a small portion of the crowd was anarchist; the majority were German workers of different political persuasions who had come out of curiosity.[27] Victor Drury and Edward King introduced Most. Drury was a French immigrant and veteran socialist who had been active in New York since the 1860s, including within the International and the Knights of Labor. A skillful English speaker, he once declared himself a "'patriot of the universe'" during a speech in Cooper Union against the Franco-Prussian War.[28] Edward King was a moderate Scottish-born reformer and positivist philosopher who lectured to radical East Side intellectuals. His ties to the anarchists strengthened when he opened a saloon in Brooklyn that served as a meeting place.

The English portion of Most's speech was rough, while his German lecture was entirely devoted to the politics of repression in Europe. A perceptive newspaper reporter noticed Most's peculiar way of orating, which to him seemed foreign and unimpressive. "As an orator, Mr. Most would not earn a reputation as he did by spitting Socialistic fire through the columns of a newspaper. His voice is pitched in a high key, there are no modulations in its tone, and when he wishes to emphasize any particular sentiment he simply screeches and grows red in the face, while the peculiar expression of his countenance as he throws his head back and shakes his arm reminds one of the boasting braggart who stands at a safe distance and calls other people hard names."[29] Interestingly, the newspaper reporter suggests that Most, and perhaps all anarchists, were merely loudmouths and somehow too cowardly for action—but anarchist action was precisely what frightened the mainstream press and its readers.

Emma Goldman remembered Most's oratory much differently. "He spoke eloquently and picturesquely. As if by magic, his disfigurement disappeared, his lack of physical distinction was forgotten." Goldman recognized Most's passionate nature once he was given an audience. "He seemed transformed into some primitive power, radiating hatred and love, strength and inspiration. The rapid current of his speech, the music of his voice, and his sparkling wit, all combined to produce an effect almost overwhelming. He stirred me to my depths."[30]

Most's "fire" during his 1882 welcome speech was directed at militarism, indirect taxation, and monopoly weighing down on the workers in Europe. Russia and central Europe received particular attention because he believed a violent confrontation was imminent. He believed in spontaneous revolt and scorned social theoreticians who rationalized revolution and its place in historical development. It is important to note that this speech was almost entirely devoted to European affairs, and in it, Johann Most publicly espoused anarchism for the first time. Three final resolutions were adopted that bestowed upon the new arrival a position of leadership—a state of affairs many anarchists would come to regret. The resolutions listed below were not binding and should not be construed as the collective opinion of the attending crowd:

Resolved: We accept that the material and spiritual interests of humankind can only be shown to advantage by anarchism.

Resolved: We greet Most as the fearless representative and apostle of anarchism and we welcome him warmly.

Resolved: We commit ourselves to supporting Johann Most in his mission to revolutionize the people of the United States.[31]

From these statements, it seems clear that the organizers and perhaps a substantial portion of the crowd had for some time made up its mind about where they stood in relation to the larger socialist movement. The shift in tone and content of *Freiheit* during the previous years emboldened them to adopt anarchist ideas. The split with the New York orthodox socialists had left this group of social revolutionaries somewhat disorganized, and the arrival of a battle-scarred rabble rouser like Most solidified the group as an essentially anarchist coalition divorced from the Socialist Labor party.

At the end of December 1882, Most embarked on an extensive lecture tour throughout the East and Midwest. He delivered speeches in crowded halls, rallying workers behind the anarchist banner. On 28 December, for instance, he spoke at the Aurora Turner Hall in Chicago, where he outlined a new society that would emerge after a social revolution. Workers responded favorably to Most's revolutionary project partly because the economic recession in 1883 threatened wages and job security. New anarchist and social-revolutionary groups were formed in cities and industrial towns across the eastern United States, with members subscribing to *Freiheit.* The American mainstream press at times devoted generous attention to Most's campaign trail but typically portrayed him as a foreign lunatic. They even printed excerpts from his speeches, to the delight of the anarchists. Curiosity on the part of newspaper editors ensured that at least part of the anarchists' message reached a relatively wide audience. During the first half of the 1880s, before these newspapers turned hostile, such exposure shows that foreign anarchists were not entirely absent from the political spectrum at the time. Some conservative religious groups took the so-called red menace seriously and staged several counterdemonstrations in Chicago, Cleveland, and Philadelphia, which only attracted more reporters. The first months of 1883 therefore constituted a publicity tour for immigrant anarchism in the United States. A lecture tour by a notorious German revolutionary suddenly put anarchism on the front page, pitted socialists against anarchists, and roused workers to form or join radical groups and emboldened them to publicly display the red flag. Most eagerly exploited the attention he received, but to many Americans, he crossed the line of polite language too many times.

A key effect of Most's arrival and subsequent propaganda tour was the establishment of *Freiheit* as the mouthpiece of German-language revolutionary anarchism, at least on the East Coast. The paper benefited from a substantial increase in subscriptions in the wake of the speaking tour. The extent of *Freiheit*'s reach can be judged from the number of agents across the country, which rose from only one in 1880 to twenty in 1883, eight of which in the New York area alone. Membership of anarchist groups in New York and New Jersey also rose during the early 1880s. A spirit of unity and solidarity and a heightened sense of revolutionary mission began to replace the previous state of isolation and inertia.

With all the hype of united anarchism, the principle of autonomy was not abandoned, and group members remained wary of central direction. They did tolerate an Information Bureau of the Socialist Federation of North America, established in April 1883 as stipulated in the Chicago Congress resolutions.

Johann Most embarked on a second propaganda tour from the beginning of April 1883 until June, this time venturing as far west as Omaha, Nebraska. He went to the Boston area and spoke in St. Joseph, Missouri. New groups popped up in Pittsburgh and St. Louis, while existing ones increased their membership. This second tour, however, lacked the enthusiasm and novelty of the first one. Even *Freiheit* refrained from overly triumphant language. Like Hasselmann in 1880, Most was perceived as a greenhorn and a newcomer. His ignorance of American culture was striking, and his ranting about American injustices was not always taken seriously.

Throughout his twenty-three years in the United States, Most assumed a leadership role as orator, editor, and publicist. In what must have been a grueling weekly schedule, he ran and edited *Freiheit,* wrote most of its articles, composed pamphlets, addressed local group meetings, attended picnics, and was invariably asked to speak at large gatherings set up for the entire anarchist community in New York. In the process, Most drew a circle of committed and talented men around him (few women can be found in the records). They played significant roles in the German anarchist movement in New York, mainly as speakers and colporteurs (agents for the anarchist press). When Most was scheduled at group gatherings, he tackled historical and practical as well as theoretical issues. He clarified the significance of the 1848 revolution in Germany, outlined the goals and methods of anarchism, surveyed the American labor movement, and railed against elections and the prison system. He also lectured for non-German groups such as the Yiddish-speaking Pioneers of Freedom (Pionire der Frayhayt) and the Russian Progressive Union.

Most always stressed the importance of social revolution and called attention to the stupidity of elections and political compromise. He was particularly fond of promoting self-defense tactics against the tyrants of the world. Slogans such as "Wake up workers! Let us place ourselves in a state of defense against our enemies," and, "No armistice between us and our enemies," were common refrains in Most's parlance.[32] In July 1886, *Freiheit* published an article called "An die Gewehre!" which had the double meaning of "to the rifles" and "let's get started!"[33] Most urged his comrades to stop spending money on bourgeois politics and instead purchase a good rifle or build a defense fund. To underscore the importance of resistance, he cited episodes of violence perpetrated or condoned by the state, such as fifty-seven lynchings that occurred in 1882. He popularized the concept of propaganda by deed, which, he cautioned, should only be engaged in if approved beforehand by the oppressed.

Most's concern about the combat-readiness of the working class was not only a rhetorical device. He felt that revolutionary workers should be knowledgeable about the means of defense. In 1884 he secretly moved to Jersey City Heights to work in an explosives factory in order to educate himself (Most also planned to send explosives to Europe). He also realized that most German anarchists were craftspeople and had no knowledge of chemistry, so he published *Revolutionäre Kriegswissenschaft* (Revolutionary war science), one of the most peculiar pamphlets in American radical literature. A manual on the techniques as well as the dangers of explosives and revolutionary warfare, this booklet helped seal the fate of the anarchist's image as terrorist. But the apparent preoccupation with explosives in the early 1880s must be placed into context. Violence by police, soldiers, and detectives against working Americans was a daily occurrence, and much of it was excessive and remained unpunished. Advocacy of the use of grenades and bullets against striking workers had been common in the popular press since the 1870s. In addition, Most was fond of drama, of rousing people in anticipation of a final act. His own demeanor was easily ignited into impetuous rage. As in Germany, the public realm was his stage, a pulpit for ideas and emotions. His public stance in editorials and speeches should therefore be viewed separately from his private opinions, which were often more nuanced. The historian Max Nettlau, who was not unsympathetic to Most, once noted that "behind the rudest words there is either a very accurate judgment or a tender feeling, that, in order to hide himself, is veiled in rudeness."[34] Moreover, Most's public rhetoric and editorship should be judged within the context of New York and of his own idiomatic-linguistic framework. In the opinion of one anarchist free-love magazine, "Herr Most writes a peculiar style in German. He excels in lurid invective. His paper can be understood and appreciated only by one who adds to a knowledge of German, a knowledge of New York life, and both German and American slang. Nobody understands and relishes pure High German better than John Most, but it suits his fancy to get up the greater part of the Freiheit in a strange macaronic tongue that is very puzzling to a newly-arrived German, be he ever so learned."[35]

In addition to editing and lecturing, Most published a series of pamphlets with a large circulation. Among the most popular where *Die Eigenthumsbestie* (The beast of property), in which he lambasted the privileged for their predatory greed and avarice, and *Die Gottespest* (The god pestilence), a rabid atheistic tract reprinted numerous times in several languages. Both were published in New York in 1883, and both were distributed in Germany by the thousands. In *Die freie Gesellschaft* (The free society), which appeared in July 1884, Most elaborated his vision of an anarchist society. His model still reflected a Bakuninist influence, a collectivist anarchism that stressed the autonomy of producer and consumer groups and the free exchange of goods proportionate to the labor involved.

After two years in America, Johann Most had become the front man of revolutionary anarchism, the uncrowned spokesperson for revolution. Most was invited to participate in a nationally advertised public debate with Paul Grottkau entitled "Anarchism or Communism?" that took place on 24 May 1884 in Chicago. The entire session, which was divided into two statements and two rebuttals, was published as a forty-eight-page booklet by the Chicago groups of the IWPA.[36]

During the 1890s, Johann Most began to temper his advocacy of revolutionary terrorism, which had cost him many months in prison already. He questioned the benefits of violence as early as 1887, when he was released from Blackwell's Island penitentiary. For all his rhetoric, Most never committed a violent crime, a fact that some extremists cited as proof of his lack of militancy. By 1890, his attention was more and more directed to the survival of *Freiheit* and the development of more efficient oral and written propaganda. No longer dismissing labor unions, he embraced a mild form of anarchosyndicalism in *Unsere Stellung in der Arbeiterbewegung* (Our position in the labor movement), published in May 1890. At the start of the new century, Most abandoned propaganda by deed as a serious anarchist tactic, but this did not prevent him from occasionally publishing provocative texts. In September 1901, he scheduled for publication "Mord contra Mord" (Murder versus murder), an article by the German radical Karl Heinzen on political murder. It appeared at the worst possible time. One day before its release, a disgruntled American claiming to be an anarchist shot President William McKinley, who later died from the wound. Most was arrested a week later and put in prison once again. At age fifty-five, he could barely suppress his agony when the judge sent him to jail; it further convinced him that terrorism was wrong and counterproductive.

Underneath Most's stubborn demeanor of a committed revolutionist hid a gentle, engaging, and at times passionate personality that could only be recognized by those who were close to him. Most's experience with his stepmother and perhaps his facial deformation, which may have damaged his sense of masculinity, combined to instill in him deep suspicions about women. In 1889, Johann Most was introduced to the twenty-year-old Emma Goldman, who had just arrived in New York. Goldman and Most, then forty-three, became friends, comrades, and for a brief period lovers (they remained friends until 1892). This appears to be Most's first romantic involvement since he arrived in the United States six years earlier. He later befriended Helene Minkin, a young Jewish woman who—together with her older sister Anna—was Goldman's roommate. Parting with Goldman was difficult. Most admitted that he sought comfort and domestic security, things Goldman made clear she could not give him. As Goldman later remembered: "A home, children, the care and attention ordinary women can give, who have no other interest in life but the man they love and the children they bear him—that was what he needed and felt he had found in Helen."[37]

Not much is known about Helene Minkin's early life; she may have been born in 1871 or 1874. She became a midwife after working long hours in sweatshops as a young woman. Most and Minkin never formally married, but on 19 May 1894, their first son, John Jr., was born, followed somewhat later by a second son, Lucifer.[38] According to John Jr., his parents' relationship was rather quarrelsome, which he blamed in part on their age difference. Most was often overworked, impatient at home, and perhaps frustrated about the fractured state of the movement in America.

During the spring of 1906, Most was again on the road for a lecture tour. In March he fell ill and was forced to rest at a friend's house in Cincinnati. The disease proved too much, and Johann Most passed away unexpectedly on the seventeenth at the age of sixty. He left behind his partner Minkin and two sons. Most's legacy lived on in the memories of countless of friends and foes, of hundreds of people who watched him perform on the stump, who read his pamphlets and subscribed to his paper. Following his death, Helene Minkin suggested publishing all of Most's papers, which to this day remains to be done.[39]

Little is known about Minkin's political convictions, but it is safe to say that she was sympathetic to the anarchist cause. Minkin should especially be remembered for running the *Freiheit* office, where she took over delivery management after Most's death. Working whenever she could to aid the operations of the magazine, she was well placed to attest to Most's utter devotion to the paper. "He did not publish 'Freiheit' in order to live," she noted, "but rather, he lived so he could publish 'Freiheit.'"[40] A single mother, Minkin's life in New York became isolated even from the movement. John Jr. remembered that "the neighbors threw insults—and sometimes rocks—at us: 'There go the filthy anarchists!' 'There's that anarchist rat family.'"[41] Lucifer Most had fond memories of attending picnics and the warm welcome they received from his father's friends. After Most's death, however, the sons were ignored.[42]

In his first summer in the United States, Johann Most, with the help of August Spies, took the initiative to organize a convention in a location somewhere between Chicago and New York. The social revolutionaries and anarchists of America—the majority of whom were Germans—had been represented at two major conventions before, one in London and another in Chicago, and most existing groups in the United States were affiliated with the IWPA. Most, who by now called himself an anarchist, was convinced that anti-authoritarian socialists in America lacked an organizational and ideological framework and proposed an American federation of the IWPA. He sought to unify the revolutionary elements under a common philosophy and organization to become more effective in combating and resisting the forces of greed and privilege. They hoped that such a convention would raise anarchism from obscurity and put it on the political map.

Johann Most invited all socialists, including the Socialist Labor party, Benjamin Tucker, the individualist anarchist and editor of *Liberty*, and the revolutionary socialists in the West led by the eccentric Burnette G. Haskell. Haskell had played a significant role in the establishment of the International Workingmen's Association, also known as the Red International (which was separate from the London-based Black International). Tucker and the SLP executive committee declined to participate, but Haskell immediately engaged in a correspondence with other organizers. In August 1883, a date for the convention was agreed upon: from 18 to

21 October in Pittsburgh (the congress would actually commence on the fourteenth). In all, thirty groups voted as to where the convention should take place: three voted for Chicago, eleven chose Cincinnati, thirteen preferred Pittsburgh, while three groups believed no convention should be held at all.[43] Pittsburgh was chosen for its geographic location, being centrally situated in the industrial belt stretching from the upper Mississippi to Philadelphia.

From the start of the convention, Johann Most was driven by pragmatism rather than dogmatism. He urged all groups and delegates to distance themselves from purely theoretical questions, which he thought threatened to drown the proceedings in endless ideological battles. Even though Most invited all socialists to participate, in reality he planned to unite all revolutionary socialists—as opposed to reformist socialists and individualist anarchists—into a sizeable force ready to act on his own ideas of social revolution. His goal of an undivided federation of anarchists met with some resistance. To some delegates, such rigid organization seemed less necessary in the American republic, where freedom of assembly and speech allowed for more openness and autonomy. Unified and secretive organization may have been the only way to operate as anarchists in Germany, but for German American anarchists such rigidity appeared to threaten spontaneous action and autonomy itself. However, a majority of delegates answered the plea to build a federative network and outline a strong declaration of principles.

A modest increase in the number of anarchist groups in the New York City area only confirmed the need to build a nationwide federative network. Prior to July 1883, when New York anarchists began discussing the "congress matter," overall membership of the German groups had been on the rise since January. At that time, only two groups existed in Manhattan: the Social-Revolutionary Club and New York Group I. Both groups increased their membership during the spring and summer, with the latter group at one time reportedly reaching one hundred members.[44] Also in the spring of 1883, New York Group II West Side (New York Gruppe II Westseite) constituted itself with twenty-five founding members on Manhattan's West Side. Anarchist groups also sprang up in Queens and Brooklyn. College Point Group in Queens was organized in the wake of the Pittsburgh convention after yet another pep talk by Most on the "State of Affairs in America."

New Jersey anarchists had since 1881 organized several tiny social-revolutionary groups, but it can be assumed that in early 1883 a renewed activity resulted in closer cooperation between radical Germans. In January, they formed the United Anarchists of Hudson County (Vereinigte

Anarchisten von Hudson County), affiliated with the IWPA, and held meetings—for all members of the constituent groups—in Kohlmaier's saloon in Union Hill.[45] Possibly because of rising membership, "local considerations" prompted the United Anarchists of Hudson County to dissolve into smaller independent groups following a loose federative model. Members argued that the meetings by the individual groups were better attended than the earlier joint meetings, especially since transportation between the towns was abominable.[46] They would still collaborate on such events as the Workers' Festival (Arbeiter-Fest), for instance, held in Union Hill's Floral Park on 5 August 1883 and organized by the Union Hill and Jersey City Heights groups. Throughout 1883, anarchists in Paterson, Newark, and Hoboken formed new, relatively small groups. Confirming their cooperative spirit once again, the New Jersey groups organized a joint meeting in which they agreed to participate in the upcoming congress.[47] Thus, even before the start of the Pittsburgh convention, local German anarchists were organized in small, autonomous groups, even setting up regional and neighborhood networks—the same model that was now being discussed for North America.

New York Group I, with Most and Schwab at the helm, took the lead in drawing up a blueprint for the new American federation a month before the convention. They invoked the example of the London Congress but insisted that a manifesto of the quintessential tenets of revolutionary anarchism was needed. Instead of reformism or other palliative solutions, the Mostians stressed the importance of self-defense, cooperation, and solidarity among revolutionary-minded workers. While agreeing to participate in the increasingly militant labor movement, the Mostians cautioned against involvement in a fight for "Cents and Minutes," as they termed it, an allusion to Most's disdain for the popular eight-hour-workday movement.[48]

A different proposal appeared in *Freiheit* shortly thereafter. It was written by Moritz A. Bachmann, possibly in the name of the Social Revolutionary Club, a group now critical of Most. Bachmann warned against centralism creeping into the anarchist ranks and instead stressed group autonomy when it came to choosing methods of propaganda. He also suggested a different name for the proposed organization: the Federation of North American Socialists (Föderation der Sozialisten von Nord-Amerika), comprised of autonomous societies, groups, and individuals who adhered to a declaration of principles.[49] Interestingly, Bachmann believed that Most's reason for building a new organization was simply to "break up the rival organization, the Social Revolutionary Club." Most's dismissal of that club as "only a baker's dozen of incurable cranks" only lends credence to Bachmann's suspicion.[50] Many anarchists saw through Most's insistence on unity of mind and action but went along with the proposal for a federation perhaps because it included more benefits than drawbacks. Comrades would not remain so accepting during the tumultuous 1890s.

Twenty-six locations were represented at the Pittsburgh Congress, which opened on 14 October 1883. According to Waltershausen, New England and the southern states were not represented, and California only sent letters of support.[51] The evening before, delegates had gathered for a rendezvous in Turner Hall in neighboring Allegheny City hosted by Joseph Frick, a senior member of the local group. A total of nine delegates representing various locations in the New York–New Jersey area participated in what would be remembered—at least by anarchists—as a milestone in the history of revolutionary anarchism in the United States.

A closer look at the proceedings of the convention reveals much about the vision, concerns, and attitudes of the revolutionary anarchists at the time. High hopes were expressed through sincere discussions that were conducted, wherever possible, along nonhierarchical principles of decision making. The first issue to be addressed was the validity of mandates from groups unable to send their own delegates, which August Spies denied. Most argued that not accepting such mandates would punish small groups with small treasuries. In the end, a consensus was reached that honored all mandates. Next was the constitution of the Information Bureau with Spies as secretary, followed by the reading of congratulatory dispatches from Italy, Britain, France, and Mexico, among other places. Afternoon lectures by keynote speakers stressed the necessity of social revolution and self-defense to protect the movement from repression. Spies was convinced that the United States was ready for a mass proletarian movement, while Most believed that American robber barons exploited workers at a faster rate than Europe's upper classes. He called for an end to monopoly and private property and the advent of a free communistic American society.

The memoranda or opinions of the groups were presented and debated as a first step in drafting a manifesto. The Chicago delegates opted for a revolutionary socialist organization based on autonomous groups abiding by a declaration of principles but objected to the designation IWPA. They insisted on arming workers and urged a strong involvement in trade unions to transform them into revolutionary cadres. New York's viewpoint (or at least Most's), which had already been published in *Freiheit* one month earlier, strongly objected to piecemeal gains envisioned by trade unions, which were viewed as not radical enough. Parsons and

Spies, however, were convinced that precisely such gains could open the door for mass support for revolutionary anarchism. Old disagreements between east and west surfaced again: Chicago's emphasis on revolutionary trade unionism—sometimes labeled "the Chicago idea"—was pitted against New York's brand of pure, unassociated anarchism. Despite such differences, at the end of the first day, committees were elected to draft a proclamation, a plan of organization, and a summation of resolutions. Most, Drury, Parsons, Spies, and the St. Louis editor J. J. Reifgraber were chosen by secret ballot to staff the proclamation committee—a perfect ideological balance.

A final draft was presented the next day—15 October—after various suggestions and amendments. H. R. Weiss, for instance, one of the older delegates and a veteran of 1848, called for the inclusion of a paragraph condemning all forms of domination, while W. Kubisch insisted on strengthening support for the emancipation of women. The organizational plan in the draft text was based on the principle of group autonomy and included guidelines for the formation of groups. A proposition for a literary bureau responsible for publishing pamphlets was quickly dismissed as too centralized.

The only task left was the presentation of resolutions, which was completed on 16 October. The Chicago delegation demanded that a clear distinction be made between Social-Democrats in Germany and socialists in North America and proposed a resolution of noninterference to guarantee the independence of the American socialists from their German compeers. Most objected, reminding them that there existed only the "socialists of the world." Then, after several corrections, the Pittsburgh Manifesto was ready for printing. It was agreed to distribute this document on a large scale in different languages: New York was put in charge of the German edition; Chicago of the English, Czech, and Scandinavian editions; and St. Louis of a French version.

At the end of the document, six principles summarized the core tenets of American revolutionary anarchism:

> "First—Destruction of the existing class rule, by all means, i.e., by energetic, relentless, revolutionary, and international action.
>
> Second—Establishment of a free society based upon cooperative organization of production.
>
> Third—Free exchange of equivalent products by and between the productive organizations without commerce and profit-mongery.
>
> Fourth—Organization of education on a secular, scientific, and equal basis for both sexes.

Fifth—Equal rights for all without distinction of sex or race.

Sixth—Regulation of all public affairs by free contract between the autonomous (independent) communes and associations, resting on a federalistic basis."[52]

The proclamation was testimony to the considerable influence of Johann Most, who had been in the United States for only nine months. Much of the language came from Most's essay "Unsere Grundsätze" (Our fundamentals), which had appeared in *Freiheit* two days before the convention. His two main objectives were organization and unity, and if this could be achieved, Most hoped to send shock waves across the elite power echelons. "'Tremble, oppressors of the world!'" one sentence read. "'Not far beyond your purblind sight there dawns the scarlet and sable light of Judgment Day!'"[53] Ideologically, the manifesto embodied a Bakuninist-Blanquist philosophy, with considerable room for anarchosyndicalism. It also contained bits of Most's thoughts on revolution and an anarchist society. His pamphlet on private property, *Die Eigenthumsbestie,* and his essay, "Freie Kommunen in der freien Gesellschaft" (Free communes in the free society), had been published during the preceding months. In them, Most compared America's corporate monopolies to Europe's grand if rusty monarchies, an analysis that preceded that of the muckrakers of the Progressive era by more than a decade.[54]

The Pittsburgh Manifesto of 16 October 1883 outlined an attempt at anti-authoritarian organization by a revolutionary movement.[55] In doing so, it paid tribute to America's historic role in the fight against tyranny. Taking up arms against British colonialism had set a precedent for the way people safeguarded their freedom and liberties. Just as the American rebels of the 1770s demanded the overthrow of colonial domination, so a century later, left-wing revolutionaries banded together in an international association to pillory the injustice and putrescence of the existing order. This comparison is not far-fetched. The first paragraph of the Pittsburgh draft invoked the famous passage in the American Declaration of Independence, citing not only the right but also the duty to overthrow a despotic government after "a long train of abuses and usurpations." The anarchists simply asked if this moment had not arrived: "'Do not the necessities of our present time compel us to reassert their [the Founding Fathers'] declaration?'"[56] By appealing to one of America's sacred texts, the revolutionary anarchists grafted their movement onto the American tradition of rebellion against privilege and despotism, even though no native-born, middle-class patriot of the 1880s would have appreciated this historical evocation. Anarchists discerned undeniable similarities between the "abuses and usurpations" of the British crown and those of the political, industrial, and financial elite of Gilded Age America. The "usurpations" of the eighteenth century simply translated into the corporate monopolies of the nineteenth, and "abuses," according to the workers, were inherent to the exploitative system of industrial capitalism and occurred daily. The anarchists were also, if not more so, heirs to a European tradition of radical agitation against the post-Napoleonic system of Restoration conservatism. In this sense, the Pittsburgh proclamation—more than the London or Chicago documents—enunciated a Euro-American ideal of freedom and democracy.

In essence, the Pittsburgh Manifesto is not so much an anarchist text as an anti-authoritarian statement and blueprint for organizing underpinned by supposedly objective observations on political, economic, and religious oppression. As Creagh observes, the delegates did not set out to author a learned treatise on the modern condition but merely sought to compose a lucid workers' statement to "galvanize the masses by presenting the Revolution as a desirable, possible, and American ideal."[57]

The effect of the Pittsburgh Congress on the anarchist movement in America was an upsurge in group activity and propaganda through periodicals, leaflets, and speaking tours. While in August 1883, thirty groups existed, by the spring of 1885, eighty IWPA groups operated in the United States with an estimated total membership of three thousand and an additional four thousand sympathizers (three thousand in Chicago, one thousand in New York), according to a Chicago anarchist paper.[58] The economic depression of the mid-1880s also enhanced the appeal of anarchism, especially in Chicago, where hundreds of factory workers listened to what the anarchists had to say. The eight-hour-day movement regained strength, and after some hesitation the Chicago anarchists threw themselves into the fray to become its most militant supporters.

Johann Most's dominant role during the convention lifted New York out of the shadow of Chicago, which had been the foremost socialist bastion since the 1870s. Chicago remained a leader in labor activism, but New York gained some salience through the work of Most, Drury, and many others. The attitude toward trade unionism and the preoccupation with sending propaganda material to Europe continued to be the main difference between the cities. The former issue made Chicago a city of anarchists participating in the workers' movement, while the latter made New York a support base for European radicals, which in turn accounted for a more congenial attitude toward revolutionary violence against oppressors.

New York anarchists opposed to Most were not always impressed by the accomplishments of the convention. Moritz Bachmann, who had objected to moving *Freiheit* to New York, once stated that the program of the 1881 Chicago convention was "far more radical and Anarchistic than the one laid down in the Pittsburgh proclamation in October, 1883."[59] The IWPA, according to him, was now more institutionalized, and the individual groups less autonomous. This was a valid point, since groups and clubs formed the locus of the anarchists' political campaign.

4 *Beyond Most: Dissent within the Movement*

Since the Unity Congress of Gotha in 1875, the socialist movement in Germany had become a considerable political force. Its leadership regarded either Ferdinand Lassalle or Karl Marx as the main fountain of inspiration despite the temporary influence of Eugen Dühring. Lasalle and Marx regarded strong leadership and ideological commitment as fundamental to a successful oppositional working-class movement. Both insisted on a rational analysis of past and current conditions based on a scientific and historical methodology, yet the majority of rank-and-file members were less involved in intellectual debates about ideology and strategy. Workers joined the socialist party simply to achieve real improvements in their working lives through collective action. They also built and enjoyed an extensive socialist subculture of family outings, mutual-aid societies, and cultural and educational organizations.

The suppression of this grassroots socialism in Germany split the movement at a time when the ideological underpinning of the party and its leaders was far from uniform. The sudden revocation of civil liberties in the Antisocialist Law of 1878 forced the movement either underground or into exile. This created ideological and strategic confusion among rank-and-file members who increasingly felt alienated from the socialist deputies Bismarck had allowed to remain in Parliament. For many, state repression became a revolutionizing experience. Ideologically, these radicalized socialists shifted from Social-Democratic ideas to Blanquism and Bakuninism, defying the state by setting up clandestine means to continue distributing propaganda into Germany and Austria from abroad. The cauldron of this radicalizing ferment was the exile community.

A peculiar atmosphere surrounded the exile colonies of German radical socialists in Switzerland, Belgium, London, and New York. A sense of fraternal community existed on the surface, but beneath the jollity of London club life a secrecy fueled by fear of infiltration seriously hampered personal relations between social revolutionaries. Spies and agents provocateurs were distressingly common. German authorities possessed extensive knowledge about the movement, though they had no inclination to eradicate it completely. Indeed, they benefited from the perceived threat of anarchism, which persuaded parliamentarians to renew the Antisocialist Law once again. Thus the exiled community, with its displaced existence, "'suffered unspeakably under this secrecy,'" as the German anarchist Gustav Landauer observed, and was shrouded by an "'atmosphere of obscurity.'"[1] Suspicion of fellow comrades did not help to build a self-sustaining and constructive community; instead, bonds of trust were weak, and mudslinging quarrels were easily ignited. Moreover, this exile community, especially in London, was ideologically immature, making it easy for strong personalities to fill the intellectual vacuum.

London social revolutionaries were wary of too much formal infrastructure, an attitude prevalent at the London convention of 1881. Leadership in itself was not unanarchistic, but the concept carried negative connotations of centralism and rigidity. In any case, the community of radicals (excluding the orthodox socialists) in London and New York during the first years of the 1880s was an amalgam of discontented, displaced, and largely antistate socialists. They included antiparliamentarians, nihilists, social revolutionaries, Blanquists, and anarchists. Positions of leadership among these radicals emerged almost exclusively in the realm of propaganda efforts rather than in intellectual endeavors. This was the result of a climate of political expediency wrought by the ban on socialist literature in Germany. And so the movement concentrated on the dangerous task of devising and maintaining a smuggling operation run by activists in the field. In London, Most and the rest of the editorial staff produced the contraband: *Freiheit,* the foremost instrument of socialist agitation in the mother country. As editor, Johann Most was in a position of considerable responsibility, which he was not eager to relinquish or share. Though initially part of the staff, he was able to gradually exert more control over this essential tool of propaganda. A close-knit *Freiheit* clique emerged, showing little hospitability to new activists. Nonetheless, all radical socialists abroad shared one source of comradeship: their common antagonism toward the Social-Democratic leadership in Germany and their mouthpiece, *Sozialdemokrat,* launched nine months after *Freiheit.*

A closer look at the German anarchist community in New York reveals not a homogenous, single-minded, well-oiled movement but rather a fractured, loosely connected, sensitive, but no less vibrant group of activists and supporters of a cause complicated by particular conditions in industrial America. Detailing points of friction among the anarchists brings to light their concerns, frustrations, and above all, their humanity. Clashes between practical solutions and ideological (and ethical) integrity were a fact of life among people who chose to set the bar of an egalitarian and autonomous existence very high.

The community of social revolutionaries in New York differed from those in London in that initially not all members were recent émigrés. Many were German Americans who had lived in America for years if not decades, such as the leading figures Justus Schwab, Moritz Bachmann, and Victor Drury. The New York Social-Revolutionary Club was perhaps anarchistic in some aspects but could by no means claim homogeneity in either membership or ideology; it was an amalgam of dissident socialists and radicals fed up with reformism and SLP hierarchy. Despite the popularity of *Freiheit* and Hasselmann's involvement in the club, it appears that this anarchistic circle did not focus its attention solely on Europe. After all, Johann Most and his followers ably kept the movement alive in that part of the world. Rather, the New York club's energy was directed toward building a radical movement in New York. Seelig had in 1881 advocated the creation of an underground press and stressed American autonomy. Also, after the London convention, New York anarchists wasted no time in discussing the possibility of holding a convention in their own city, and during the Chicago meeting only journals produced in America were chosen as official organs.

It is no surprise, then, that one of the first disputes among New York's social revolutionaries and anarchists revolved around the decision to relocate *Freiheit* to New York. Many club members felt with some justification that as the sole German propaganda organ, it had no business operating in the United States and should remain in London. Most and his supporters instead argued that England or Switzerland were no longer safe after the crackdown of 1880–82; there was no choice but to relocate across the Atlantic. This dispute resulted in the first of many splits within the movement: between a Most faction and the Social-Revolutionary Club, which appears to have developed its own newsletter.[2] Immediately following the split, club members also produced and distributed a scathing four-page pamphlet, financed, according to Rocker, with money initially collected for *Freiheit.*[3] Bachmann and Seelig, two of the more vocal club members, feared that efforts to build an American movement would be thwarted or even co-opted by Most and his "Euro-centered" paper. Both men later denounced Most and moved to Philadelphia, where they engaged in producing a rival weekly, *Die Zukunft* (The future). By July 1885, all ties between *Freiheit* and Bachmann were broken; the latter by then subscribed to Benjamin Tucker's individualist publication *Liberty.*[4] The coming of *Freiheit* in 1882 was clearly seen by some as an intrusion and a distraction that pulled East Coast German-speaking anarchists away from creating their own anarchist movement in urban America.

Despite some German American radicals' misgivings, it is probable that Johann Most moved his paper solely for pragmatic reasons. Once in New York, he was able to secure its survival by creating a network of supporters who subscribed and contributed funds to *Freiheit.* Several former members of the Social-Revolutionary Club—Justus Schwab and Carl Wölky, for instance—joined New York Gruppe I, the circle dominated by Most. At some point, Most and Schwab realized that *Freiheit* would have to shift to accommodate its American subscribers if it was to survive in the future. After all, no anarchistic German-language paper existed on the East Coast, with the possible exception of the left-libertarian *New Yorker Abend-Zeitung,* which folded in 1874. Until 1885, *Freiheit*'s intended readership consisted largely of workers in Germany and Austria, but it now was set to fill the vacuum of anarchist journalism in New York as well.

Freiheit would become one of the longest-running anarchist periodicals in the United States. It is remarkable, although some would say unfortunate, that the paper was run by one man, Johann Most. It bore his imprint and reflected changes of the man himself. The paper came to America with a revolutionary zeal, releasing fiery articles, unabashed declamations of class warfare, and relentless accusations against the capitalist system. However, it gradually tempered its rhetoric of revolutionary terrorism. In February 1885, for instance, the editor distanced himself from the Irish nationalists and their tactics, and in 1892 Most published an essay rejecting individualist acts of terror. By July 1885, *Freiheit* appeared with eight pages (including a four-page European edition) and contained numerous advertisements from local artisans, saloons, parks, and breweries, most of them owned by Germans. It also changed its subtitle to *Organ of German-Language Anarchists* (Organ der Anarchisten deutscher Sprache). But many found the new paper bland, diluted by meekness and commercialism.[5] *Freiheit* was forced to return to four pages. An enlargement fund was soon set up, but it wasn't enough.

A tighter budget also delayed an 1884 proposition to launch a daily to complement *Freiheit.*[6]

The 1890s witnessed the slow decline of the paper. Circulation dropped, and funds were ever more scarce. In 1890, peddlers or colporteurs distributed some eight hundred issues in New York and environs, but the previous year the account books showed nearly a thousand dollars in outstanding debts by subscribers, mostly from foreign and Chicago comrades.[7] Eventually, the paper faced a lack of colporteurs in New York, which kept circulation low. In overall expenditures, the paper went from an eleven-dollar surplus in 1889 to a $340 deficit four years later, mainly due to rising printing and shipping costs.[8] From August 1897 until the next summer, Most resided in Buffalo to save his paper by teaming up with a local labor paper. On 15 June 1895, two years before the move to Buffalo, anarchists opened the new issue of *Freiheit* to discover a modern-looking paper completely in Latin script (instead of Gothic letters). The editors chose this script not only because it signified modernity but also because it "will make it easier for those who are not native Germans to read printed material in German."[9] In other words, it would make it more accessible to second-generation comrades.

Johann Most's position as editor of *Freiheit* provoked questions among New York anarchists about individual autonomy and leadership. Many saw the paper as useful, but its position and the attitude of the editor reeked of monopoly. Some comrades likened Most's position as editor to that of an autocrat. Most argued that the survival of *Freiheit* depended on his strong editorial management, even if that meant contributions could be rejected if he saw fit. Tensions regarding management and editorial responsibilities had also surfaced in London, where rivalries were common. Most complained of disingenuous or incompetent collaborators who did nothing but "rummage about" without producing strong contributions. Sometime after the move to New York, a London office was set up to coordinate shipment to the rest of Europe. Most repeatedly complained about the inability of his London contacts to reimburse promptly, while they charged that funds sent back to New York paid for unnecessary luxuries.

Josef Peukert, an Austrian anarchist born in Albrechtsdorf near Gablonz in northern Bohemia, voiced the strongest criticism of Most's editorial conduct. Peukert would become Most's arch-enemy for life. Like his German rival, Peukert had been scarred by an uncaring stepmother but overcame his childhood insecurity to become a leading figure in the movement.[10] Trained as an interior decorator and attracted to socialism at an early age, he moved to Paris in 1877 to help organize a German anarchist group. Fluent in French, Peukert immersed himself in the new tenets of communist-anarchism and helped disseminate it among German-speaking radicals. In 1881, he traveled to London as a delegate to the International Congress of Social-Revolutionaries, where he raised the issue of editorial responsibility within a revolutionary movement, mainly in response to Most. After the congress, he returned to Vienna, where he gained notoriety as a speaker and later as labor editor. As in Germany, the Austrian worker's movement was divided into a moderate and a radical wing. Despite the immense popularity of *Freiheit,* Austrian radicals launched their own paper, *Die Zukunft,* in 1879; Peukert became its editor sometime in the early 1880s and according to him achieved a fivefold increase in circulation. Most and Peukert cultivated a personal in addition to an ideological animosity toward each other well before Most arrived in New York. In 1880, when *Freiheit* was not yet an anarchist paper, Most rejected an article by Peukert on the grounds that it did not denounce suffrage. Peukert accused Most of being doctrinaire and dismissive of dissident voices. For the Austrian, the socialist press was to be an "open and free tribune," and its editorial staff should consist of temporary workers who refrain from controlling the content of the paper. "The temporary editor," Peukert once wrote, "cannot morally be made personally responsible for everything in a Social-Democratic paper."[11] Any attempt to do so would be an imposition of personality over the independence of the party. According to Peukert's recollection, he proposed the establishment of an editorial committee after Most's arrest in March 1881, an idea that found many supporters. This committee was to select articles for publication in *Freiheit* rather than leaving decisions solely to the editor.[12] Most dismissed such schemes as the product of Peukert's frustration over his inability to secure an editorship himself.

During the early 1880s, Peukert enjoyed considerable popular support in Austria and the Bohemian provinces and continued to have a following in London. Most warned his followers that Peukert's influence reached as far as New York's Lower East Side, probably a reasonable assumption. Sometime in 1883, an Austrian Revolutionary League (Österreichisch-revolutionäre Liga) was formed, perhaps in the wake of a unitary congress of social revolutionaries in Vienna in 1883. Austrian authorities proceeded to crack down on radicals after a series of violent crimes committed by men influenced by the extremes of anarchist philosophy. The situation in Austria prompted many activists to emigrate. It is unclear if Peukert had a hand in the establishment of the Austrian League in New York, but the group was in disagreement with Most, to say the least. Most further claimed that Peukert had collaborators within the Social-Revolutionary Club and that this club was in league with the Austrians.[13] Unfortunately, little information on group allegiance exists beyond the subjective accounts of leading polemicists. German anarchists in New York enjoyed great intellectual and social mobility within the movement and were most likely not seriously affected by the bickering of Most and Peukert. Leo Kochmann, a member of the Austrian League, for instance, collected money for the "Free Speech and John Most" defense fund, set up after Most's arrest and conviction in 1891.[14]

Tension mounted, however, when a debate on the diversity of the anarchist press was organized in New York, similar to the one instigated by Peukert in London. Organized by the Social-Revolutionary Club, some twenty people gathered in October 1884 to discuss their position regarding *Freiheit* and Most, who was invited but declined the honor. The members stated that a labor paper did not need an editor and that everyone should be free to contribute to it. Most then decided to take the gloves off. He scorned the club and called the attendants "crazy rowdies" and "filthy fellows."[15] His utter dismissal of this event was founded on his loathing for Peukert, of course, whom he believed was behind the opposition. When six or seven members of the Austrian League sought to join New York Group I, Most, rather than welcoming them, was convinced they were instructed by Peukert to make trouble.[16] This internal strife continued through the end of 1884, when several Austrians were expelled from Most's group.

A distinct ethnic tension between Germans and Austrians colored the anarchist movement in New York. The historian Max Nettlau notes that a different development of revolutionary socialism in the two countries explains this rivalry.[17] Whereas German radicals were muzzled in 1878, radical socialists in Austria remained relatively free to operate until as late as 1884. They even succeeded in gaining influence among the workers in Vienna and the industrial regions of Bohemia and Silesia. Still, though Austrians were less consistently repressed than their German counterparts, occasional prison terms were often harsher, with sentences ranging from ten to fifteen years for relatively minor offenses. Nettlau, an Austrian, pointed to resentment on the part of Austrian radicals regarding the unequal punishment meted out to them compared to Germany's master smuggler Johann Neve, for instance, who received "only" six months in prison upon his arrest near Frankfurt. In January 1884, Austrian authorities decided to crush the revolutionary movement by passing an exception law (Ausnahmegesetz) similar to the 1878 German edict, causing many to flee the country. Nettlau noted that these emigrating social revolutionaries and anarchists, while outlawed, nevertheless had a wider following than orthodox socialists. They arrived in London and New York with a "joy that progress was made" prior to exile. This contrasts sharply with the experience of German exiles, whose hard work in Germany was mired in bitterness and perhaps defeat. This difference in mood was undoubtedly at work in the internecine feuds within the New York anarchist community during the last decades of the nineteenth century, an added factor to the increasingly thorny issue of pluralism within the movement.

Most's control of the German-language anarchist press in New York stemmed in part from his belief in the need for a degree of uniformity within the anarchist ranks. But the advocacy of uniformity was not as pertinent in the United States as in the oppressive, tight-lipped atmosphere of London or Switzerland. Most's fear of division might have been another's celebration of diversity. More than once, New York anarchists launched projects that met with a particularly uncivil opposition from Most, who was prone to ridicule any alternative views, perhaps a residue from his Marxist past. Dissent was immediately perceived as opposition. In an 1885 letter, he vented that the entire labor movement was populated by "inflated frogs" and that humanity resembles "an extraordinarily vulgar species of apes."[18]

The German anarchist press in America during the early 1880s was flourishing, and Most realized (or feared) that as an anarchist center, New York would soon witness a proliferation of anarchist papers. He had long given up on curbing the growth of midwestern papers, but he viewed competition on the East Coast as detrimental to the health of his own paper. In 1884 Philadelphia anarchists started *Die Zukunft,* and in the following year the IWPA Group New Haven (Connecticut) purchased the *New England Anzeiger* and transformed it into an anarchist mouthpiece. Interestingly, Most considered taking over this paper to publish it as a daily in New York, thereby co-opting the efforts of his New Haven followers.[19]

Another episode of bashing competitors occurred across the Hudson in New Jersey, where local German anarchists had fashioned their own movement beginning in the early 1880s. In April 1884, the anarchist groups of Hudson County announced in *Freiheit* the launching of the *New Jersey Arbeiterzeitung,* a weekly newspaper headquartered in Jersey City Heights.[20] The paper was edited by Moritz Stern and published by Charles Kurz. Only a year before, Kurz had been the Jersey City Heights agent for *Freiheit,* but he was suddenly replaced by Otto Nicolai. Stern had been a member of New York Gruppe I but had apparently moved to New Jersey.[21] A week after the announcement, Most's agent in neighboring Hoboken denounced the project, stating that the new paper had been founded without the knowledge and approval of the respective groups and that it "strives to sow discord."[22] The agent further accused the founders of swindling and warned local workers not to support this "bogus" publication. Stern in particular was labeled a renegade and an unsophisticated neophyte. It is unknown what became of their paper, since *Freiheit* refrained from including any references to "rivals." Most likely, it did not remain afloat for long, although the project was not abandoned entirely. It reappeared in 1887 not in Jersey City Heights but in Newark, perhaps due to Most's more relaxed or jaded attitude.[23] A rather condescending review appeared in *Freiheit,* deeming the paper useful but not exactly in line with the IWPA's standpoint. This attitude turned many German (and other) anarchists away from the IWPA.

It didn't take long for enterprising anarchists to launch a rival paper in the lion's den, New York City. In 1886, Wilhelm Hasselmann, perhaps in cooperation with Austrian social revolutionaries, launched the *Amerikanische Arbeiter-Zeitung* (American workers' newspaper), apparently published at a comrade's house on Second Street not far from Schwab's saloon. According to Rocker, this publication was expressly aimed to compete with *Freiheit.*[24] Even though the paper lasted only six months, it is worthwhile to listen to what it had to say. As the title suggests, the *Amerikanische Arbeiter-Zeitung* focused its assault on American conditions. In the first article, "To the Men of Labor," it called on American workers to arm themselves and prepare for a social upheaval against the "robber society." It also encouraged the establishment of more labor papers and reminded editors of their duty to pillory the shameless deeds of the oppressors. Moreover, since the paper sought to become the mouthpiece of revolutionary workers, no editor or manager would be employed, a hint at the ongoing debate about the anarchist press. "Every worker can, without censorship and with responsibility for the content, publish relevant articles, space permitting, in the columns of this paper."[25] This statement, signed by the "United Publishers," was clearly a response to the perceived undemocratic policies of the *Freiheit* staff, and specifically to Most. Hasselmann wrote a piece denouncing any kind of personality cult, again implicitly referring to Most's self-important stance among New York anarchists. Another feature that set this paper apart was its close cooperation with the Federated Unions of New York (Föderirte Gewerkschaften New Yorks), a federation of German trade unions whose delegates met every Friday at Lauda's Halle on East Fifth Street. It included machinists, tailors, turners, painters, metal workers, and perhaps even the Social-Revolutionary Club.[26] There is no evidence to suggest that the Federated Unions were anti-Most, since many of their member unions advertised in *Freiheit.* It is certain that at this time Most did not espouse unionism as a proper anarchist tactic. He had said as much during a meeting with the Chicago anarchist August Spies in 1885, in which he dismissed anarchist involvement in the growing eight-hour-day movement.

If Most was not interested in union activism during this time, he certainly championed the idea of propaganda by deed, which he put forth as the sole mission of the anarchist movement. This idea, widely believed by the mainstream to be the official anarchist tactic, caused serious divisions within the anarchist movement and specifically between the Mostians and the rest. Most's obsession with violent insurrection, which was reflected in *Freiheit,* partly stemmed from his time in London and his enduring ties with European activists faced with repression and humiliation. A large part of *Freiheit*'s subscribers, for instance, were German and Austrian workers. For Most, New York had always seemed like a safe staging ground to continue his assault on Europe's ruling classes. He dreamed out loud about extralegal means to overthrow the system and sought to instruct willing activists in the methods of revolutionary terrorism.

A defining incident in 1884 forced the German movement in New York to seriously reevaluate their stance on violence. Several men—allegedly members of the New York Group I and the Social-Revolutionary Club—devised a scheme in which they insured their tenements for enormous sums before setting them ablaze with kerosene lamps to collect the insurance money, presumably to benefit the cause. It was perhaps unavoidable that a handful of fanatical revolutionaries and ordinary criminals, some appropriating the anarchist label, put some of Most's subversive reflections to use. Several of the perpetrators were apprehended and sentenced. This would have been the end of the so-called firebug story if it wasn't for Benjamin Tucker, who in 1886 published "The Beast of Communism" in *Liberty,* linking the episode explicitly to New York's two foremost German anarchist groups. Seven to eight fires in 1884 and twenty in 1885 yielded profits of thousands of dollars, according to the paper. One woman and two children had reportedly died in one of the conflagrations.

The breaking of the firebug story exacerbated the already sour relations between Tucker and Most, but what is more important is the upheaval it caused within the already fractured German movement. When confronted with the truth, Most refused to denounce either the actions or the offenders. Most's biographer, Rudolf Rocker, has suggested that he was financially dependent on these criminals to keep his paper afloat, but Most denied ever having employed criminals as his lieutenants. His refusal to denounce the affair caused consternation among rank-and-file anarchists, leading many to dissociate themselves from him. Justus Schwab was the most conspicuous of Most's companions to break ties when he demanded that Most choose between the perpetrators and himself. Most ignored Schwab, who in turn refused the perpetrators entrance to his popular saloon. As a result, Schwab was branded a coward, and Most's followers even instigated a boycott of his tavern. In the end, it was Johann Most who became more isolated, at least until the time he definitively rejected propaganda by deed. Justus Schwab, distressed by the whole affair, clarified his position in an eloquent letter of 10 April 1886 to the Detroit anarchist editor Robert Reitzel:

> My dear Robert,
>
> Before these lines reach you, you have probably been enlightened through Liberty as to how I stand with Most. As for myself, I have so far amended the Jesuitical maxim: "The end justifies the means," as to say that the means must not desecrate the end. I regard myself as a member of the International Working People's Association,—first, because I stand upon its ground principles, and, secondly, because, as far as my conception of integrity sanctions, I fulfill my duties to the same. I am no party man, in the narrow sense of that term. May I also be preserved in the exercise of an independent judgment over all deeds that come to my view! I hate orthodoxy in any form. Behind the scenes there are people from whom I am minded to turn away, on account of their peculiarities. However deeply I may be involved in the whirl and confusion of citizen life, I have not yet lost my conceptions of love, honesty, and decency. So be it well, if former "friends" choose to attack me: I can bear it, in the consciousness of never having proved recreant to the highest good and welfare of society.
>
> *Vive l'Humanité.*
>
> With hearty greeting, thy
> Justus H. Schwab.[27]

In May 1886, a day before the Haymarket explosion, the liberal *New York Sun* published an even lengthier article on the firebugs, naming several members of Most's group. Most immediately blamed Moritz Bachmann for informing the bourgeois press with slanderous lies, since Bachmann had been critical of Most and the Pittsburgh Manifesto from the beginning. Even August Spies went so far as to accuse Bachmann of being a Prussian spy. Bachmann clearly believed that Johann Most and his followers had irrevocably misrepresented anarchism to the public by condoning and advocating violence. When the American anarchist Joseph Labadie sought to educate the public about who the anarchists were, Bachmann wrote to Labadie that it would never be possible to make anarchism "'fashionable, or at least not objectionable,'" as long as people like Most existed within the ranks.[28] In an attempt to dissociate himself from New York Group I, Bachmann sketched an autocratic atmosphere within the group (he never was a card-carrying member):

> "Then and there I found out that it requires a certain prominence in such organizations to influence others. I gained some prominence, but, in order to accomplish that, I had to keep silent where I ought to have spoken and to take part in a great many doings which a sober second thought obliged me to condemn. I was allowed to write for the journals of the International Working People's Association, but I had to modify and shape my words, not according to my conviction, but to suit the test and the ideas of an indistinct majority of its members. I stood all this for a while, but gradually I was compelled either to sink my entire individuality in the flattening sea of collectivism or to rebel. After a battle with myself, I chose the latter course."[29]

This is the testimony of two veteran German American radicals—Schwab and Bachmann—both of whom had lived in New York for more than a decade before Most and many other hardline exiles arrived in the mid-1880s.[30] Both men slowly drifted toward a more individualist anarchism, not unlike Reitzel's style of literary irreverence. The condemnation by anarchists of the incident, and especially of Most's behavior in the aftermath, shows the extent to which the role of violence within the movement was not taken for granted, as mainstream opinion would have it. Most German American anarchists were not absolute pacifists; resistance was believed to be valid, but reckless violence was rarely, if ever, tolerated.

Dissent within the movement was not only the result of issues pertaining to press freedom and ideology. Questions of organization, integrity, and unity played a cardinal role in the workings of the movement, and disagreements in this area often spilled over into the realm of the personal. A personality like Johann Most's, with his powerful voice and biting pen, was bound to be absorbed by genuine discussions about how the movement operated. Since the early days of Most's career, unity and the collective spirit of a movement carried a high premium for the former Marxist and dissident exile. He urged his American comrades to never lose sight of this when he initiated a convention at Pittsburgh and authored much of the resulting proclamation. Most was indeed wary of dissension and impotence on the part of anarchists, who, according to him, should carry a clear and convincing message to the workers of the world. In short, he wanted to build a strong anarchist movement free of internal strife that was able to retaliate against the established order that had demonstrated its willingness to use violence against the working class as a matter of policy. Dismissing and purging dissident comrades was his way of upholding the illusion that the revolutionary anarchists could remain an undivided force. Ironically, his actions caused less unity and more dissent among anarchists.

The following episode illustrates Most's failure to bring together all anarchists despite ideological differences, but it also provides a glimpse of the real problems facing an insular, much-maligned, oppositional movement in turn-of-the-century America. On 14 July 1889, Bastille Day, a conference of all eastern IWPA groups was organized in a beerhall on East Fourth Street. It was clear that the principal organizer was Most, whose circle of friends in New York, though all tireless activists, had grown thin after instances of intimidation toward rival papers and the firebug revelations. Nonetheless, some 150 people attended to discuss the state of propaganda efforts among anarchists. However, several communist-anarchist groups were refused admission. They were told at the door that only internal affairs were being discussed. In retaliation, the excluded groups published a "protest" in the socialist *New Yorker Volkszeitung.*[31] According to *Die Autonomie,* a London-based paper, Most alone had issued valid admission tickets, and the paper further reported that the meeting was held behind closed doors.[32] This episode again illustrated Most's unilateral actions, highlighting the rift between Mostians and the others. Typically, Most stressed the need for a "more systematic agitation by anarchists in America."[33] To that end, he proposed the establishment of a permanent Committee of Agitation (Agitations-Komite), endowed with funds from all groups to conduct methodical oral and written propaganda (deeds were no longer mentioned). Furthermore, individual groups were allowed to set up their own propaganda treasuries, although available funds had to be reported to the committee. All conference delegates approved the proposal and chose New York as the location. Nine committee members were promptly elected, and all were close associates of Most who were active in the production and distribution of *Freiheit.* Most himself declined a seat as a committee member.

The Committee of Agitation dissolved two years later, in April 1891. Committee members complained that individual groups ignored the committee and instead donated money directly to *Freiheit* and that committee meetings went unattended for months. Johann Most accepted the dissolution of the Committee of Agitation, but his reaction revealed an essential intellectual dilemma. On the one hand, he acknowledged that "anarchist groups are autonomous, and do not need a body that even resembles that of an executive or centralization."[34] He admitted, for instance, that forced contributions to the committee resembled taxes. But on the other hand, he pointed to the futility of an underfunded propaganda organization that lacked the power of initiative. This was one of the principal problems of anarchist organization.

At the root of these seemingly petty disagreements lay a fundamental difference of approach as to how and when an anarchist society should exist. One view held that an anarchist society was not possible at this moment, and activists should organize to bring about the conditions that would allow an anarchist lifestyle later. This view implied suspending certain notions of freedom now for the good of the cause, and it was this belief that caused Most to clash with an "immediatist" approach, which believed that one could live according to anarchist principles in the here and now without reneging on the revolutionary mission for the future: the movement itself therefore should embody an anarchist society in miniature. Demands for autonomy and pluralism within the movement were not, as Most would say, frivolous but rather essential to preserving the integrity of the movement.

This tension between efficiency and autonomy spawned many inter- and intragroup disputes and is still relevant today. Rivalries are therefore not always a tedious footnote in the historical record but often reveal serious attempts by political dissenters to live a principled and meaningful life outside the capitalist sphere. This is not to say that all disputes were intellectual in nature; often they seem more about clashes between personalities. Separation or disbandment usually followed, and not always on amicable terms. To remedy this problem, an anonymous writer in *Freiheit* offered a solution. Before constituting a group, comrades should ascertain that they share key philosophical views and commit themselves "to freely subordinate the Ego to the interest of the cause."[35] If personal disagreements should erupt, the writer continued, the opposing faction must separate immediately to form a new group. The writer criticized the practice of groups attempting to overcome discord by implementing majority-rule methods. This artificially imposed unity, the argument continued, would eventually lead to a more bitter separation in which rival groups would compete with each other even in the realm of anarchist propaganda. One such group, calling themselves the Independent Revolutionists of New York, broke ties with Most's circle in 1889, but not on friendly terms. Richard Braunschweig, the leading figure in the group and an erstwhile disciple of Most, openly denounced his former mentor. To many dissidents, it sounded like an old refrain. Braunschweig called Most a traitor and "corruptionist" and was able to rally the other attendants behind him.

Most's obsession with unity and control affected personal relations on many occasions. Indeed, a demand for party discipline and loyalty often resulted in autocratic behavior on the part of leading anarchists. For reasons mentioned above, Most certainly displayed an unattractive intolerance toward pluralism inside the anarchist ranks. This intolerance and self-involvement was not uncommon among persecuted, beaten, or exiled radicals, many of whom regarded loyalty as vital to survival in the face of repression. Moritz Schultze, for example, a prominent anarchist speaker and able compositor for *Freiheit,* experienced a degree of ostracism because he veered toward social democracy during the 1890s. His treatment by other anarchists illustrates that even highly respected comrades could become victims of a purge. Schultze was chosen as interim editor of *Freiheit* during Most's imprisonment in Blackwell's Island penitentiary. Throughout the 1880s he was known as an indefatigable lecturer in New York. His reputation, at least among Mostian anarchists, was such that in 1889 he was chosen as IWPA delegate to the socialist congress in Paris (the St. Louis and Chicago groups also endorsed his nomination).[36] A year later, however, Schultze seemed to have left New York to join the socialists in Chicago. His apostasy prompted a barrage of criticism denouncing him as a slanderer and informer, despite his previous service among the anarchists.[37]

It is no surprise, then, that for many German and Austrian anarchists in New York, the Mostians had diverged from the anarchist spirit. Most's autocratic behavior, together with the firebug investigations, caused numerous anarchists to distance themselves from the International, causing "several secessions."[38] Outspoken critics like Moritz Bachmann found nothing redeeming about Most's clique of revolutionaries: "The members of the New York German Group of the International have become rude and devoid of all the better and more refined qualities of mankind." He claimed that these radicals failed to see the unjust consequences of their blind revolutionism. A "spirit of rudeness and fanatical unreasonable desire for merciless cruelty" pervaded their activities, according to Bachmann.[39]

Around 1885 a new philosophy—communist-anarchism—began to manifest itself in New York with the formation of an autonomist movement, which further drained the ranks of Most and the Internationalists. This time, battle lines between the anarchist groups were drawn according to ideology, mostly overlapping earlier personal and ethnic divisions.

The German anarchist movement in greater New York—small as it was—did not constitute an ideologically homogenous community. The movement was an amalgam of revolutionaries united in their opposition to the state, church, and the moneyed class but otherwise in disagreement over methods of action and a vision of how an anarchist society should function. Anarchist convictions were constantly subjected to new ideas and cannot be studied, let alone judged, as a monolithic doctrine, as some contemporary and modern observers have done. Ideological divisiveness was an illustration not only of anarchism's versatility but also of the transatlantic character of the movement during the last quarter of the nineteenth century.

Autonomists were Austrian and German anarchists who embraced communist-anarchism while criticizing Bakuninist, and by extension Mostian, anarchism. They received their name from the Autonomy Group (Gruppe Autonomie), founded by Peukert and his friends in the summer of 1885 with a separate clubhouse in London. A year later they launched *Die Autonomie,* which ran until April 1893. Rather than cooperating, the two distinct camps among the German exiles (apart from a few individualist anarchists) harbored a minimum of mutual trust for each other. Autonomists favored direct action, individual autonomy, an uncompromising equalitarianism, and the philosophy that the anarchist movement should act according to its own principles as if it presently constituted a miniature anarchist society. They were a growing segment within the German-language anarchist diaspora and deserve their own discussion, because the ideological divisions in the movement were compounded, especially in New York, by personal and ethnic rivalries. Autonomists came to dismiss Most's leadership and instead sought to build a much less centralized movement. For this reason, it is worthwhile to explore autonomist organizations and periodical ventures because they reflect a different approach to anarchism than the infrastructure set up by Most and his associates.

First of all, autonomists were communist-anarchists, and this was enough to raise suspicions with Johann Most, who was uncertain about his own anarchism but cognizant of his position as principal editor of *Freiheit.* Starting in the 1870s, two philosophical camps emerged within European anarchism: collectivist (or Bakuninist) anarchism and communist-anarchism. The ideas of Mikhail Bakunin dominated at first and provided an alternative to the socialist doctrines of Karl Marx and Ferdinand Lassalle. Bakunin's ideas gained a substantial following during the Russian's fight with Marx in the International, which subsequently split the socialist movement. Communist-anarchists such as Kropotkin introduced the principle of need in distributing the necessities of life. They also recognized that to build a free society, all instances of authority and inequality must be eliminated. The autonomy of the individual or group was essential to create a harmonious and ethical society based on human dignity and justice.

From the beginning, Johann Most knew little about communist-anarchism, and when its influence grew within the London exile community, he did not think much of it. For much of his life, Most's radicalism was influenced by an amalgam of thinkers, including Marx, Lassalle, Blanqui, and Bakunin. Political repression in Germany had engendered in him and many others a virulent antistatism first and a militant anticapitalism second, as the historian Ulrich Linse has argued.[40] Wilhelm Hasselmann and Johann Most were among the better-known activists who became social revolutionaries without completely abandoning certain Blanquist or Lassallean traits. Perhaps for that reason, Most's anarchism would always remain eclectic. As late as 1887, Kropotkin commented that the anarchism espoused in *Freiheit* was full of Blanquism.[41] Nettlau, in fact, believed that for years Most's affinity with anarchism was tenuous and that it matured slowly.[42] Up until the 1890s, Most continued to ridicule what he saw as Kropotkin's pie-in-the-sky vision of human goodness and spontaneity. The New York autonomists would receive the brunt of his ridicule.

German-speaking radicals who were directly influenced by communist-anarchism tended to operate outside the Reich's borders in such radical centers as Geneva and Paris. They considered the collectivism of Bakunin an outmoded theory. Otto Rinke and Josef Peukert were the two main exponents of communist-anarchism among German-speaking revolutionaries. Rinke was born in the town of Schmiegel in the Prussian province of Posen and learned the trade of locksmith. With little formal education, Rinke entered the fledgling labor movement of southeastern Germany. He refused to fulfill his military service and deserted to Switzerland, where he cofounded a pioneering revolutionary paper. He moved to Paris and continued his propaganda efforts with occasional forays into Germany. It was in the French capital in 1880 that Rinke and Peukert became friends. Peukert was one of the first activists in German-speaking Europe to spread the new philosophy among Austrian and Bohemian workers. Rinke and Peukert read *Le Révolté,* the foremost communist-anarchist journal in Europe launched by Kropotkin in February 1879 (incidentally, only one month after the first issue of *Freiheit* rolled off the press).

By the spring of 1884, after Austrian and Swiss authorities successfully crushed revolutionary movements, the center of activity for German-speaking radicals shifted to London. An influx of Austrian radicals, including Peukert, arrived in the British capital. Once settled in London, German and Austrian anarchists formed their own sections within the Communist Workers' Educational Society (Communistischer Arbeiter-Bildungs-Verein; CABV). Ideological divisions became more apparent. Old tensions between the Most and Peukert factions quickly surfaced, revolving around the role of periodicals. In April 1884, *Freiheit* openly adhered to Bakunin's anarchist principles, while *Der Rebell* had associated itself with communist-anarchism several months earlier. In addition, Most published a pamphlet, *The Free Society* (Die freie Gesellschaft), in July with the subtitle, *Treatise on Principles and Tactics of the Communist Anarchists* (Eine Abhandlung über Principien und Taktik der kommunistischen Anarchisten). Peukert was incensed. He immediately denounced it as a disgraceful misrepresentation of communist-anarchism, since Most had in fact written a treatise on the principles of collectivist anarchism, and proceeded in muddying the waters of anarchism. "'As producer,'" Most wrote, "'everyone will receive their share according to real labor performed.'"[43] This share would be granted by a consumer organization loosely connected to other organizations, which would all replace the state, according to Most's tract. This was textbook Bakunin, and he proceeded in questioning the viability of a communist-anarchist society. In particular, he was concerned about what he called "unproductive parasites" that would appear in a communist-anarchist system, since all goods were distributed according to need instead of earned labor. Most's hatred of the privileged classes may have had something to do with his deep suspicion of the practicability of Kropotkin's theories.

Given Most's preoccupation with unity in the face of repression, he and his friends considered it unfortunate that two anarchist periodicals in the German language were being distributed in Central Europe. This competition, as they saw it, threatened the oneness of the movement and could paralyze propaganda activities. Peukert and Rinke argued that *Freiheit* was too American and had lost touch with European workers. Finally, in the summer of 1884, in an attempt to resolve the issue, the editors of *Der Rebell* were urged to cease publication for fear it would split the movement. A conference was organized to discuss the matter, but Rinke vehemently refused to shut down his paper. The split that was feared all along was now a reality. It became official when, in May 1885, Peukert and his associates were thrown out of the CABV. Not long after this, they set up their own group.

Underneath this battle for ideology and control simmered a deeply personal enmity between Peukert and Most that dated back to 1880. Both men came of age in a working-class environment and as young men assumed leadership positions in the labor movement of Austria and Germany. Both were acclaimed public speakers and editors, and both had faced the wrath of their governments. But differences in personality were perhaps more striking. Most had won the hearts of thousands of workers through his superior oratory skill, his exuberance and zest on the podium. Peukert was an introvert who valued an intellectual dimension to his anarchism, presenting himself in a didactic and somewhat donnish way. This difference in style is even more apparent in their writing. Most's language is straightforward and brash, his texts laced with brazen wit and humor. Peukert wrote discourses, theoretical exposés that often seemed dull and professorial. He sought to appeal to the reader's intellect, while Most worked the emotions. "Peukert was grave, pedantic, utterly devoid of humor," remembered Emma Goldman. "He lacked the vivid personality [of Most]."[44] Karl Schneidt even called Peukert "characterless" and judged him vain and not very industrious. But Schneidt worked for *Freiheit* and was perhaps biased when he stated that Peukert's vanity had been the cause of the split in the movement.[45] The American journalist John Gilmer Speed, who met Peukert in a Manhattan saloon in 1892, noticed that his "eyes are small and black, and every time I have seen them they looked angry. Peukert has probably never laughed much in a wholesome day."[46]

Amid this atmosphere of distrust, a tragic episode poisoned the relationship between the factions for good. The capture of the German smuggler Johann Neve by police was not shocking, given the climate of intense surveillance of radicals and increasing cooperation between police forces across Europe, but what is significant about this episode is the way that an already fractured movement proceeded to blame fellow comrades for admittedly serious mistakes, aggravated by the fact that Neve never left prison alive. A tireless and admired activist, Neve stood on somewhat neutral ground during the ongoing disputes and had traveled to Belgium in November 1885 to organize the extremely risky undertaking of smuggling *Freiheit, Der Rebell,* and later *Die Autonomie* into Germany. He quickly raised the suspicion of the German and Belgian police, who launched a joint campaign to arrest him. Neve felt uneasy and immediately urged Peukert to send two replacements so that he could evade arrest and the smuggling could continue without interruption. In December 1886, Peukert decided to travel to Brussels himself, taking with him Karl Theodor Reuss, a new convert. This proved to be a cardinal mistake. Reuss had been under suspicion of being a police spy (which he was) and had been expelled from the Socialist League earlier that spring. Victor Dave finally exposed Reuss to the entire anarchist movement in London. Since the Mostian camp had condemned Reuss without any hearing, Peukert—perhaps blinded by hatred toward Dave—foolishly refused to accept the facts. In January 1887, Peukert and Reuss traveled to Brussels and on to Verviers, where they met Neve. The visit was short, and both men returned to London the same month. But on 21 February, Johann Neve, who had been warned by others of foul play, was arrested by Belgian detectives and handed over to the Germans. The entire smuggling operation for the German anarchist press instantly collapsed. What was worse, a detailed, unsigned article on the affair appeared in *Der Sozialdemokrat,* the Social-Democratic organ, pointing the finger at Peukert, who in turn suspected Dave of authoring the article. Emotions took the upper hand. The Mostians, with some justification, called Peukert's trip to Belgium irresponsible, but they did not leave it at that. They blatantly accused Peukert of betraying Neve, a charge that ruined Peukert's position forever. Neve was eventually sentenced to fifteen years in prison, where in 1896 he died of tuberculosis in the "lunatic" section of the prison.

In the spring of 1887, with Neve behind bars and propaganda efforts crippled, the movement sought clarity about what happened in Belgium to deflate conspiracy theories. On 22 May, three months after Neve's apprehension, a commission organized by the Autonomy Group investigated the affair and found Peukert not guilty of the charges. Most and Dave, however, saw no reason to exculpate the Austrian and continued their relentless assault. Peukert may have acted recklessly, but he never intended to blow the whistle on the movement's most effective activist. Most seemed not to care that throwing around a charge of betrayal during an intensely repressive political climate was uncalled for. Indeed, Most was so blinded by hatred for Peukert that he blamed all autonomists for the capture of Neve and the disunity that ensued. He once proposed house searches and confiscation of printing material to teach the London autonomists—whom he also accused of not paying for *Freiheit*—a lesson.[47] To outdo his earlier claims, Most made the outrageous charge that *Die Autonomie* had been financed with police funds. Such statements incensed many anarchists, and in March 1889 a London commission, which included Kropotkin, found Most's claims unsubstantiated.[48]

The Neve affair and its aftermath ripped apart the movement at its seam. Personal and ideological tensions now lined up perfectly and were manifested in New York as well as in London. The initial split had occurred when Peukert and his followers—mostly Austrians—were expelled from the CABV and founded their own club that provided the communist-anarchists with a physical address. Activists elsewhere were encouraged to organize. Chicago, the city with the largest concentration of German-speaking anarchists, became the leading center of communist-anarchism in the United States. New York soon followed suit, with the emergence of a small network of autonomist venues and organizations operating alongside Mostian groups in relative calm.

In 1890, Otto Rinke and Josef Peukert arrived in New York, and their presence not only strengthened the autonomist anarchist community but reanimated old tensions. Peukert arrived penniless in New York in early June after wanderings in France and Spain. "My only goal was to come clean with Most," he later wrote, "and to save as much as possible in order to set out on my return voyage."[49] But Peukert had a premonition that peaceful reconciliation with Most was out of the question. In a letter published in *Freiheit,* he challenged Most to present evidence for his allegations to a committee of ten or twelve independent comrades. Speaking in the name of the IWPA, Most bluntly dismissed Peukert's request, stating that "for us Peukert is long dead (alas only morally)." Not for nothing did the American writer James Huneker remember Most as "an intelligent and stubborn man, if ever there was one."[50]

While in New York, Peukert began working for the anarchist cause in a city divided—at least among anarchists. He delivered speeches to autonomist meetings in New York, Brooklyn, and New Jersey and possibly joined the Radical Workers' Association. He may have had a hand in the formation of the umbrella organization Autonomous Groups of America (Autonome Gruppen Amerikas). This suggests that a clear organizational split between Mostians and autonomists was now a reality. The Mostian camp was afflicted by dissent, and many left to join the autonomists. One of them was Alexander Berkman, a young and impetuous Russian who worked in the *Freiheit* office. Berkman met Most in the beginning of 1888 and became one of his most ardent disciples. Like so many, Berkman felt the ghost of the Neve affair obstructing any joint propaganda efforts and proposed a final resolution at a conference of Yiddish-speaking anarchists, but all good intentions came to nothing. He joined the autonomists in 1891.

On 23 July 1892, Berkman shot but did not kill Henry Clay Frick, the industrialist who brutally suppressed a strike at the Homestead plant near Pittsburgh. This deed was the only truly anarchist-inspired act of violence against a member of the elite in American history. In fact, more than any other, this seemed a textbook example of propaganda by deed. But anarchists in the United States were not united in their support for this act. Like the firebug incident, the attempt on Frick's life by a young comrade caused intense debate among anarchists, especially in New York. And like the Neve affair, Berkman's deed ripped open old wounds that had never properly healed. To the astonishment of all, Johann Most, who had made a career as propagator of revolutionary violence, condemned Berkman's act (and Goldman's defense of Berkman) as reckless and proceeded to dismiss such violence altogether. "America is not the place for assassinations," he remarked in an article calling such acts suicidal for the anarchist movement.[51] But what really infuriated Goldman was Most's suggestion that the entire episode had been a stunt to provoke sympathy for Frick. At his next lecture, Most was publicly challenged by Goldman to provide evidence for his allegations. When he dismissed her, she stepped onto the stage, drew a horsewhip, and struck the stunned German, then broke the whip and threw it into his face before leaving the hall. The incident became a news item. Goldman later regretted her behavior.

Most's attitude is not simply explained by his condescending demeanor toward young autonomist anarchists. He was genuinely troubled by the role of violence in the revolutionary anarchist movement in the United States. Max Baginski, a young, broad-minded German anarchist sympathetic to Most, alluded to the latter's alienation in a foreign country. "In the United States Most was out of his element," Goldman remembered Baginski saying, "without the inspiration and impetus that come from the life and struggle of the masses. Most, of course, had considerable German support in the country, but it is only the native element in a country that can bring about fundamental change. It must have been the helplessness of his position in America and the absence of a native anarchist movement that caused Most to turn against 'propaganda by deed' and, with it, against Sasha [Berkman]."[52] Whatever his reasons, autonomists lambasted Most's apparent change of heart regarding revolutionary tactics. In a convention later that year, they stated that Berkman's assault was "purely revolutionary and anarchist."[53] Saverio Merlino, the well-known Italian communist-anarchist, believed that Berkman's shot—while not killing Frick—had hit at the heart of the system of exploitation.

To some extent, Berkman's act constituted the end of an era. The beginning of the 1890s brought the beginning of the end of sturm und drang in the German anarchist circles of New York. After this period, only a few anarchists advocated terrorist propaganda, although the rise in assassinations in Europe sparked great interest among Italian and Spanish immigrant radicals. Most himself hinted at a change in attitude when he urged a greater anarchist involvement in trade unions. His pamphlet *Der kommunistische Anarchismus* (December 1889) even adopted communist-anarchist tenets. Internationally, communist-anarchism became the dominant philosophy of the movement, and the effects of this shift were visible in the streets and cafés of the Lower East Side. Immigrant anarchism in general became a more intellectual movement. New immigrants such as Russian Jews and Italians began to fashion their own movements, often in cooperation with Germans.

Despite these developments and the economic depression of the mid-1890s, the Neve affair remained unresolved. Peukert, desperate to lift an intolerable burden, pressed for a final exoneration. Above all, he sought a reconciliation with Most. The majority of German-speaking anarchists had long accepted his innocence, though they had never forgotten his recklessness. In September 1893, Peukert traveled to Chicago, then hosting the dazzling World's Columbian Exposition, to attend the International Anarchist Conference as a delegate for the united autonomist groups of New York. He had been wanted by the New York police for approving Berkman's attempt on Frick's life and so decided to settle in Chicago. One of the conference's main objectives was to devise a plan for efficient propaganda in the English language.[54] Most and his *Freiheit* associates strongly opposed such a plan; they saw the production and distribution of anarchist propaganda and newspapers among native-born workers as futile and extremely costly. Some twenty delegates participated, among them representatives from New York and Brooklyn. Times had changed since the first anarchist conference in America a decade ago: a severe economic depression was wreaking havoc among working families, and very few donations found their way to the anarchist cause. The Spanish anarchist Pedro Esteve reported that at the gathering spirits were high, but, unlike Pittsburgh, no coordinating organization emerged from it.[55] It was probably Peukert's final important public appearance within the anarchist movement. Two months after the conference, the Chicago Debating Club, one of the few German groups still active in the city, elected a six-member investigative committee to present all the evidence—domestic as well as international—pertaining to the Neve affair. A year later, the committee concluded that all allegations against

Peukert were slander based on lies. The committee also recommended that Most come to Chicago and acknowledge the results in public and in the presence of Peukert, but Most was unmoved. He refused to accept the findings and even proceeded to throw suspicion on the committee itself. He also refrained from publishing the findings in *Freiheit*. Nevertheless, the 1894 declaration of Peukert's innocence provided closure to the affair, reducing Most's continued attacks on Peukert to hot air. On 3 March 1910, Josef Peukert died "in comparative obscurity and poverty," as one obituary had it.[56] He was only fifty-five.

The majority of the men and women in the autonomist anarchist community in New York were not caught up in the personal vendetta between Most and Peukert, although Berkman characterized the Mostians and Peukert's circle as being "chiefly concerned" with the matter.[57] The movement they built allows us to observe a communist-anarchist culture all its own, and quite different from that of the Mostians. It is an illustration of how ideology obtains meaning through human agency, how it becomes visible in relationships, cultural expressions, and the cultivation of solidarity and cooperation. In terms of their public campaign, many autonomists expressed an ultra-radicalism and even utopianism that distinguished them from the older German anarchists belonging to the International Working People's Association, the federation created by Most and Spies. Autonomists believed in the immediate destruction of the established order and cared less about gradually building a support base among workers. On the level of day-to-day anarchist living, they strove for all-out decentralization and small group action and upheld the primacy of the individual. Any formal organization was denounced as an embryo of authority, including the central committees of the IWPA. To the autonomists, the IWPA was outdated and came too close to a centralized party. Anarchism and communism were not antagonistic, they argued, but complemented each other in a free society; personal freedom and collective ownership of goods went hand in hand. This free society should be reflected in the movement itself, and anarchists must practice here and now what they envision for the future.

True to their philosophy, autonomists founded their own groups and launched their own activities outside the IWPA purview. The Austrian Revolutionary League was possibly the first German-speaking communist-anarchist group in New York. It existed in Manhattan throughout 1884 following the emigration of dozens of Austrian and Swiss radicals. The Radical Workers' Association (Radikale Arbeiterbund), founded in

1885, became the foremost autonomist circle in New York. The designation "Radikale" was a reference to the early social-revolutionary party in Austria (the Radikale Arbeiterpartei). The Radical Workers' Association consisted mainly of Austrian and Hungarian anarchists who—ironically—had become radicals by attending speeches by Most in Austria in the late 1860s.[58] In his anger, Most could not resist playing the nationality card by ridiculing the intimate bond between the Austrians. "I used to have a very high regard for the Austrians (comrades)," he wrote in a letter to Dave. "My enthusiasm has nearly dropped to a freezing-point."[59] In turn, the autonomists publicly criticized Most's purported authoritarian attitude toward other periodicals within the movement. One instance involved the English-language anarchist paper *Alarm,* which reappeared in 1888 and which Most demanded be published in New York instead of Chicago, where it had initially appeared.[60]

The autonomist anarchist community of New York, which was smaller than the one in Chicago or St. Louis, increased its membership and activities between 1885 and 1900. Like anarchists before them, autonomists created their own alternative sphere within the city's neighborhoods in which they could discuss, celebrate, and live their version of anarchism. The Radical Workers' Association organized free discussion evenings, with topics ranging from free love and socialism to revolutionary tactics and propaganda by deed. They staged labor festivals with roots in Bavarian and Austrian proletarian culture and infused with specifically anarchist sensibilities. For example, the March Festival (März-Feier), probably a commemoration of the revolutionary March days of 1848, was a family gathering accompanied by singing, speeches, stage performances, and at the end, a ball.[61] The Vintage Harvest Festival (Weinlesefest) was a characteristic annual event. Scheduled sometime in September, it was traditionally celebrated with dancing, food, and drinking. The autonomists introduced this wine festival in 1885, when the group was founded, while the last gathering—its twelfth edition—took place in 1897.[62] The Austrian Peasants' Ball (Österreichischen Bauern Ball) was another typical event organized by the members of New York's Workers' Association. Starting in 1892, this dance fair was held every February at a large taproom in Clarendon Hall.

The New York autonomists also boasted their own cafés and restaurants. These gathering places acted as infoshops, discussion forums, and locales for pleasure and recreation. Ordinary places were effectively refashioned into anarchist spaces through decorations, ownership, or dedication of function as headquarters or clearinghouses. During the latter part of the 1880s, most autonomist anarchists could be found in the Manhattan neighborhood around the intersection of East Fifth Street and Second Avenue in places like Herzog's or Ritter's saloon. Soon they began frequenting At Rough Mike's (Zum groben Michel), a popular saloon on 209 East Fifth Street, which soon became the "headquarters" of the German-speaking communist-anarchists in New York. The saloon quickly attracted undercover police agents, who kept a watchful eye on the area around East Fifth Street. One of the reasons for the increased surveillance may have been the seizure in 1892 of anarchist literature in Philadelphia destined for one of the neighborhood saloons on the Lower East Side.[63] Ignaz Neumaier's Viennese restaurant on Allen Street also attracted autonomists, and the place sold tickets for many of the festivals in the neighborhood, another function that distinguished it from non-anarchist venues.[64]

The 1890s saw a proliferation of autonomist groups in spite of a wrenching economic depression in 1893 accompanied by widespread unemployment, hunger, and protest across the country. Josef Peukert's arrival in New York in 1890 and subsequent lecture tour renewed the activism of the autonomists. Initiatives followed, as had happened in the wake of Johann Most's tour in 1883. For instance, the early activism of an independent anarchist group in Brooklyn was inspired by Peukert. "The performances of the lecturer, Comrade Peukert, have made a deep impression on the attendants," reported *Der Anarchist,* "and led many to a better understanding."[65] The German anarchists of Newark illustrate the life of a group in the flux of ideological change. Since 1888, they organized themselves into a citywide association and were affiliated with the IWPA. They held discussion meetings and invited speakers to their lecture evenings. The exclusion of this association from a regional conference dominated by Mostians in 1889 changed everything. Even before the arrival of Peukert, members began to openly support *Der Anarchist,* a communist-anarchist organ in St. Louis. The Newark Workers' Association changed its name to Radical Groups of Newark (Radikale Gruppen Newarks) and remained quite independent.[66] Other autonomist groups were founded in Elizabeth, Paterson, Jersey City Heights, and West Hoboken.

The most obvious handicap for New York autonomists was the absence of a New York–based communist-anarchist periodical. The issue of a diverse anarchist press had been a source of enmity within the movement ever since the arrival of Johann Most. *Freiheit* virtually ignored all autonomist activities during the second half of the 1880s, inadvertently highlighting the need for a separate local autonomist organ. The appearance of *Der Anarchist* in Chicago in January 1886, one of the first communist-anarchist periodicals in America, provided a forum for autonomists, but the paper collapsed after Haymarket.

Since newspapers provided not only a mouthpiece for anarchists, a vehicle for propaganda but also a tool for fostering community and identity, it is important to analyze the autonomist papers. Moreover, as a result of the fights with Most, autonomists came to adopt a different approach to running an anarchist newspaper and an anarchist movement in general. Anti-authoritarian principles were reflected in the workings of the editorial committee and the role of the editor. Despite the ever-present fear of financial ruin, an argument Most repeatedly invoked to justify his strict management style, autonomists never turned their backs on a new periodical venture.

The first communist-anarchist periodical in New York came about a year after Peukert's arrival in the city. On 8 August 1891, the fourteenth issue of *Der Anarchist* was published in New York by the Autonomous Groups of America. The relocation was prompted by the fact that financial support in St. Louis was drying up, while autonomist ranks were growing on the East Coast. "Especially here in the east," observed an editorial, "has the autonomist idea enjoyed ever greater dissemination."[67] Claus Timmermann, a young, energetic activist and poet, had sought to revive the spirit of the moribund Chicago *Anarchist* and produced several issues in St. Louis. In the summer of 1891, he moved to New York, where he shared a Lower East Side apartment with Emma Goldman, Alexander Berkman, and the Jewish anarchist illustrator Modest "Fedya" Stein. "He had considerable poetic talent and wrote forceful propaganda," Goldman remembered. Timmermann became intrigued with Berkman's plan to kill Frick in July 1892 and eventually helped draft a manifesto rallying the workers of Homestead to destroy the wage system. "'He was a likable fellow and entirely trustworthy,'" Goldman wrote, "'though a considerable drinker. We felt that Claus was the only person we could safely draw into our plan. He caught our spirit at once.'"[68] Timmermann was indeed an advocate of armed resistance against the capitalist oligarchs. He deplored the reckless use of violence by the robber barons against working people and took no issue with the use of dynamite as a defense against the Gatling guns of the capitalists. He further criticized the double standard used by the mainstream press when reporting on violence committed by workers against captains of industry. "Only the reactionary forces are to blame for the fact that the use of dynamite by the people in social struggles will play an important role," Timmermann argued, "since the Reaction itself forces them to use such methods."[69] Underneath the ardent rhetoric resided a more gentle and perhaps troubled personality. Luba Benenson, the daughter of Fedya Stein, remembered Timmermann as a heavy drinker, a skilled carpenter, and above all a caring friend: "'Though Claus earned very little, every time he got paid he sent some money to Emma and Sasha [Berkman] in France.'"[70]

While Timmermann settled in Lower Manhattan, it was the Austrian émigré Karl Mazur (also spelled Masur) who became the new editor of *Der Anarchist.* A shoemaker from Silesia, Mazur immigrated to New York in 1884 as a political exile.[71] As an editor, Mazur was committed to the idea of personal autonomy and stated that the mission of the paper was not only to battle the existing coercive political system "but also . . . to prevent any personal authority or tutelage within our own ranks, and to habituate ourselves today to live and act free and equal."[72] The anarchist movement was thus not only seen as the champion of an anarchist society for the future but also as an example of one in the present—the entire anarchist community embodied the anarchist ideal here and now. After two years, the paper changed leadership, a policy in sharp contrast to the editorial structure at *Freiheit.* Nicolaus Mauer, the new editor, had been administrative secretary for *Der Anarchist* and had been involved as an investigator in the Peukert-Neve affair in the late 1880s.[73] He personally experienced the Mostians' recalcitrance to accept the findings. Puzzled by Most's continued attacks, Mauer wrote "dozens" of letters to inform Most of the results.[74]

Through the able guidance of these editors, *Der Anarchist* positioned itself as a counterpart to *Freiheit.* The paper sought to balance the monopoly position of Most by providing an alternative outlet. Its carefully stated mission was twofold: it offered a free forum in which anarchist theory and its relevance in human society could be analyzed, and it vowed to publish all opinions and ideas uncensored. In the spirit of Peukert's ideas, the task of the editor and publisher was designated as purely "technical," consisting of composition, managing the flow of correspondence, and financial responsibilities. Decisions regarding the content of the paper were made according to principles of free discussion and consensus. Each individual had the right to publish his or her opinions, even when that person could not demonstrate any writing skills.[75] Furthermore, weekly publishers' meetings (open to anybody) undertook the management of the paper. Various functionaries were elected at these meetings, and occasionally the autonomist groups of the New York City area organized a general publishers' conference.

The last two years of *Der Anarchist*—from the summer of 1893 to the summer of 1895—coincided with one of America's worst economic depressions. Thousands found themselves out of work, and many were evicted from their homes and wholly dependent on charity. A great many took to the streets to demand relief and vent frustration. Anarchists and socialists appeared on street corners, squares, and saloons to speak to desperate men and women; they organized rallies, distributed pamphlets, and told workers to defy the law and take what is theirs. Timmermann and Goldman, for example, spoke at unemployment rallies, and both were arrested for urging workers to take bread if no relief was coming. Despite this renewed activism, despair and poverty dampened the spirit of working-class New Yorkers, including anarchists. "The continuous unemployment of the self-sacrificing comrades in New York and Brooklyn," lamented an anarchist editorial, "as also the wretched state of business in general have drained the last willing powers."[76] From February 1893 on, editors appealed to subscribers to pay their dues, reminding readers that there would be no victory without a fight and no fight without sacrifice. No payment was ever returned for the hundreds of copies sent to Europe. High printing costs combined with a decline in sales skewed the balance sheets. The cost of printing forty-five issues of *Der Anarchist* in 1892 amounted to 72 percent of the total cost of the magazine (seventeen dollars per issue—each sold for only three cents!), and the cost kept rising the following year.[77] Carelessness on the part of subscribers to pay arrears remained a constant irritation for the editors. The last issue appeared on 22 June 1895, with a notice that unless financial support increased, *Der Anarchist* would suspend publication.[78] No further issues have been found, and it is believed the paper folded for good. Around the same time, another, more obscure German-language paper, *Anarchisten*, appeared in New York from 1893 until 1895. No issues have been found, and it is not clear if it adhered to communist-anarchism, to the Mostians, or perhaps to individualist anarchism.

The activities of Claus Timmermann continued during the second half of the 1890s and illustrate how independent activists attempted their own enterprises in a time of economic hardship, rapid change in the ethnic makeup of New York, and increasing antagonism between the haves and have-nots. Timmermann's ventures reflect the changing attitude of many young anarchists seeking to break out of their own ethnically (and linguistically) circumscribed movement. Still considering themselves communist-anarchists, it is clear that activists like Timmermann and Goldman had lost appetite for the petty club life of either the Mostians or the autonomists. They sought to connect their anarchist beliefs with a wider audience, with different neighborhoods, cities, and causes. Personal autonomy, gender equality, and ideas about sexual freedom cannot be underestimated as factors in this rebellion of the young. Goldman's public humiliation of Most dramatizes this division between the older male guard and the younger, mostly emancipated male and female activists.

A month before Mauer became editor of *Der Anarchist,* Timmermann went solo and launched *Die Brandfackel* (The torch), a paper that lasted only until January 1895.[79] It appeared irregularly, even though its subtitle labeled it a monthly. Timmermann's new undertaking breathed the zeitgeist of the 1890s: a renewed hope for revolution during hard times, a romantic rebelliousness that contained both anger and the promise of salvation. An editorial written in typically colorful language introduced the first issue: "May [it] give light to the many oppressed and blast away the bastions of reaction, may it destroy a good deal of lies and prejudice."[80] Times of unemployment and the suppression of strikes and demonstrations were always a source for scathing and high-toned anarchist opinion pieces. Such language was typical of anarchism's public discourse: it was deliberately bombastic, threatening, and idealistic.

Fluent in English, Timmermann soon realized that what was needed for a successful anarchist campaign in America was English-language propaganda. This assessment was shared by a large number of anarchists coming of age. Leaving the insular world of the older German movement, Timmermann connected with other ambitious, cosmopolitan activists such as his friends Goldman, Berkman, and Stein. Goldman, of course, was on her way to becoming an American radical, which may have inspired Timmermann. Also, in 1894, the British anarchist Charles Wilfred Mowbray arrived in the United States for a lecture tour and managed to rouse an audience of English-speaking workers. As he admitted himself, all these developments caused Timmermann to abandon *Die Brandfackel* and instead allocate his editorial skills to the making of English-language propaganda. "It is a fact," he wrote, "that here in America the anarchist publications in the German language in number significantly surpass those in English, even though the latter are much more useful and necessary."[81] Using the same printing press, he now ran pamphlets by Kropotkin and Elisée Reclus in translation.

Despite Timmermann's newfound commitment to propaganda in English, he ventured one more time into German journalism. In November 1897, he launched *Sturmvogel,* of which he was the main contributor, typesetter, printer, and colporteur. In his characteristically lyrical language, Timmermann introduced the reader to his magazine by invoking the metaphor of a gathering storm. The title itself is a reference to the storm petrel, a type of long-winged seabird "that soars like an arrow over troubled water and whips the waves with its wings." The petrel stood for the "small pioneer of freedom" flying forward while braving the roar of the tempest.[82] Timmermann chose "Lewwer duad üs Slaav" as his motto, an ancient Frisian battle cry meaning "rather dead than a slave." The first issue appeared on 1 November 1897, with Justus Schwab's saloon as its business address. But shortly after the new year began, the paper was already in trouble. Problems with typesetting, illness, and complications with postal requirements suspended production. Timmermann apologized to his readers for the delay, but Schwab humorously (and in good spirit) remarked that no one would ever believe the ridiculous chain of events that had befallen the paper and that it would have been easier for Timmermann to admit drunkenness during that period.[83]

Timmermann's *Sturmvogel,* which folded on 16 May 1899, endorsed the immediate liberation of the working classes, by violent means if necessary. Liberation without force was viewed as impossible, since the state itself was based on violence and employed it repeatedly to quell the demands of the oppressed. The present social struggle was about people, *Sturmvogel* asserted, people who resist slavery and servitude and are capable of love but also of hatred; people who "aspire to the freedom of the individual and the highest joy of life."[84] In line with Timmermann's conviction, the paper sought to transcend ethnicity and reported on non-Germans and the growing activism of middle-class American radicals and their clubs. In this sense, despite its low circulation, *Sturmvogel* formed a bridge between younger German anarchists and the broader noninstitutional progressive movement.

The German anarchist ranks in New York during the late 1890s had declined, and many once-prominent clubs seem to have been defunct by 1898. The sharp divisions between the Mostians and the autonomists also vanished. Since communist-anarchism had become the prevalent philosophy among immigrant anarchists (apart from some individualists or syndicalists), autonomism as a faction was rendered obsolete. Starting in the late 1890s, young German anarchists, often in concert with Jewish and American comrades, started to engage in a more intellectual movement that lasted until the eve of the First World War. Others retreated from the movement or grew disillusioned. Some old-timers saw Timmermann's ambitions for anarchist propaganda as overly optimistic and even futile.

Antagonism between the Mostian IWPA groups and the autonomists from 1885 to 1900 undoubtedly inhibited propaganda efforts into the broader mainstream society. But this divide should not be dramatized as an all-consuming trench warfare between German and Austrian anarchists. After all, they shared the same language and were united in their opposition to the state, church, and capital. At no time was a spirit of solidarity more prevalent than during periods of political repression. In the wake of the Haymarket explosion (4 May 1886), American authorities launched the first nationwide red scare. Anarchists were at the top of the list, and they knew they had to stand together. In July 1886, for instance, the IWPA groups, the united autonomists, and the Social-Revolutionary Club organized a large picnic in Hudson County Park, New Jersey. "Again the revolutionary elements of New York gave occasion to a day of recreation and of harmonious cooperation," printed *Freiheit.* The tone of the account was markedly sincere, expressing optimism that all anarchists would live in a "spirit of union" and cultivate "brotherliness among New York revolutionaries."[85] However, this mood could reverse dramatically once milder political times returned. In January 1889, a short piece in *Freiheit*—possibly penned by Most—was again deriding the Radical Workers' Association and the Social-Revolutionary Club as "bogus organizations."[86]

Much of this ideological mudslinging appeared in periodicals and pamphlets and most likely was portrayed as graver than it actually was. It is impossible to gauge what effect these polemics had on the hundreds of ordinary German-speaking anarchists and sympathizers. Aside from debating weighty matters of ideology and strategy, anarchists also socialized expressly to leave such matters aside, to forget society's ills. When Goldman invited a cantankerous Most out for a drink "for old friendship's sake," they chose a café never frequented by anarchists. "His changed mood would transport me to a different world," she wrote, "a world without discord and strife, without a Cause to bind one, or opinions of comrades to consider. All differences were forgotten."[87]

Discord among members of the German anarchist movement had many causes. Among the less obvious, perhaps, was a generational conflict that began to drive a wedge between the older guard of activists born during or before the 1840s and a younger generation born in the 1860s or after. During the 1890s, when many of the younger comrades reached their twenties, age divisions became more visible within the movement. As early as 1887, New York Group I organized a meeting for "older members" only—for those who had been active during the years 1882–86, often seen as the heyday of German American anarchism.[88] When in 1904 Goldman was asked to speak at a meeting dedicated to the fifty-eight-year-old Most, members of Most's circle, including his partner Helene Minkin, strongly objected. "I had no desire to intrude," replied Goldman, "but the younger comrades in the German ranks, as well as many of the Yiddish anarchists, insisted on my speaking."[89] Sometimes both generations cooperated within the same group, as when Newark's seniors (Alten) and juniors (Jungen) held a joint meeting in 1895 to streamline propaganda efforts.[90] Still, amid the ideological changes of the late 1880s and 1890s, age was often another dividing line. Among the youngsters who collided with Most were Timmermann, Goldman, Berkman, and Stern, to name a few. These young adults joined the autonomists and later steered an independent course within New York's (and the nation's) multiethnic anarchist movement.

*Entrance and interior of Zum groben Michel, or Tough Mike's Saloon. (*Harper's Weekly, *20 August 1892)*

*Wilhelm Hasselmann in Williamsburg, Brooklyn, around 1900. (*Philadelphia Times, *17 December 1899, in Ramus Scrapbook, Pierre Ramus Archives, International Institute for Social History, Amsterdam)*

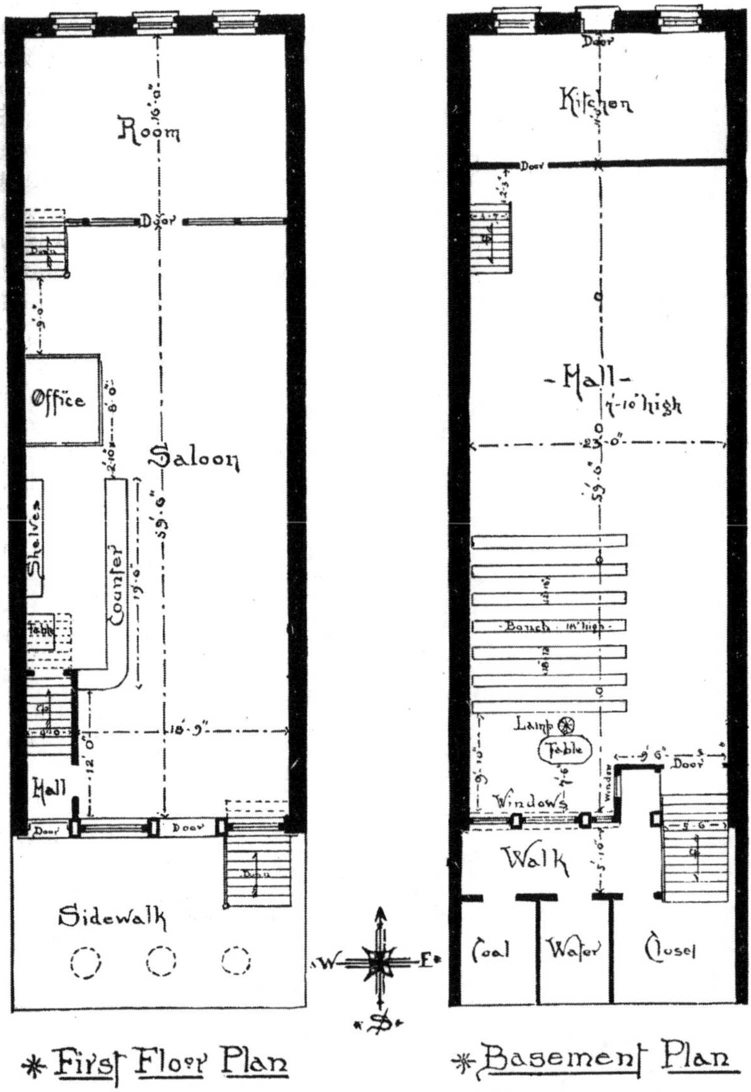

Floor plan of Greif's beerhall in Chicago. (Schaack, Anarchy and Anarchists, *440)*

Neff's beerhall, Chicago. (Schaack, Anarchy and Anarchists, *136)*

(Below) Interior view of Neff's beerhall, Chicago. (Schaack, Anarchy and Anarchists, *111)*

*A Jewish anarchist meeting in Military Hall on the Bowery, New York. (*Harper's Weekly*, 20 August 1892)*

Max Metzkow. (Special Collections Library, Labadie Collection, University of Michigan)

Johann Most in 1883 or 1884. (International Institute for Social History, Amsterdam)

*Johann Most addresses a meeting at Cooper Union, 1887. (*Frank Leslie's Illustrated Newspaper, *16 April 1887, 133)*

Clara Hänsch in Leipzig, Germany. (International Institute for Social History, Amsterdam)

5 *Facing America: German Anarchists' Political Culture in New York*

The alternative space that the German anarchists in greater New York created for themselves went beyond saloons and lecture halls to encompass propaganda groups, discussion and reading clubs, theater and musical groups, picnics, and public demonstrations. This political culture was not entirely isolated from the mainstream; its spatial borders touched and conflicted at many times with the larger society. The movement culture that will be explored in this chapter reveals a dual purpose: on the one hand, it served the anarchists' need for a separate, ideologically fulfilling sphere of action in which they could nurture an anarchist lifestyle, and on the other hand, it was designed to critique—and occasionally oppose—mainstream capitalist society. In it are contained the elements of defiance and resistance. This chapter will further show that anarchists were not occupied with desperate or indiscriminate violence against their enemies. Their movement culture was not a sideshow to support alleged criminals; it was anarchism in action. They may have been dreamers, but they also built their own world by carving out space and, where possible, challenging the norm.

An overview of the organizational structures of the movement and its historical precedents will make the various anarchist cultural expressions more comprehensible. The importance of organization to the members cannot be overstated, and this statement alone counters a prevailing misconception—then and now—that anarchism equals chaos. It is the type and scale of the organization that is crucial in understanding anarchism. Furthermore, a closer look at membership size, the role of women, and the different approaches to activism can fill in much of what is not widely known about immigrant anarchists. An analysis of German anarchist cultural groups shows not only a creative and imaginative side but reveals myriad forms of resistance to and defiance of the dominant culture, all existing in a defined space. Like the editorial arrangement of the autonomist paper *Der Anarchist,* many cultural organizations adopted anti-authoritarian models to run their affairs in such a way as to reflect an anarchist spirit of cooperation, respect, and autonomy.

Club Life and Activism

A central concern for revolutionary anarchists in New York was organization, which was seen as a platform from which effective propaganda could be launched. Without proper organization guided by anarchist principles, no coherent and sustained public campaign was possible. It is important to stress the role of organization because it is precisely on this topic that mainstream society utterly misunderstood what anarchism was about. Since anarchists spoke forcefully about the abolition of the established order, it was believed that they opposed any form of order—that anarchists were nihilists believing in nothing but destruction. "The anarchists' method of reforming the world is to pull down everything that exists," wrote the Christian editor Arthur T. Pierson in 1901, two months after President McKinley was assassinated by a deranged man claiming to be an anarchist. "Destruction is the first step and construction is secondary," Pierson continued. "Whether there shall be left anything to reconstruct does not appear to have absorbed much attention."[1] The socialists were also eager to point out the alleged backwardness of anarchism. "Their dissolution of society into individuals, their destruction of any organization and any cohesion is not progress, but a regression," wrote the socialist Gabriel Pierre Deville in a pamphlet.[2] The fact that anarchists did not have a conventional political structure with party headquarters, election committees, and a centralized executive office with an official street address forces us to examine fragmented geographic space as the location of a relatively stable anarchist organizational network.

The vast majority of anarchists throughout history, however, have gone to great lengths to propose alternative models for organizing people and society. Even Johann Most, who reveled in the language of revolutionary violence, composed several pamphlets on the workings of an anarchist society. The Pittsburgh Manifesto (1883) highlighted organization and unity as essential for the success of a revolutionary movement. This was not simply a slogan to rally a roaming anarchist class of laborers; it expressed the idea of a permanent presence of anarchist groups in all major American cities. Moreover, anarchists claimed that the capitalist state itself equals disorder—that it is a system based on exploitation, disrespect, and unabashed materialism, a negation of freedom. Anarchism would not entail the advent of chaos but rather the restoration of a harmonious society based on justice and human needs. Once freedom and justice were restored, harmony and order would follow, or as the individualist anarchist paper *Liberty* summarized this idea in its masthead: "Liberty: Not the Daughter, but the Mother of Order."

A SHORT HISTORY OF ANARCHIST CLUB LIFE

Small, autonomous groups that met regularly and advanced the cause through propaganda were of central importance to an anarchist movement in urban America. Those were the units that anchored anarchism to the urban geography. Groups had an address and a regular time schedule, just like the workplace. This regularity helped invest the meeting place with a sense of purpose, strength, and homeliness. It was important to show the outside world that each anarchist group had a known address to dispel the prevalent opinion that anarchists constantly engaged in secretive, conspiratorial activities, vanishing into the shadow of the ghetto after committing an act of subversion. Regardless of mainstream anxieties, German anarchists set up a decentralized network of autonomous clubs. August Sartorius von Waltershausen, an astute observer of socialism, criticized this model of "free associations" as impractical and prone to erupt in dissension and inaction. He could not envision an organization of strong-minded people without the guiding force of a majority will. While his majoritarianism may have been a bias, Waltershausen was correct in his warning against factionalism among the anarchist groups.[3] That said, German anarchists not only formed agitation groups but also trade unions, self-defense groups, ad hoc committees, and publishing associations. All these organizations were engaged in the public campaign to promote anarchism among the workers and citizens of New York.

This group-centered form of activism has its origins in the revolutionary movements of Europe. In speaking of impediments to anarchist organization posed by state and church, Mikhail Bakunin once wrote, "There exists a power which is capable of overcoming all that. It is the collective." "By being united and by organizing your own forces," he continued, "being led by common thought and common attitude, and by striving toward a common goal, you will be invincible."[4] Bakunin envisioned this collective or group (Gruppe) as a political-action or propaganda unit, small in size and cemented by strong bonds of solidarity and trust, all working toward a common cause. Bakunin's collective became a mainstay for anarchism's political campaign and remains so today, although the concept has undergone numerous modifications. German immigrant anarchists combined the group model with the recreational dimensions of a typical German workers' association.

In Germany, workers formed their own organizations as early as the 1840s. Members of the same trade or artists of similar talent banded together to increase their leverage in a rapidly industrializing society. Skilled workers organized craft associations (Fachvereine) and grew more vocal in their advocacy of workers' rights. This segment of the working class championed class-consciousness and would later turn to socialism and anarchism. The workers' associations (Arbeitervereine) became the building blocks for a labor movement that was further enriched by protective, mutual-aid, and various cultural and educational societies. These blocks literally created an alternative space.

Bismarck ended all this in 1878. In effect, space instantly became homogenized and dominant. Alternative fragmentation of social space was denied, and radicals had to adopt new ways to use space. Radical socialists and anarchists such as Most and Hasselmann opted for a secretive mode of organization: an underground network of autonomous groups. Four to five persons sufficed to form a group. Each of the groups appointed a confidant, who remained in touch with and conveyed information to the confidants of other groups. This way, none of the members knew the names of members of other groups, a scheme that supposedly offered the greatest protection against rampant police infiltration. This model of organizing sprang from the climate of repression in Germany at the time. Spatial occupation on the part of these radicals could never be permanent; it was temporary, even itinerant at times, with leading organizers and smugglers traveling the land and stopping at crossroads only briefly. This movement was literally based on movement: travel, improvisation, and secrecy. Sometime in 1880, this "cell organization" fell apart due to resourceful police tactics and the capture in December 1880 of Victor Dave, an important field organizer.

In New York, the anarchist movement was a small community that succeeded in obtaining a sedentary presence with none of the nomadic existence of hunted activists in Bismarck's Germany. Exactly how small it was is difficult to determine, given the anarchists' aversion to central authority and the lack of any reliable sources. "They cannot be counted," wrote a sympathetic writer, "since they are organized in independent groups."[5] This does not mean that they were irrelevant or nondescript. To arrive at a reasonable estimate, it is first necessary to distinguish among anarchist activists, sympathizers, and a substantial number of curious people. The first category typically consisted of group members, lecturers, writers, or people working for the anarchist press. The second category included politically minded people who were not fully committed to any anarchist organization but felt uneasy among orthodox socialists. A large number of workers and other citizens were simply curious about what anarchists had to say or merely attracted to the movement's colorful personalities and events. This explains why large meetings organized by anarchists sometimes attracted thousands of attendees.

The *New York Times,* an otherwise biased source, offers one of the few helpful statistics concerning the number of anarchists for April 1883, a time when Germans made up the majority of revolutionaries. The paper was certainly less sensationalist than Joseph Pulitzer's *New York World,* and in the years before Haymarket, the *Times* treated anarchists more as a curiosity than as a threat. In 1883, the paper made a distinction between "revolutionary Socialists of the Johann Most type" and "the milder type" (the "anarchist" label was not yet in vogue). Of the former, the paper reported "on good authority" that no more than two hundred resided in New York. Of the latter type, eight hundred to a thousand lived in the city, excluding New Jersey.[6] These numbers rose quickly during the remainder of the decade but declined afterwards. Even by November 1883, a month after the Pittsburgh convention, the number of Mostian anarchists may have doubled. A meeting in February 1884 to commemorate an Austrian anarchist-terrorist was attended by five hundred Germans and Austrians.[7] A contemporary New York anarchist and professor, Mezeroff, estimated that in 1886 some ten thousand anarchists lived in the United States, concentrated in Chicago (five thousand) and New York (2,500), with the rest dispersed throughout the country: Milwaukee (seven hundred), Pittsburgh and Philadelphia (both 250), Cincinnati (two hundred), St. Louis (150), and Buffalo (one hundred).[8] The reporter John Gilmer Speed stated that between three and four hundred anarchists lived in New York in 1893, which is almost certainly an underestimation.[9] These figures do not include occasional sympathizers or curious workers, who were among the thousands attending protest meetings organized by anarchists. These crowds often consisted of many nationalities and included a large number of women. Women interested in radical politics did not stay home on the evening of a major event, though they were rarely seen on stage.

The organization of anarchist groups in America was laid out in detail during the Pittsburgh Congress of 1883. It was the exact purpose of the delegates to provide a framework in which a durable anarchist presence could be created in any town or city. This presence was personified by a representative (usually a contact person for *Freiheit*) who actually lived there, not by an itinerant organizer. All groups were now affiliated with the IWPA and adhered to its proclamation of principles. These IWPA groups were no longer secret, however. Typically, anarchists from the same neighborhood or town constituted a new group and elected among themselves a chairperson, a corresponding and recording secretary, a treasurer, and sometimes a librarian or archivist, all short-term, rotating positions. Lecturers of well-established groups, such as Most and Peukert, often embarked on speaking tours to inspire locals to form new groups in different neighborhoods or towns. Sometimes new groups formed after breaking off from larger ones, a process that the historian Bruce C. Nelson has likened to mitosis or cell division.[10] Nine persons were authorized to set up a group. When several groups operated in the same town, a central committee—without executive powers—was put in place, staffed with delegates from the constituent groups to coordinate joint action. The individual groups could recall their delegates at any time, and decisions by the committee were made on a consensus basis.

In all, some seventy-eight German anarchist groups existed at one time or another in the greater New York City area from 1880 to 1914. They were either affiliated with the IWPA or adhered to the autonomist creed, and after 1900, most were independent. Often groups disbanded shortly after their founding or suspended activities for months or even years until better economic or political times. Nearly half of these groups were founded on the island of Manhattan, and more than a third were established in the northern New Jersey industrial belt. Half of them were active during the tumultuous 1880s, while still more than a third persisted into the 1890s.

The 1880s stand out as the most energetic decade in which a spirited and audacious anarchist movement came to life after Johann Most's lecture tours and the Pittsburgh Congress of 1883. But the decade's momentum was broken by the execution in November 1887 of four anarchists wrongly convicted of complicity in the Haymarket explosion. It brought the entire movement to a halt. Chicago was instantly deprived of its prominence as an anarchist center. A disheartening mourning period caused anarchists all over the United States to cease group activities, to disband, or to retreat into the shadow of the metropolis. However, the tragic events in Chicago did not herald the demise of anarchist activity in the United States, as some believed. It was a moment of repression that did not eliminate the spatial organization of anarchism; only the visibility and audibility of the activists diminished for awhile. Many sympathizers were converted to anarchism in the wake of the executions, notably Emma Goldman, Voltairine de Cleyre, and a host of newly arrived Russian Jewish socialists in Lower Manhattan. Starting in 1888, a year that began with a murderous blizzard, a post-Haymarket revival in anarchist activism occurred. New groups sprang up in Bushwick, Manhattan's West Side, and downtown areas. In Yorkville, which saw its German American population increase, the new Agitation Club Forward (Agitation-Club Vorwärts) launched its first meeting. The following year, several Newark groups joined to form the General Workers' Association of Newark (Allgemeine Arbeiterbund Newark).

The increased activity during the late 1880s was not necessarily a sign of a rise of anarchism's influence on America's working classes. More likely, it was a reaction of leading activists and speakers to an overall decline in enthusiasm among rank-and-file members. The Social-Revolutionary Club, for instance, the pioneer anarchist circle in America, was last mentioned in May 1886. A period of relative economic prosperity after the Haymarket affair further reduced the appeal of radical philosophies among ordinary workers. "The agitation of our comrades in America up to now leaves much to be desired," read an editorial in *Freiheit.*[11] The printed word especially failed to be widely distributed. Financial difficulties plagued the movement following the sacrifices made on behalf of the Haymarket defense fund for the accused. Debts incurred by groups triggered petty infighting. "The German revolutionary movement lies completely fallow," wrote a Newark comrade lamenting the fact that resources were not used to good advantage, and squabbles invariably hindered constructive action.[12]

The role of public speakers within the German movement can hardly be overstated. To a large extent, they were the promoters of the movement, the spellbinders with the power to turn lethargy into militancy. No wonder many felt that the vitality of the movement depended in part on itinerant speechmakers. The anarchist Bruno Reinsdorf wrote that "the living word penetrates to the heart more than the dead letter," praising the value of lectures and discussions especially for uneducated newcomers. The lecture evening in the club's home base was the cornerstone of weekly anarchist group activity. It comes as no surprise that well-spoken anarchists were deputized as scouts with a duty to energize scattered activists. Their responsibility was such that the failure of a group to stay active was sometimes blamed on the "laziness" of the speakers. "The movement would have shown more success today, if the agitational forces did their duty," wrote one group secretary.[13] German anarchists outside Manhattan sometimes complained about the trouble of procuring first-rate orators, since New York's finest speakers resided in Manhattan.

During the 1890s, immigrant anarchism showed the first signs of a shift from a militant to a more intellectual movement still rooted in the physical clubs and lecture halls of the city. This shift reflects the course of American society leading up to the turn of the century. Historians of the decade have interpreted it as a transitional period bridging the frenzied society of the Gilded Age with the more innovative rationality of the Progressive era. After Berkman's failed assassination attempt in 1892, the German anarchist movement gradually abandoned the rhetoric of martial heroism, denouncing individual acts of violence as harmful to the movement. Johann Most and others devoted more attention to syndicalism and cultural propaganda such as theater and poetry. A kind of ethnic bohemia emerged in the cafés and reading rooms of immigrant New York a decade prior to the better-known Greenwich Villagers of mostly native-born Americans. The presence of books, magazines, decorations, and the organization of reading and discussion sessions around town conceptualized these places into alternative zones. However, the share of Germans among all immigrant arrivals dropped from 28 percent in the 1880s to 14 percent in 1890s, while a new wave of eastern and southern Europeans, mostly Russian Jews and Italians, rapidly transformed the ethnic makeup of Lower Manhattan once again.[14] As a result, the significance of the Lower East Side as a stronghold of German anarchism also declined. Many second-generation Germans moved to Yorkville on Manhattan's Upper East Side or outlying areas in Brooklyn and Queens. More German anarchist groups emerged in the Yorkville neighborhood during the 1890s than on the Lower East Side. The Antisocialist Law in Germany was repealed in 1890, bringing the influx of German radicals to a standstill; or as Karl Kautsky put it, "the well dried up."[15] This development led to renewed anarchist activism in Germany, especially by the youth movement called Die Jungen.

In and around New York City, several new clubs were founded in entirely new areas during the first years of the 1890s. Groups were formed in Harlem, Morrisania, Maspeth, and Long Island City in Queens as well as in West Hoboken. This activity on the periphery reflected the general trend among Germans to move out of the overcrowded tenement districts of Lower Manhattan. It also meant that Russian Jews and Italians accounted for the bulk of anarchist and socialist activity in Manhattan.

In 1893, the United States underwent one of the severest economic depressions in its history, with a record seventy thousand New Yorkers out of work and another twenty-five thousand destitute in Brooklyn during the winter of 1893–94, according to a police report.[16] Many anarchist group members were among these jobless men and women, and a host of groups were forced to suspend activities, sometimes losing meeting places in the process. The otherwise active Bakers' Discussion Club, for instance, was never heard of after October 1892. During the years 1893 to 1895, *Freiheit*'s coverage of group activity was noticeably less than in previous years. In spite of the widespread misery, several new clubs appeared, and old ones were reactivated. The Paterson Group, one of the veteran anarchist circles, regrouped and remained active for at least eight more years. In the middle of the depression winter of 1893, Newark anarchists organized a Workers' Educational Society (Arbeiter-Bildungsverein).

Despite these initiatives, overall German anarchist club life was on the decline in the years leading up to the new century. The IWPA structure of groups slowly eroded. Long-standing anarchist circles disappeared from the record. One of them was New York Group I, a circle that had grown to be the foremost German anarchist presence in New York, operating for at least thirteen years. The autonomists also faded from the record. Their main guild, the Radical Workers' Association, was last mentioned in September 1897. The close relationship between group activity (and discipline) and the physical location of its meeting place was such that when group members left or showed up only occasionally, the backroom meetings themselves did not materialize, and it was time to call it quits. The saloon simply lost one of its regular gatherings. The few sparks of activity in the beerhalls of Yorkville and Brooklyn could not reverse the downward course of the German movement. Social mobility among all Germans in New York accounts for some of the decline. Many erstwhile radicals found a measure of economic success as saloon keepers, brewers, proprietors, or independent artisans and either abandoned their ideals or simply withdrew from the movement. Those who remained increasingly directed their interests to purely recreational activities within the anarchist community. "If a group or club occupies a saloon as a favorite pub with hall," complained a Milwaukee anarchist, "the money is usually spent on drinking, smoking, and gaming, whereas half of it would otherwise have been allocated to agitation."[17]

Aside from open associational club life, there has been some speculation about the existence of secret groups, especially during the more reckless 1880s. It is not unthinkable that within a radical movement—fed on ideas of Bakunin and Blanqui—secret societies could have been active in New York. Waltershausen was certain that even before the Pittsburgh Congress a host of underground anarchist "agitation clubs" existed, even increasing their number after the congress. These groups did not come into the open, and no meetings were announced or reviewed. Not all anarchists believed in the permanent invisibility of secret organizations, however. "A secret society that does not know to make a stir is a dead body," some argued. "In order to thrive it will always and permanently have to appear publicly—without being seen, so to speak, but perhaps being audible and palpable."[18] Waltershausen mentions from hearsay a secret organization named the Black Hand (Die Schwarze Hand), which may simply have been the notorious Spanish group Mano Negra, who published some letters in *Freiheit*. In one of those letters, the Black Hand profiled itself as an international secret organization and seems to have been operating in various countries. They styled themselves as a vanguard revolutionary circle set on strengthening ties "on both sides of the ocean."[19] The New York chapter, of which Moritz Bachmann allegedly was the leading member, broke with the editorial circle of *Freiheit*.[20] Waltershausen spoke with certainty about a Secret Association (Geheimbund) in St. Louis, formed in the autumn of 1885 and presumably acting as a model for similar endeavors elsewhere. Only five to ten members were needed; their contributions were voluntary. Members were designated by numbers, and no written records were kept. Each member was required to set up a secondary group. Traitors faced death.[21]

HOW THE MOVEMENT MOVED: THE BUSINESS OF ANARCHIST CLUBS

One way anarchists conceptualized their club space was to impose some order and regularity to it, attributes that were never associated with anarchism in the public mind. The fact that meetings were scheduled regularly and conducted according to an agreed-upon process ensured not only that the organization ran effectively but also that locality was as much part of the movement as ideology. All clubs encoded some form of bylaws, which provided not only internal stability but a sense of creative independence, as is true for any voluntary association. An organized movement of independent clubs united by ideology also enhanced the sense of an otherwise elusive concept of alternative space. It structured that space and gave it legitimacy, at least in the eyes of the anarchists. The main purpose of an anarchist political group or club was propaganda and fundraising. Initially, it is true, rhetoric of violent revolution dominated the anarchists' public campaign, in part to gain more press and notoriety.

However, oral and written propaganda disseminated among ordinary workers was of paramount concern. When a new group constituted itself, the members scheduled weekly business meetings (Geschäftssitzungen) restricted to card-carrying members. Large clubs also held quarterly meetings in which new functionaries were elected, and other topics such as recruitment, briefings of various committees, and the state of propaganda efforts were discussed. Some groups suspended weekly meetings during the hot summer months or reduced their schedule to once a month only to resume a full schedule in the fall and winter.[22]

In addition to business gatherings, agitation groups arranged weekly discussions and open lecture evenings. The Social-Revolutionary Club, for instance, invariably invited "friends and opponents of anarchy," who were guaranteed freedom of speech. If a room could be filled with members and sympathizers, the lecturer—often a familiar face in the anarchist community—attempted to persuade newcomers and rejuvenate older members with an exposé on current conditions or historical events. Herein lies another reason why physical venues carried so much importance for the movement: it was easy to invite and accommodate an interested public to scheduled events with a street address. Recently immigrated comrades were invited to update New Yorkers on the labor movement in western and central Europe. Such gatherings were popular and served to strengthen international ties. By periodically receiving firsthand news from Europe, the New York anarchists had an opportunity to evaluate conditions in America and draw transatlantic comparisons. Most lectures held in New York, however, addressed events in America or tackled social, cultural, and philosophical issues. The range of lecture topics is impressive. Subjects such as "Clericalism and Bigotry in America," "Darwinism and Socialism," "The Place of Humans in Nature," "The Australian Electoral System," "Modern Marriage," and "Women and Girls among the Proletariat" are but a glimpse of what stirred the hearts and minds of this radical intellectual milieu in New York.

To attract new members, anarchist clubs sought to advertise activities and ideas to a wide working-class audience. Announcing meetings in *Freiheit* and other anarchist periodicals was not enough because outsiders—let alone non-German readers—could not be reached. To remedy this, the Bushwick anarchists decided to announce their meetings and lectures by distributing handbills throughout the neighborhood, a much more direct way of making contact with local workers. Perhaps because of this, they remained the strongest German anarchist circle in Brooklyn throughout the 1890s. Other groups urged members to announce meetings to coworkers and persuade them to bring along friends to a club meeting. Once new members were admitted, they agreed to pay dues, usually ten cents a month during the 1880s. A member could be expunged when he or she failed to pay for a period of three months, except in case of unemployment or illness. In times of political repression, such as during the Haymarket trial, club members proceeded with caution when admitting newcomers. In St. Louis, for example, the integrity of potential neophytes was deliberated during an ad hoc meeting. Furthermore, a two-week surveillance period was required before actual membership was possible, and new members could only be admitted during official business meetings. There is no evidence that such a procedure was standard practice among German anarchists in America, although the last stipulation seems to have been common.

Finances were the constant worry of all anarchist groups. Money was essential to the movement's goal of production and distribution of propaganda and for keeping afloat its precious periodical literature. Chronic lack of funds could easily cripple or even ruin an entire publishing venture. For instance, Claus Timmermann's *Sturmvogel* was forced to fold due to excessive printing costs, and *Freiheit* merged with a Buffalo paper for a while to regain financial viability. The need for financial health inevitably connected the anarchist movement to New York's capitalist marketplace; the movement, after all, was not a utopian colony but a consciously alternative and urban community of idealists who were at the same time wage earners and consumers. Large groups elected auditors (Revisoren) who periodically reviewed the bookkeeping of its operations. Typically, printing costs and travel expenses for lecturers were the heftiest expenses on an anarchist group's ledger, with postage and office supplies as secondary expenditures. The balance sheets—published in *Freiheit*—of the Committee of Agitation, the nine-member body that only existed for one and a half years, reveal that printing costs comprised 56 percent of all expenses, and travel money another 42 percent.[23]

The only source of income for the anarchist movement in New York consisted of contributions from anarchists themselves. Self-sufficiency was a staple anarchist tenet. There was a sense of integrity and empowerment in knowing that the movement was supported by the members themselves. Donors included individual members, sympathizers, other anarchist groups, or proceeds from special events. Fundraising was therefore the motor behind the movement's infrastructure. When in 1898 the Berkman Defense Association raised a little over one thousand dollars from anarchists nationwide, German-speaking comrades from the New York area contributed 38 percent of it.[24] Social and cultural events organized and attended by anarchists kept the movement alive in the most basic sense: it filled the coffers. It also established and maintained bonds of mutual support so vital in times of economic stress or political reaction.

Anarchism in New York (and in any large city) was not simply an idea or temporal entity; it was also a self-sustaining community that existed spatially, a community that was at the same time American, German, and international—even transnational. Indeed, the network of contributors and correspondents to *Freiheit,* while mostly comprising persons in the United States, stretched as far as Switzerland, Belgium, France, England, Hungary, Italy, Canada, Norway, Argentina, Brazil, Australia, and even one person in Africa.

THE WOMAN QUESTION

The German anarchist movement in New York and environs was largely a men's affair, even though women were not entirely absent. Contemporary sources offer little information to clarify the role of gender in the movement, but it seems that German anarchist families tended to retain traditional patterns of family relations, gender roles, and perhaps child rearing. The older generation of radicals struggled with conflicting notions of gender and equality. On the one hand, activists like Kubisch and Hasselmann championed women's rights in the social and public realm while displaying a reluctance to alter their views on gender roles within their own households. This more conservative sentiment may have had its origin in two closely related traditions. First, the patriarchal culture in nineteenth-century Germany prescribed for women a heroic mission involving mastery of the three K's: Kinder, Küche, and Kirche (children, kitchen, church). Second, nineteenth-century German radicalism was opposed not only to the ancien régime but also to bourgeois culture and its excesses. In this context, an indulgence in feminist ideas was seen as a middle-class frivolity unworthy of serious thought.

Perhaps for these reasons, older German anarchists frowned upon early discussions of free love, sexual orientation, and alternative lifestyles. They did not deny that marriage was an institution sanctioned by state and church, but neither did they see matrimony as inherently exploitative or without benefits. They could agreed that love and sexuality were personal matters that should be detached from politics or religion, but they failed to see that the personal was political, especially for millions of women trapped in unhappy and unequal relations. Men like Johann Most, who mistrusted women from an early age, were not ready to accept free-love ideas within the movement, ideas they often interpreted as permission for promiscuity and adultery. Emma Goldman, referring to Most's unenlightened views, once said that his intellectual field was limited to "social and political subjects."[25] What prompted Goldman to horsewhip her old mentor is as much explained by her anger at his arrogance toward women as by his insinuations about Berkman's integrity in the Frick shooting. On the occasions that Most did address the liberation of women, it was situated in the future, as a process instead of an immediate issue. "Women's confined sphere of home, sweet home, will *gradually* disappear," he wrote in 1884, "every calling *will* be open to them; matrimony *will* no longer be the sole channel through which women may seek happiness."[26] The historian Margaret Marsh has shown that most anarchist men believed that the Woman Question was less of a priority than issues of economic and political justice.[27]

Throughout the pages of the anarchist press, especially *Freiheit*, there are occasions of gendered language that correlated masculinity with workers' pride. Offensive stereotypes of women occasionally made it into the press as well. In March 1889, an elderly woman complained to the editors of *Freiheit* for using disparaging slang for women and for treating them as a separate caste. The editors duly apologized.[28] Perhaps the special treatment of women at the box office of social events hints at Victorian attitudes. Some anarchist festivities offered free entrance or had reduced prices for women, although this was not standard practice. Although not explicitly stated, one gets the impression that most women connected to anarchist men performed a supportive role within the movement. The impressive attendance of women in the audience at large gatherings—a fact always noted by newspaper reporters—confirms the sense that wives, daughters, and companions were not "hidden" whenever the movement made a bold public appearance.

Emma Goldman's brief relationship with the Austrian anarchist Edward Brady illustrates a general attitude of many male anarchists. Brady was a Bohemian-born, well-educated activist who in the early 1870s took a job as collector at a Vienna radical magazine. He quickly became immersed in the socialist movement, where he was employed as an editor and publicist. When, in January 1884, Austria passed the Exception Law suppressing all radical activities, Brady continued to distribute pamphlets in Vienna and Budapest. His defiance landed him in prison for twelve long years.[29] Upon his release, he was expelled from Austria, traveled to Hamburg, then London, and finally arrived in New York in late 1892, where he met Goldman at a meeting.[30]

Brady was something of a scholar who was fond of English and French literature, a passion he shared with his romantic companion, Goldman. She described him as "tall and broad, well built, with soft blond hair and blue eyes."[31] Their relationship cooled ("a rude awakening"), however, when Goldman learned about Brady's opinion of Maria Roda, a young and eloquent Italian anarchist speaker, millhand, and mother of eight whom they had heard at a gathering. Brady believed all Italian women matured early and that their energy deteriorated after childbirth. Goldman countered that Roda could have remained childless if that helped her pursue her ideals. "'No woman should do that,'" Brady bluntly retorted. "'Nature has made her for motherhood. All else is nonsense, artificial and unreal.'"[32] This reaction reminded Goldman of similar interactions with German male anarchists. "His conservatism roused my anger," she wrote later. "I demanded to know if he thought me also nonsensical because I preferred to work for an ideal instead of producing children. *I expressed contempt for the reactionary attitude of our German comrades on these matters. I had believed that he was different, but I could see that he was like the rest.*" She was instantly reminded of her failed relationship with Most. "Perhaps he, too, loved only the woman in me, wanted me only as his wife and the bearer of his children. He was not the first to expect that of me, but he might as well know that I would never be that—never! I had chosen my path; no man should ever take me from it."[33] Goldman eventually broke with Brady, but they remained friends. He died unexpectedly of a heart attack in 1903. Her experience with German men in the anarchist movement must have been consistent and apparently left a mark on her memory. In a 1929 letter to Berkman, Goldman repeated the charge that German radicals had not advanced in terms of gender equality. "[The Germans] remain stationary on all points except economics. Especially as regards women, they are really antediluvian."[34]

It is true that the overwhelming majority of German anarchists belonging to a group or organization were men, at least during the last two decades of the nineteenth century. In general, women rarely participated in the weekly business meetings, organizing or propaganda committees, or the running of the press. Many had factory jobs or worked from home while at the same time being responsible for child rearing and a host of backbreaking household duties. This permitted little free time to attend meetings. They did attend large gatherings and invariably joined their partners in social and cultural events such as theater performances and outings. To be fair, there were some anarchist couples where both partners were loved as equals, and both were active in the movement. In a few instances, male-dominated affinity groups reached out to women activists, who were referred to as "female comrades" (Genossinnen).[35] For example, the Bushwick anarchists printed the following announcement: "Since for the time being only two meetings per month will take place, comrades should make it their duty not only to show up themselves, but to bring along the women, and where possible, friends."[36] The New York group once described its festivals as especially suited for bringing "the women and the youngsters" into the ranks.[37] New clubs assured the neighborhood that not only men could join but also women, although the fact that an announcement was needed only confirms how male-centered club life had grown to be.[38] An 1884 lecture on "Woman and Anarchism" further indicates that the issue of gender equality in the movement was certainly not shunned but rather that much work remained to be done.[39]

All things considered, women were far less active than men in the German anarchist movement, a reality that is perhaps less acceptable for a self-proclaimed liberationist movement. But no evidence of outright dismissal or barring of women has been found, and the realities of economic survival and child care prevented many committed women from actively participating. Many men were also unable to give all their free time to the cause. That said, most propaganda groups and committees—all venues considered influential—distinguished themselves by an embarrassing absence of women. The movers and shakers of the movement were overwhelmingly male. Given the importance of public speaking in the movement, it is surprising that so few women speakers took the stand. On a few occasions women did appear on stage at commemorative gatherings or to orate a prologue to a play. Emma Goldman was by far the most noteworthy woman speaker in the early German movement, but there were others. Emilie Baudisch, an Austrian immigrant anarchist and actress, shared the Cooper Union stage with Johann Most.[40] In 1889, Mrs. Heinrich Wilhelmi (as she was addressed in *Freiheit*) spoke to a gathering of Paterson anarchists.[41] Martha Krause was an actress and delivered a declamation at the 1890 November Eleventh commemoration.[42] Large events in which many nationalities participated could count on some exceptional, but mostly non-German, women activists such as Voltairine De Cleyre, Lucy E. Parsons, Marie Louise, Maria Roda, Ida M. Van Etten, and Sarah Edelstadt Palm.

ARMING AND SELF-DEFENSE

German anarchist rifle clubs are another illustration of an alternative space in which anarchist ideas could be put into practice. Martial prowess expressed through shooting practices, banners, and uniforms allowed anarchists to release their anger at society and perhaps indulge in harmless violence that was inconceivable outside the club. These hidden desires and frustrations could not always be safely expressed in public. In this context, these clubs can be see as spaces where what James Scott calls the anarchists' "hidden transcript" could be expressed. Short of going into battle against the capitalists, anarchists cultivated their own sense of combative revolutionism, an expression of resistance and to some extent a clear provocative defiance of established order. Anarchists created their own order, their own martial response to outside threats. Rifle clubs played a recreational as well as a political role, but they were undeniably part of the overall anarchist imagery. To a large degree, it was the existence of such clubs that fueled the stereotype of the anarchist terrorist so prevalent in mainstream society, and some anarchists were not necessarily bothered by that inference, viewing it instead as a badge of honor.

Apart from political affinity groups, German anarchists joined defense and educational associations (Lehr-und-Wehr Verein) with a mission to protect activists in the public arena. Historic precedents for such groups can be found in the Turner associations, the Swiss military organization Help Yourself (Hilf Dir), founded in the 1860s to fight for a German republic, and the various ethnic battle units during the American Civil War. The existence of such groups had been a controversial topic during debates between socialists and anarchists. Socialists were opposed to bringing arms into the movement, while anarchists simply felt that workers had a right to defend themselves against overzealous police officers, guardsmen, and corporate detectives rather than relying on the police or courts for protection. During the nationwide labor uprising of the 1870s, law enforcement committed numerous brutalities against striking cabinet makers in Chicago, for example. In Maryland, ten workers were killed and many wounded, and in Reading, Pennsylvania, thirteen workers were shot dead and twenty-two wounded. Pinkerton detective guards shot dead in cold blood six men and six women in St. Louis without ever being indicted or convicted. Similar killings happened during labor rallies in Milwaukee and Pittsburgh.

Arming workers was a popular goal among German anarchists in America, especially in Chicago. Indiscriminate violence was always denounced by organized anarchists, but violence as a result of self-defense they believed was justified. Some extremely militant comrades seem to have approved of offensive violence only if it benefited a higher cause and if approved by the proletariat. "Now I'd like to go along with the objection that it is unanarchistic to inflict violence on others," editorialized one paper. "Indeed, violence is always reprehensible and inimical to freedom where it does not appear as resistance or the removal of oppression. The desire for self-preservation, the right of resistance and self-defense, which is—nobody will deny—implied in anarchism, sometimes demands with absolute necessity the use of crude violence."[43] The few anarchists adhering to an absolute pacifism were scathingly labeled as "precious anarchists" (Edel-Anarchisten).

By combining the rationale for self-defense and the advocacy of social revolution, anarchist orators and editors incurred the wrath of mainstream society, a society that otherwise ignored the demands for reform from workers. When Johann Most urged workers to purchase a weapon after news of the Haymarket incident, he was promptly arrested and charged with inciting to riot. He believed that his utterances were simply an acknowledgment of the constitutional right to bear arms. "The servants of the capitalists are armed," he reasoned, "and why should not workingmen be armed?" "Witnesses have said that I advised the audience to join a rifle club. Why not?" His trial eventually led to a one-year prison sentence.[44] Aside from the often exaggerated ranting about insurrection of some anarchist orators like Most, the issue of arming workers was a sincere reaction to intimidation, humiliation, and ubiquitous police violence against workers during labor rallies, strikes, and demonstrations.

With membership ranging from ten to seventy, rifle clubs held meetings in their own saloons and, like other groups, created their own environment by adopting insignias, flags, and uniforms. These marksmen met regularly for business meetings and participated in parades and festivities involving the wider movement. They also scheduled several hours for weapons training and drill exercises. Waltershausen asserts that a "technical club" existed in New York before the Haymarket incident with the purpose of training revolutionaries. He advised against taking such rifle clubs too seriously. Some groups evolved into hunting or sports clubs, which members joined to practice target shooting and not necessarily to prepare for revolutionary or conspiratorial activities.[45] Also, for many anarchists rifle clubs were confraternities, offering an occasion for male bonding similar to a game of pool at the local beerhall.

Other gun clubs were staunchly political. They not only fashioned their own uniforms, banners, and flags but also appropriated images or personalities from a revolutionary past. The Andreas Hofer Defense Company 2 (Andreas Hofer Schützen-Compagnie 2) appropriated the name of an Austrian patriot and militia leader during the Napoleonic wars. The International Defense Association of New York (Internationale Schützenbund New York) was the most active defense organization in New York during the 1880s. It is not clear whether it eventually acted as an umbrella organization for other German workingmen's rifle companies or if it operated on its own; it is certain that it was affiliated with the IWPA. According to Waltershausen, only persons who were "convinced that the social question can be solved through violent means" could join. A sample of bylaws adopted by the Schützenbund, however, reveals a much more defensive approach. The first statute, for example, stated that the "'Association seeks to promote the arming of the workers by all means so that the proletariat will be able to resist with vigor any assault on the common welfare.'" As a cooperative organization, "all weapons purchased by the Association remain the property of the organization." Moreover, as anarchists, members sought to eliminate the element of profit making and maintained an egalitarian atmosphere by a decree that stated that "'the Association must, if a member so desires, supply weapons at their cost price.'"[46]

During the 1890s, a new defense federation, the German American Defense Association (Deutsch-Amerikanische Schützenbund), seems to have been active in suggesting cooperation among several clubs. The autonomist anarchists apparently had their own self-defense organizations, such as the Elizabeth Sharpshooting Society (Elizabeth Scharfschützen Gesellschaft).[47] Despite the existence of such colorful groups, no incident of violence by an anarchist rifle club has been found, even though they were feared as the stormtroopers of the coming revolution. Instead, these groups should be viewed not only in the context of a real need for self-defense during the last quarter of the nineteenth century but also in connection with anarchist folklore, workers' pride, and the doctrine of self-management.

It is telling that immigrant radicals organized groups with a mission to protect themselves against the ruling elite of their adopted country. Such organizations, whether German, Irish, or Czech, were more an expression of class-consciousness than of ethnic identity; these radical immigrants declared their disgust with and disloyalty to the capitalist system dominated by robber barons and accommodated by a corrupt national and local polity. Of course, the designation "radical immigrants" is itself culturally and politically biased. Class-conscious immigrants regarded America's corporate elite as "radically" conservative, ruthless, and even inhumane. The choice of adjectives, like language in general, is always affected by prevailing power relations within society. If industrialists thought socialists and anarchists radical because they envisioned a free, cooperative society, it was equally justified for the latter to view captains of industry as extreme because they implemented sweeping changes in the way ordinary people earned a living. Anarchists can be said to cling to the original meaning of the word "radical" because they incessantly hammered away at the root causes of society's ills, namely greed, coercive authority, and relentless competition.

TRADE UNIONS AND PUBLIC DEMONSTRATIONS

Anarchists fashioned their own social space in which they moved from home to workplace to recreation without hiding or compromising their convictions and customs. Anarchist trade unions became one more venue for comradeship, another alternative space that could be extended into the workplace separate from management, non-union workers, and the socialists. All anarchist progressive unions held regular meetings, organized picnics, concerts, and donated money to anarchist campaigns, defense funds, the press, or mutual-aid associations. Typical functionaries within the organization included a protocol secretary, a financial secretary, a treasurer, and auditors.

By 1880, trade union membership for German skilled workers had become something of a tradition in America and Europe, and this was no different for the vast majority of German and Austrian anarchists in New York. Ever since the middle of the nineteenth century, artisans and skilled workers had associated along craft lines to protect themselves and their trade against mechanization and concentration. The transition from independent artisan to wage earner (skilled or unskilled) was one of the most dramatic, though gradual, developments of the nineteenth century and one that caused much anxiety among native and immigrant artisans. Anarchists had come to understand this development as something that should be resisted by all means precisely because anarchists imagined the restoration of a self-governing producer class of independent artisans. Educated in the Jacobin tradition—from François-Noël Babeuf and Proudhon to Marx and Bakunin—German anarchists realized that economic concentration meant proletarianization, a permanent dependence on wages, a loss of autonomy and control (and perhaps masculinity), and ultimately class struggle. They offered ethical and historical reasons for combating industrial capitalism and wage labor.

German anarchists in New York and New Jersey did not distinguish themselves by widespread union militancy. The eight-hour-day movement, which had so mesmerized the Chicago anarchists, was hardly visible in New York. Johann Most's dismissal of the eight-hour-day movement as potentially revolutionizing hampered union activism by New York anarchists for years to come, although Rudolf Rocker points out that Most never intended to sabotage the labor movement but merely sought to prevent reactionary elements from compromising the unions' true revolutionary mission.[48] Most may have agreed with the Chicagoans about the principle of revolutionary unions, but he disagreed about the practicability of such an approach in the United States. Even so, Most changed his views on the role of trade unions around 1890, when he realized that small affinity groups were not enough to make a difference. In an article on trade unions, Most denied that anarchists (that is, his followers) were against unions. Some of the goals he believed essential for revolutionary trade unions included "systematic opposition to capitalism in the context of contemporary society, no matter what means, offensive or defensive," and the "promotion of the class war in any form." Trade unions were to "pave the way for a new social system, in which economic and all other human relations would be governed not by the state or any privileged class or any dominant power but by free associations of the able-bodied each according to different spheres of activity."[49]

German anarchists called their trade unions "progressive unions" to distinguish them from socialist organizations. They were usually small and adhered to revolutionary principles as opposed to the prevailing reformism of most socialist unions. Among the most important anarchist trade unions were those of the bakers, cabinet makers, tailors, typesetters, brewery workers, machinists, and cigar makers. These trades had been dominated by German skilled and semiskilled workers since the 1850s. Like their non-anarchist counterparts, these unions counted several branches across the New York–New Jersey area, and some set up federative bodies, such as the United Machinists or United Cornice makers.

Most of these revolutionary unions stayed aloof from the larger development of labor activism in the city. The main vehicle for unionism in New York during the 1880s was the Central Labor Union (CLU) of New York, one of the nation's largest urban trade federations. Founded in 1882, this body included Anglo-Irish workers connected to the Land League, Knights of Labor locals, and German and American socialists. By the mid-1880s, CLU New York comprised over 120 independent unions and local assemblies with a total membership of forty thousand workers.[50] It is not certain how much, if any, influence German anarchists had within the CLU. Socialists by no means dominated the CLU, but since a large part of its membership were Germans, socialist speakers were welcomed. What's more, New York's foremost socialist newspaper, the *New Yorker Volkszeitung,* became a mouthpiece for the CLU. By 1884, CLU membership stood at sixty-seven thousand.[51]

Opposition to mainstream political activities such as elections constituted the main cause for the rupture between the CLU (together with the SLP) and the anarchists. The CLU had participated in municipal elections in 1882 and 1883, but the New York mayoral election of 1886 united an otherwise strife-ridden CLU to endorse the reformer Henry George on a platform of practical socialism. While numerous German American unionists, mostly cigar makers and furniture workers, collected signatures from East Side residents, the German anarchists repudiated the entire affair, charging that elections were a fraud and served only the powerful. The decision to distance themselves from any political action not only drove a wedge between German socialists and anarchists but also between German anarchists and the majority of working-class Germans in New York, who overwhelmingly supported George. The anarchists perhaps failed to see that the George campaign transformed a scattered progressive movement—divided along ethnic and craft lines—into a class-conscious political movement.

During the late 1880s and the early 1890s, labor politics in New York was in disarray. Some antipolitical unions asserted their independence and endorsed a revolutionary (anarchist) stance. In January 1887, the Brooklyn Progressive Cabinetmakers (Brooklyn Schreiner Progressive Union), for instance, was formed when it broke away from the socialist Furniture Workers' Union 7 (Möbelschreiner Union 7). The immediate cause for the split was an evening of lectures presented by three German anarchist cabinet makers. They were able to convince a portion of the members of the need for revolutionary unionism. The anarchists were instantly accused of pseudo-radicalism, but one of them countered that even if no revolutionary acts followed, at least a revolutionary spirit reigned among the workers.[52] This statement shows again that anarchists were not only focused on planning and preparing for a future revolution but were equally involved in creating an oppositional space or spirit here and now. As a result, the CLU refused to admit the progressive cabinet makers on account of their anarchist affiliation.[53] The CLU of Newark was even less tolerant and proceeded to ban all socialists from its parade as well as forbidding red flags.[54]

It was not long before the radical unions organized their own federation in the spring of 1889. The Central Labor Federation (CLF), set up separately from the CLU, included thirty-two organizations embracing what Waltershausen termed "the radical German tendency."[55] A few months later, the CLF of New York announced plans to launch an English-language weekly trade journal, but nothing else is known about it.[56] Not all radical unions were affiliated with the CLF, which moved to reconcile its differences with the CLU. Some accused the CLF of centralism and appealed to other progressive unions for financial support. The charge of centralism seems to have confirmed Most's concern about anarchist involvement in trade unions. Many radical unions were also affiliated with the Socialist Trades and Labor Alliance (STLA), formed in the early 1890s. The STLA was a national federation of urban labor bodies including, among others, the CLF of New York and Newark and the United Hebrew Trades. The STLA openly advocated industrial unionism in reaction to the growing conservatism of the mannered American Federation of Labor (AFL).

The battle between the Brewery Workers' Union and the brewing manufacturers during the late 1880s and 1890s was one episode in which German anarchists were unusually active. The Brewery Workers' Union was one of the earliest and most successful illustrations of German radicalism in an American industry. Strongly infused with socialism, the German-dominated union was able to radicalize American and Irish journeyman brewers who toiled for meager wages in unsanitary conditions. The union teamed up with the *New Yorker Volkszeitung* to spread its message advocating industrial unionism and later founded its own paper, *Die Brauer-Zeitung,* edited by William E. Trautmann. Moreover, the union was successful in forging bargaining agreements with the employers, raising salaries, and significantly improving conditions in the malt houses of America. They even established closed shops in which only union members could be employed. Unionization also prompted advertisements for beer in socialist and anarchist papers, including *Freiheit*—a much-needed source of income. Ever since the introduction of German lager beer (as opposed to English-style ales), American brewing companies were engaged in a fierce competition. They soon understood, however, that the formation of cartels (or pools), price fixing, and extravagant advertising could boost their market power. By the mid-1880s, the American brewing industry was dominated by a powerful manufacturers' association ready to take on the union.

In the fall of 1887, when a lockout was imposed on brewery workers in Milwaukee, a nationwide battle between the union and the manufacturers began. Employers argued that the union wielded too much power over the hiring process and that workers should accept that standardization was the way of the future even if it eroded artisanal skills. The union threatened a citywide boycott, whereupon the employers locked out the workers. On 1 April 1888, manufacturers in New York, Brooklyn, and New Jersey ungraciously terminated all labor contracts and announced that they would enter into new ones only with individual (non-union) workers.[57] New York's CLU quickly responded with a nationwide boycott of beer brewed by any of the cartel or pool manufacturers. Such a boycott was not to be taken lightly, since working-class Americans, especially immigrants, had become the principal consumers of beer. Workers who frequented saloons serving "pool beer" were accosted or, in the case of union members, fined. Vigilante committees roamed the streets to stop women who made beer runs for home gatherings to ensure that the right kind was fetched.

German anarchists stood squarely behind the boycott. *Freiheit* published names and addresses of noncompliant businesses and called for a boycott of them. The radical German Brewery Workers' Union 1 successfully appealed to other anarchist groups for support with the result that at recreational events, anarchist organizations frequented only parks that did business with unionized breweries, such as Joseph Eppig's brewery in Brooklyn. They would only consume "union beer." The slightest suspicion of the presence of pool beer could disrupt an entire picnic. This happened in August 1889, when members of the anarchist machinists' union congregated at Anton Heil's park in Fort Wadsworth, Staten Island. When someone yelled, "Pool beer!" it was discovered that Heil had lied to the organizers about serving only union beer. "In less than five minutes," reported *Freiheit*, "beer taps were discontinued and a real migration over hill and dale ensued. There goal was [nearby] Bechtel's Brewery." The event proceeded with much jollity, even as it frightened some local residents.[58]

In the end, the beer boycott failed to harm the cartel, partly because the boycott was not adhered to en masse, and partly because the non-cartel breweries and drinking establishments possessed so little market share that they were unable to satisfy the drinking needs of so many. This proved to be crucial in the victory of the brewing industry. The practice of manufacturers combining their power to enlarge market share and crush union representation would become widespread and a rallying cry for progressive reformers and radicals, eventually leading to a toothless antitrust law.

German anarchists—union members and others—frequently participated in public parades and demonstrations in the streets and squares of greater New York. These locations could temporarily be transformed into radical spaces that were as much part of an anarchist geography as the less-visible beerhalls. Union Square was by far the most popular public arena for labor demonstrations in New York. May Day and Labor Day parades had been a tradition in the labor movement since the early 1880s. The first Labor Day parade in the United States took place on 5 September 1882 and was organized under the auspices of the New York CLU.[59] Both holidays became a forum for the labor movement to show strength and voice complaints and demands. It quickly became a stage for the eight-hour-day movement. Johann Most and his followers shunned this movement because it focused on immediate goals that did not alter the fundamental system. The autonomist anarchists, however, did participate and marched along the streets of Manhattan in the 1889 Labor Day parade.[60] The following year's parade in Newark numbered about 1,400 workers after the local CLU had banned socialists and anarchists, who simply organized their own march.[61]

It is impossible to know how many German anarchists typically marched in such parades, but it is certain that leading anarchists often criticized such events for their meekness and reformism. The 1886 May Day demonstration in New York, for instance, was deemed "the most harmless of all labor demonstrations ever."[62] The police, who saw to it that the different groups kept a safe distance from each other, carefully mapped out the trajectory for them. More meaningful were mass protest gatherings, especially of New York's unemployed during the economic depression of 1893. Overall, the participation of German anarchists in the public labor movement in New York was limited, partly due to a strong animosity between socialists and anarchists and sometimes among the anarchist groups themselves.

In one instance, the misunderstanding between socialists and anarchists escalated into a small riot. On 2 February 1884, a fight broke out between anarchists and socialists, mostly Germans, in the auditorium of Concordia Hall on Avenue A. It began with the news of a recent terrorist attack in London by Irish nationalists. The event touched a nerve with anarchists as well as socialists. The anarchists, tired of being lumped together with such extremists, condemned the affair. The socialists decided to organize a meeting to denounce terrorist tactics. The anarchists announced that they would also attend; they suspected the socialists would take the opportunity to denounce all anarchists, who were widely perceived as terrorists. In fact, the Executive Committee of the SLP did just that. It is not clear whether any plan to disrupt the meeting had been concocted beforehand, but as soon as Sergius Schevitsch, a prominent Russian socialist, announced the anti-anarchist resolution, "chairs and beer glasses came hurtling on to the stage," according to one eyewitness. The entire hall was transformed into a brawl, prompting someone to call the police.[63] At the end, Justus Schwab was arrested for inciting to riot when he battled with a police officer (as he had done in 1874); he was released shortly thereafter. This culture of animosity between socialists and anarchists was as much a part of the movement as was the struggle against capitalist exploitation. It shows that anarchists were as troubled by stereotypes as they were sometimes flattered by them. Irked by misconceptions about anarchism in mainstream society, anarchists were especially resentful of a deliberate campaign of distortion on the part of their ideological cousins, the socialists.

Hoch Die Anarchie! Music, Theater, and Picnics

In his social history of the Chicago anarchist movement, Bruce C. Nelson concludes that they created and maintained a "self-consciously visible, vital, and militant movement culture." "Without its club life, press, unions, and culture," Nelson asserts, "the ideology of that movement is unintelligible."[64] Any meaningful discussion of anarchists in New York must investigate its cultural landscape. Together with the beerhalls, cultural organizations illustrate the extent and nature of an alternative space created and conceptualized by anarchists. That cultural practices of German anarchists in New York were so elaborate, colorful, and often symbolic also attests to the nonviolent character of this movement. It is important to note that German anarchists viewed music and theater groups and picnic events as anarchism itself, not merely as diversions or recreational sideshows. Ideology, pleasure, and identity were interwoven in much the same way as inside the anarchist beerhalls.

This "movement culture," as historians of the German working class have termed it, was not synonymous with New York's socialist culture, which is too broad and pluralist. German anarchists, affiliated with the IWPA or the autonomists, infused their associational life (Vereinsleben) with revolutionary proletarian culture, tempered with some American elements. This anarchist culture was not unique to New York. Chicago, Cleveland, St. Louis, and a host of other immigrant cities harbored similar subcultures.

Three cultural institutions—music, theater, and picnics—occupied a prominent place (and space) in the daily lives of German anarchists in New York and New Jersey. Of course, these institutions were much older than either anarchism or socialism; the anarchist community simply reinvented or restyled and radicalized them—an important theme in the creation and conceptualization of their social space.

Music was of particular importance for German anarchists in New York. German working-class culture was steeped in the creation and enjoyment of music, and music played an important role in the early labor movement in Germany. In America too, socialists and anarchists of many ethnicities organized musical groups that enlivened gatherings and festivals while strengthening group identity and cohesion. Anarchists formed orchestras and singing societies with a distinctly anarchistic flavor. The musical groups adopted statutes in accord with their anarchist principles and rehearsed primarily an anarchist or revolutionary repertoire that emphasized a sense of progress, justice, and freedom. It is interesting that no anarchist musical organization carried the appellation "anarchist" in its title. Instead, they gave the groups evocative names like Progress, Forward, or Freedom. For many activists, singers, and conductors, the word "anarchist" may still have been too derogatory or deemed unsafe, although similar terms were used profusely in the movement press. Or perhaps members of such groups simply viewed "anarchist" as too limited and political a qualifier for conveying what they saw as a broader ideal of a free human spirit. In other words, they may have sought to avoid the perception of sectarianism and instead styled themselves as enlightened, progressive, and freethinking citizens of the world. In contrast, some singing societies affiliated with the socialists did feature titles such as Socialist Singing Society of New York (Sozialistische Liedertafel New York) or Karl Marx Singing Society.

A close study of the movement reveals a remarkable energy among German radicals who translated their beliefs into song. No less than forty-two German singing societies, affiliated with the anarchist movement, existed at one time in New York and New Jersey. Most societies stayed active for several years, while a few lasted for over ten years, and one remained active for twenty-seven. The majority of vocal music groups existed during the 1880s and 1890s; only a handful still performed during the first decade of the new century. Membership averaged twenty to thirty people. The popular groups Lassallea-Ottensen Singing Society (Gesangverein Lassallea-Ottensen) and Herwegh Men's Choir (Herwegh-Männerchor) together were reported to mobilize more than two hundred singers.[65]

Anarchist singing societies (Gesangvereine) were proud, well-organized associations that attested to the value German anarchists bestowed on organization, leisure time, and community. Like the propaganda groups, singing societies held weekly business meetings, although these were overshadowed by the need for weekly rehearsals held in their favorite beerhalls. In these consciously anarchist organizations, members worked under a system of mutual agreement with persons holding rotating positions of responsibility. Depending on the size of the group, the following functionaries were elected at quarterly meetings: a corresponding (or protocol) secretary, a finance secretary, a treasurer, a conductor, a beer collector, a beer treasurer, an archivist, auditors, and a standard bearer. Smaller groups sometimes combined the secretary and beer positions. The larger singing societies also elected a music committee (Musikkomite) to take on its artistic direction, and one even featured an arbitration committee to mediate internal disputes. The archivist was responsible for the storage and care of musical scores, correspondence, and newspaper subscriptions to, for example, *Freiheit.* Most singing groups required monthly dues, although the autonomist Workers' Singing Society Forward (Arbeitergesangverein Vorwärts) refrained from mandatory dues and instead decided on voluntary donations by members. This decision was in accord with the communist-anarchist principle of giving according to one's ability and receiving according to one's need.[66] The old cultural format of communal singing was infused with anarchist principles.

Singing societies also organized themselves into a federative body, the New York Workers' Singing Association (Arbeiter-Sängerbund New York), which included socialist as well as anarchist groups. Not surprisingly, animosity between the two factions threatened its continued existence. By May 1889, the association decided to continue as an independent federation abstaining from any involvement in festivities organized by either the Socialist Labor party or the IWPA; only constituent groups could decide to participate.[67] In 1890, an apparently anarchist umbrella organization, the United Workers' Singing Societies of New York (Vereinigte Arbeiter-Gesangvereine New Yorks), organized large concerts and balls involving several ethnic groups. One such concert in April 1890 featured German vocalists and a Scandinavian choral group as well as poetry recitations, comical sketches, and a lecture by Johann Most.[68]

The singing societies were not only organized along anti-authoritarian lines; more importantly, their music aspired to be anarchist and revolutionary. Just like the beerhalls, content was as important as form in producing a genuine anarchist space. Singing societies described their mission as aiding anarchist propaganda intellectually, spiritually, and financially. "Our strength and perseverance are essentially based on the conviction that for that elevated ideal communist-anarchism we must give everything we can that is necessary for an organization of action . . . that aids and always will aid propaganda spiritually and financially to the best of its ability."[69] This was accomplished by the spirit and conviction of its members and by the selection of appropriate songs. An autonomist singing society stated as its key objective that "in the perfect spirit of consensus, members will organize toward a common goal."[70] In other words, anarchism should be practiced presently in a "sphere of free action," to quote Goodman again. Johann Most said as much when he pointed to singing societies, turner associations, and sporting clubs as voluntary organizations based on the free contract functioning without state intervention.[71] Music was anarchism in practice. "Anyone should be able to say of himself, 'I fought back!' and the satisfaction of that will not be wanting," wrote G. Kupferschmidt, treasurer of a singing society, in a plea to solicit support in times of unemployment.[72]

With this philosophy and structure, anarchist singing societies maintained a busy schedule of concerts, numerous support appearances, and outings for their own members. All political gatherings of anarchists included musical and sometimes theatrical performances. Large gatherings such as Commune festivals could bring together as many as twenty choirs with orchestras from different nationalities. For example, in preparation for the celebration of the centennial of the storming of the Bastille in July 1889, a singers' conference was organized to put together a mass choir. In addition to four German societies, Bohemian, Hungarian, Russian, and Italian choral societies attended—more than 150 singers in all.[73]

The most popular songs came from the large arsenal of proletarian ballads, revolutionary songs, hymns to workers' pride and struggle, drinking songs, and traditional German folk songs. Titles such as "Die rote Fahne" (The red flag), "Das Lied von der Kommune" (The song of the commune), "Hoch die Anarchie!" (Long live anarchy!), or Johann Most's "Arbeitermänner" (Workingmen) were repeatedly performed at celebrations or political gatherings. The Marseillaise was a mainstay at all radical gatherings, while the Internationale was by far the most widely known—across ethnic boundaries—and one of the most frequently performed pieces of music in the anarchist community. Communal events were usually concluded by a powerful rendition of this song, written in 1874 by Eugène Pottier in honor of the Paris Commune (set to music by Pierre DeGeyter in 1888). Songs from the homeland were also featured at such festivities, such as "Die Wacht am Rhein" (The watch on the Rhine), as well as excerpts from pieces by Richard Wagner, Frederick Chopin, and Giacomo Meyerbeer.

No singing would be complete without instrumental accompaniment. German anarchists in New York formed several orchestras and music bands that played at numerous events and concerts. Carl Sahm and Fritz Sundersdorf were the best-known figures in German instrumental music in radical New York. Sahm was a well-known conductor and composer of a number of proletarian songs for men's choir. The Fritz Sundersdorf Orchestra was one of the most sought-after ensembles at German anarchist festivities during the 1880s. When Sundersdorf died in September 1889, a memorial concert was staged by several singing societies in a beerhall on East Fourth Street.[74]

Poetry was another creative outlet for the anarchist community. Poems by German American anarchists appeared in published collections, in the anarchist press, or were recited at festivals, commemorations, and other gatherings. All German anarchist periodicals in New York featured poetry from well-known German poets, socialist authors, and local bards. A host of German authors from the prerevolutionary but nonetheless radical Vormärz period (1815–48) also found their way into New York anarchist journals: Ferdinand Freiligrath, Georg Herwegh, Karl Ludwig Pfau, Alfred Meissner, and Alfred Heinrich Strodtmann. In addition, German socialist writers such as August Geib, Robert Seidel, and Jakob Audorf were readily available to German anarchist readers. Respectable local writers and poets were also published, including Georg Biedenkapp, Martin Drescher, Edna Fern, Emma Clausen, Hans Stromer, Otto Sattler, and Martin Schupp.

Biedenkapp was by far the best-known anarchist poet-activist in New York. A member of the New York group, he became a regular speaker at meetings and festivals. His poems "Glück Auf!" (Good luck!) and "Bergmannslied" became favorites for recitation. In August 1893, his best poems were collected and published in West Hoboken, New Jersey, as *Sankta Libertas,* which became an instant success.[75] He was a prominent speaker at a memorial meeting for Robert Reitzel, another icon of German American radical literature who had founded and edited *Der arme Teufel* in Detroit; he died on 30 March 1898.

Martin Drescher, yet another man of letters, was a friend of Reitzel. He was born on 8 May 1863 in Thüringen. He started studies at Göttingen University but traveled to the United States at a young age. There he lived as a day laborer, wandering from place to place and composing numerous poems—his so-called tramp days. Eventually, he met Reitzel and became an assistant editor at *Die arme Teufel,* which he continued after Reitzel's death. During 1901–2, he launched several small literary-anarchist papers such as *Mephisto* and *Der Zigeuner* in Chicago and *Wolfsaugen* in St. Louis. Drescher by this time was something of a luminary within the German-speaking movement. When he fell ill, friends organized the Martin Drescher Foundation. He moved back to Maspeth in Queens, where he died in March 1920.[76]

German anarchist poetry in the United States reflected the ideology of the movement at large with proletarian ballads, songs ridiculing Victorian society and morality, and poems attacking corporate America. The proletarian ballad was a highly popular form that could be found in every German radical paper in the United States during the last quarter of the nineteenth century. The main goal of these ballads was to create political awareness and class-consciousness within the German ethnic group and the working class in general. It is striking, however, that almost none of them depicted real life. It was more the expression of a growing, autonomous culture of radical immigrants engaging in an emotional appeal for socialist ideals. The main ingredients were sarcasm, emotional sincerity, strident anticlericalism, and often an interest in shocking outsiders with blunt statements. Anarchist poets attacked and ridiculed Victorian American values as part and parcel of the bourgeois republic and the puritan moralism that surged during the late nineteenth century. Another ingredient in anarchists' poetic expression was a relentless anticlericalism, a mockery and indictment of religion and superstition. But the main target in German American anarchist poetry was corporate America, especially after Haymarket. For anarchists, the economic and political elite did not differ much; they ran an autocratic regime behind the facade of a democratic republic.

Theater's potential for provocation under the guise of innocent performance has always rendered it risky in the eyes of moral guardians and explains why the stage as an art form has had to battle against prejudice longer than any other form of entertainment. For a minority group such as anarchists, theater was much more than entertainment. It proved to be an excellent tool for propaganda, a venue where an otherwise "hidden transcript"—desire for retribution, hope of rebellion—could be expressed openly. Stage productions by the anarchist community therefore helped conceptualize the social space of that community. Theater offered anarchists a metaphorical space (the stage) inside an already re-created space (the theater auditorium). Theater's potential for subversion and trickery had been recognized since the sixteenth century; the anarchists simply used a powerful cultural form to act out their own political message. It bolstered ideological and ethnic identity while at the same time projecting that ideology to a (potentially) wider audience.

German anarchist theater in New York was rooted in German as well as German American culture. Like vocal and instrumental music, anarchists adopted an older art form and restyled it to reflect their own values. The German theater in general had been a venerable institution in New York since the 1860s. New immigrants during the 1880s and 1890s helped sustain its reputation for high quality and artistic independence. There were respectable "high art" stage productions, and there was the proletarian theater concentrated on the Bowery, where other nationalities performed alongside German productions. Yiddish theater, for instance, became one of the most distinctive cultural expressions during the 1890s on the Lower East Side. During that decade, Germans had already begun to move out of the neighborhood to areas uptown. German theaters such as Irving Place Theater and the Germania were located in the Union Square district, in between working-class Bowery and respectable, middle-class Broadway.

German anarchists, however, did not so quickly abandon the playhouses on the Bowery, an entertainment strip that was once the heart of Little Germany. The old German Thalia Theater was the beating heart of German immigrant drama during the 1880s. Gustav Amberg, who was the first manager in 1879, named it.[77] It ceased to be a German house in 1888, and three years later Thalia Theater opened its doors as a Yiddish playhouse, although German-language productions did not disappear altogether.[78] German anarchists continued to stage productions for the movement there.

Amateur dramatic clubs of German anarchists formed as early as 1883 in the wake of the foundation of the IWPA. Outside Manhattan, Newark demonstrated the most active theater scene among German anarchists with at least three dramatic societies being organized during the second half of the 1880s.[79] Auditions were held for anybody interested in becoming an actor. On 22 October 1887, *Der Deserteur* was performed during a workers' festival in Newark probably by the Puck Company, with well-received performances by John Baudisch and his daughter Emilie—recent immigrants from Austria.[80] During the early 1890s, several small anarchist dramatic clubs existed in New York. These troupes mostly performed short pieces and farces with dance and music. Other than plays, one or more actors, such as Gustav Bauer and Justus Schwab, performed comic sketches at anarchist events.

Sometime in the spring or summer of 1894, Johann Most—who had always harbored a love for the stage—founded the amateur theater company Free Stage of New York (Freie Bühne von New York), which grew to forty-one members.[81] The title followed the example of the independent Free Stage Theater in Berlin, built in 1889 and run as a socialist cooperative committed to promoting the new realist and naturalist drama. Leaving tactics of propaganda by deed behind, Most realized that theater could be a far better means to promulgate a revolutionary philosophy. The play that particularly resonated with him was Gerhard Hauptmann's naturalistic drama *Die Weber* (The weavers), a powerful portrait of the harsh working conditions and abject poverty of weavers in Silesia. It featured a rebellion, street fighting, and vandalism and was immediately targeted by the German censors for its potential to incite rebellion among workers. It premiered in Berlin on 26 February 1893. According to John C. Blankenagel, Hauptmann did not write as an agitator but rather composed his story from newspaper accounts.[82] The German anarchist and native Silesian Max Baginski, who later immigrated to New York, had provided background information about the region's dire conditions to Hauptmann. Anarchists and socialists in Europe and America viewed the performances as an opportunity to spread their revolutionary message. During the first performance in Brussels in October 1894, anarchists threw leaflets amidst the spectators.

German anarchists in New York and Newark were responsible for the first American production of Hauptmann's play, although Most was more interested in producing his version of *Die Weber.* It was the perfect play to take advantage of so intricate a combination of ideology and spatiality. A social revolution unfolded on stage within the temporarily revolutionized space of the auditorium located in the oppressor's most fragmented city. The first performance took place on 8 October 1894 in the Thalia Theater, starring Most in the role of the weaver Baumert.[83] A review in a socialist daily acknowledged the dedication of the actors but regretted the lack of intensity required to portray ruthless poverty.[84] The reviewer was particularly irked by the fact that Most had altered the original text, adding explosive sentences to Jäger's speech in which he lambasted the industrialist Dreißiger. The Thalia Theater crowd, however, greeted these additions with applause.

By the end of October 1894, Most's theater group made preparations to perform in Brooklyn, Newark, and Paterson.[85] The spatial dynamic of staging this play in a restless, working-class town immediately became apparent to the officials. The Newark municipal authorities forbade its staging for fear that ongoing strikes might turn violent. The fact that a known rabble-rouser like Most would be playing a major role was seen as too risky—apparently more so than when Most would simply (and not as an actor) deliver a speech at an anarchist club. According to a socialist newspaper, the Newark police captain explained that "'in the 4th precinct there are 1000 workers out of a job for nine weeks, their families starving, therefore I regard it as dangerous to allow an agitator like John Most to incite them even further.'" "'If he [Most] dares to come here and speak,'" he continued, "'I will arrest him.'"[86] Most was asked to hand over the text to a censoring commission, which included the mayor, the police chief, and the district attorney. The mayor described Hauptmann's piece as "crass and tasteless" and invoked his role as moral guardian of the city. The district attorney proceeded to insult his New York colleagues by calling them "dumb" for having allowed the play to be performed twice.[87] The night the performance was to take place, sixty-five mounted police appeared in front of the theater, an episode that received some media attention: "Police Censorship of the Stage," read one headline.[88] Hauptmann's play returned to the New York stage in 1904 in what was probably Most's final appearance before his death in 1906. He performed alongside a number of second-generation Germans, some sons and daughters of his old comrades.[89]

It is clear that Most and his associates regarded Hauptmann's play, to which he added material, as an excellent vehicle to convey revolutionary propaganda. "I believe in the drama as the most effective propaganda," he once told the *New York Times*, "and last but not least, it is a business venture."[90] Anarchists hailed the new social drama that chose the life and times of working people as its subject. In an article entitled "Der Klassenkampf auf der Schau-Buehne" (The class war on stage) in *Sturmvogel*, the editors praised the kind of drama in which the playwright holds a mirror to society.[91] Works such as Emile Zola's *Germinal* (1885) and *Les Mauvais Bergers* (1897) by the radical dramatist Octave Mirbeau received exhilarating reviews because the topic of anarchism played a positive role.

Apart from *Die Weber*, a number of other plays and farces were acted on the anarchist stage in New York. One of the first popular social-revolutionary plays in America was *Die Nihilisten* (The nihilists), a four-act play celebrating the assassination of Czar Alexander I in 1881. Written by the anarchist editor August Spies and performed at the 1882 Commune Festival in Chicago, the first act relates how the nihilists organize themselves and discuss Russia's future after czarism is defeated. The second act shows the upper classes in their resolve to crush the conspirators. In the third act, the nihilists are caught and brought to trial. But in the final act, their comrades rescue them, proclaiming that the czar has been liquidated. Interestingly, Spies and Oskar Neebe, who would both "reenact" this role during the Haymarket trial, played two of the roles.[92] *Die Nihilisten* was popular in Newark as well, although no performance announcements in New York have been found during the 1880s and 1890s. However, an unknown theater group staged this play in a playhouse in the Bronx as late as April 1905.[93] Other plays included *Der Jongleur* (The juggler) by Emil Pohl, *Die Ehre* (Honor) by the well-known playwright Hermann Sudermann, and *Gebrüder Bock* (The brothers Bock) by the Berlin Freie Bühne playwright Adolph L'Arronge.

Summertime excursions to parks and groves on the outskirts of town were a popular pastime within the labor movement, especially for the German proletarian culture in the United States. As soon as warmer weather arrived, German workers flocked to the gardens of the larger beerhalls or organized picnics to accentuate the value of leisure and solidarity. These outings were family affairs as much as they were community or political affairs. They were held not only outside the urban setting but also away from police patrols, although in a few cases officers kept an eye on anarchists lying in the park.

German anarchists in greater New York fashioned a picnic culture all their own. A political dimension was added, combining recreation with a display of solidarity and defiance. Again, anarchists regarded recreation as part of an anarchist philosophy, and it will be necessary to connect these seemingly mundane activities with an appreciation of how space, power, and identity intersect, especially for anarchists. Socialists could visualize and vocalize political opinion through the medium of party conventions and election rallies; anarchists had no such forum. Their theater of action coincided with everyday recreation and socializing. It is therefore essential to view outings and other types of leisure as an integral part of immigrant anarchism.

The meaning of anarchist picnics can be broken down into several layers. To start off, picnics meant an escape; they were an obvious choice to get the family out of sweltering tenements and into the lush parks, groves, and seaside recreation areas. This was no different for most working-class men, women, and children—anarchist or not. The most popular parks and groves in the New York area were located on Staten Island, northern and eastern Queens, the Bronx, and along the Hudson River in New Jersey. All these sites required Manhattanites to take a ferry. Many of these parks or recreation areas frequented by German anarchists were privately owned—nearly all by Germans—and featured picnic tables, concert podiums, dance pavilions, shooting galleries, fishing and boating amenities, and, of course, prepaid kegs of beer. Rarely did anarchists venture into public parks, and (not surprisingly) never were anarchist activities recorded in Central Park. Most anarchist holiday outings were held by several groups across ethnic and occupational lines. Individual groups often organized small family excursions for members only. The most common occasions for anarchists to get out were May Day, the Fourth of July, Midsummer Night, Labor Day, and numerous family and workers' outdoor festivals. These excursions were well organized. Once a decision was made to hold an outing, an arrangement committee was elected that would reserve a spot at one of the picnic grounds, print tickets, organize a raffle, and publish announcements in the anarchist press. The autonomists once posted an "Autonomie" sign near the entrance of the picnic grounds to signal trolley riders when to get off. Many park owners specifically catered to workers' organizations. Harmony Park, located in the Grasmere area of Staten Island, offered two locations in Lower Manhattan where organizing committees could obtain park information—one a saloon, and the other a barber shop on First Avenue.[94] Picnics by socialists and anarchists in Chicago before Haymarket drew from two to four thousand people. New York outings were smaller: an 1898 picnic listed 850 tickets sold.[95]

Outings organized by German anarchists were always family affairs. Trade union, workers' fraternal, or holiday outings began in the afternoon, usually by two or three o'clock, and could last well into the night. Most family outings (Familien-Ausflug), however, started early in the day, usually at ten in the morning, when whole families headed for the ferry terminal. This allowed especially children to escape the filth and dangers of New York's streets and alleys. Children's games were always part of such gatherings.[96] The most popular games included ninepins or skittles, sharpshooting, target shooting for children (Vogelstechen), throwing rings (Ringwerfen), and egg-in-spoon running (Eierlaufen). Prizes could be won in ninepins and shooting games. Unless organized by multiple groups with lavish amounts of food and beer, families simply packed up lunches and ordered one beer keg per family. At one Fourth of July picnic in a private park in Fort Wadsworth in 1896, a *New York Times* reporter noticed that by six in the evening, eighteen kegs had been consumed.[97] All-male excursions were also organized. In June 1899, two anarchist singing societies brought the men out for a laid-back Sunday excursion to Silver Lake in Staten Island.[98]

Besides socializing and merrymaking, outings offered an excellent way to raise funds for the anarchist press or a defense fund for incarcerated comrades—an integration of politics and leisure. The 1898 picnic in New Jersey with 850 tickets sold yielded a respectable $121.65 in revenues. Assuming that the average family counted five members, some 170 families attended the picnic. As gleaned from the published expense account, it is interesting that four in five of the attendants purchased their tickets in advance, and not at the entrance booth of the park.[99]

But a closer look at the activities during an anarchist picnic and the language used by anarchist reviewers reveals a second layer of meaning: the creation of an oppositional space. Anarchists not only fashioned their own space wherever they could; they also thought of it as such. Picnics can be seen in the same way. Not only was the park grounds a real space, but anarchists conceived (or imagined) it as an anarchist space in which their ideals could be practiced in the here and now. Implicitly, anarchism was not merely something planned for the future but also something that could be attempted presently in a defined space.

Several descriptions hint at this potentially revolutionary meaning of picnics. For instance, in praising the success of a wine festival in Manhattan, one anarchist paper wrote: "Everyone thoroughly enjoyed a few hours of unrestrained joy of life," an obvious reference to an anti-authoritarian agenda.[100] In 1887, an anarchist review reveals an interesting pun: "Everywhere groups of comrades who came with their families lay down on the vast park grounds in order to combine the relaxation of the outdoors with serious discussions about current events." The original text for "relaxation of the outdoors" reads "die Erholung im Freien," which has the double meaning of "outdoors" and "in the wild."[101] The best description of a picnic by a participant in which an anarchist spirit and the notion of oppositional space are interwoven comes from a review in 1898:

> Kröbel's large park, including the giant dance pavilion, could of course by no means be filled, but even so, a splendid crowd of men and women appeared. And, the main thing was that there existed an altogether *anarchist harmony.* Arrangements were not "well planned" but instead instantly improvised so that everything proceeded like clockwork, and a spontaneous order prevailed. There was no program, so the various conversations never stopped. Sunday drinking laws were flouted, and the police was conspicuous by its absence.[102]

It is interesting that several key points about anarchism and the typical working-class aversion to bourgeois morals and capitalist regimentation in this review should be addressed to a readership already familiar with these tenets. Perhaps it was important to reiterate the very potential of picnics to become an anarchist space, or a segregated "moral climate" (as Robert Park would say[103]), in the midst of a world ruled by money, time, and competition. In this sense, this paragraph may have been designed to train anarchists in how to produce space in politically meaningful ways—to perform publicly and successfully their seeming contradictions between "spontaneity" and "order." There is also hidden in this excerpt a celebration of quality over quantity: Even though the park could not be filled numerically, it was the splendidness and harmonious nature of the crowd that mattered.

Let us now further observe how a day in the park unfolded and what meaning we can derive from the various activities. As soon as everyone was settled down, organizers began preparations for certain political activities. Anarchist picnics always featured an element of performance. Picnics were as good an occasion as any to stage a politically subversive exhibition, to state the groups' oppositional character in an open space, and to display solidarity and defiance. As the socialist historian Friedrich Sorge observed of the radical movement in Chicago, "[E]very appropriate event in public life was used to shake up the people, the workers, and to bring them to a realization of the condition and also, certainly, to frighten the philistines and politicians."[104] Anarchists regarded recreation as part of an anarchist philosophy not only in terms of creating an anarchist space but also by setting up a pulpit to harangue their detractors. Their theater of political action and everyday socializing complemented each other.

A good illustration of the performative nature of these picnics was the role of music. Anarchists of all ethnicities had numerous vocal and instrumental bands specializing in revolutionary and labor songs. At picnics, anarchists could let the radical tunes travel free through the air instead of being confined to a labor hall or saloon. All picnickers would often join in a chorus to sing the Marseillaise, and the Germans never failed to gather for a recital of the nostalgic "Wacht am Rhein." Another important aspect of the outdoor anarchist pageant, at least with German and Bohemian anarchists, was a full-fledged, military-style flag ceremony (Fahneweihe) performed with grace and pride on the park grounds. It was an elaborate dedication in which trade unions and agitation groups unfurled and dedicated their flags and banners or paid tribute to fallen comrades from the Haymarket debacle. If such open-air spectacles confirmed the identity of the participants, they also sent a message to onlookers and, in several instances, police officers who kept an eye on the proceedings.

The highlight of a typical anarchist outing was the stump speech, every bit as impressive for its theatrical value as for its political focus. Anarchist speakers were considered the foot soldiers of propaganda, often managing a hectic weekly schedule of engagements during after-work hours. Speeches affirmed the commitment to anarchism, but the indictments against the state and big industry were also directed to the world outside the group—they did not simply preach to the choir.

The dynamic of oppositional politics played out at these outdoor gatherings of anarchists worked both ways. The outsiders did on more than one occasion become the audience for the anarchist performers, and if they were not always an active audience, they certainly were curious observers. Newspaper reporters nearly all sent back grossly distorted stories of bloody shootouts and public drunkenness. Anarchists commenting on their own recreation events frequently noted the presence or absence of police officers. Picnics were rarely broken up by police, but for anarchists surveillance by cops was often worse. That the mere presence of law enforcement could spoil the fun, even if no incidents occurred, is evident from the link anarchist reviewers made between the exalted atmosphere and the absence of patrolmen. To some extent, however, anarchists savored the attention and publicity they received from police and press. It was at such specific standoffs that resistance and defiance was shown, carrying substantial meaning for the anarchist community.

Intimidation and harassment by locals was a nuisance as well as an opportunity for resistance. Some of these locals may have been provoked by the sight (and noise) of dozens and sometimes hundreds of anarchists with their families celebrating revolution while displaying red and black flags. Even worse, anarchists consistently broke Sunday drinking laws, and the chanting of rebellion songs while drinking proved too much for conservative onlookers. When in 1879 the Bohemian Sharpshooters, a Czech anarchist defense society, began their picnic in Chicago's Silver Leaf Grove with a recital, a gang of Irish men attacked the grounds by throwing stones, causing a melee at which gunshots were fired.[105] A well-attended picnic of several radical organizations in Weehawken, New Jersey, was targeted by a gang "vagabonds of the American specialty," as *Freiheit* called them, who attempted to force their way into the park. When that was prevented, they threw stones, while one even fired shots at the picnickers. According to the reviewer, one of the intruders was apprehended by anarchists, given a beating, "and thrown over the fence."[106] The fence is the perfect metaphor for the anarchists' sense of identity forged in a temporary radical space—the space of the picnic ground they occupied and made their own, if only for an afternoon. Anarchists maintained the integrity of their space and in doing so defied and if necessary confronted intruders.

In the end, what does the emotional and political experience of space mean for the study of dissent and resistance? Is this experience in the minds of organized anarchists perhaps a manifestation of some form of revolutionary consciousness? In the context of the dominant (capitalist) organization of urban space, the question becomes: Did anarchists actually subvert capitalist normality by creating their own space in the parks and groves of suburban New York? Social theorists are divided on this issue: some say space can never truly become revolutionary; others say space is always open to being "produced" and fragmented. Some practices at anarchist picnics, however, suggest that they consciously created a noncapitalist space. Consumption of beer was a market transaction that was transformed into a community function by using prepaid tokens for payment. The insistence on union beer as opposed to pool beer was in keeping with nonmarket values and strengthened solidarity with brewery workers. Elements of competitiveness, such as the shooting contests, were relished, yet the ultimate goal remained the raising of money for a higher cause. It goes without saying that picnics and other recreation served as an excellent way to raise money for the movement and reinforced mutual aid and self-sufficiency. The evidence shows that anarchists may not have created an enduring revolutionary space, but they were aware of the revolutionary possibilities of such space appropriation.

Ferdinand Schaffhauser.
(Illustriertes Wiener Extrablatt
147 [28 May 1884])

Moritz A. Bachmann.
(International Institute for
Social History, Amsterdam)

Josef Peukert, ca. 1901. (International Institute for Social History, Amsterdam)

Eduard Brady. (International Institute for Social History, Amsterdam)

*Georg Biedenkapp. (*Freiheit*, 26 December 1903)*

(Below) Announcement for Die Weber, *starring Johann Most. (*Freiheit*, 26 December 1903)*

A PICNIC OF THE "REDS" AT SHEFFIELD.

Scenes from a picnic of German anarchists, pejoratively depicted by a former police officer. (Schaack, Anarchy and Anarchists, *453)*

A group of the Lehr-und-Wehr Verein, Chicago. (Schaack, Anarchy and Anarchists, *352)*

"Underground Rifle Practice: A Meeting of the Lehr-und-Wehr Verein," Chicago. (Schaack, Anarchy and Anarchists, *289)*

Helene Minkin. (International Institute for Social History, Amsterdam)

John Most Jr. and Lucifer Most in 1907. (International Institute for Social History, Amsterdam)

Johann Most in 1903. (International Institute for Social History, Amsterdam)

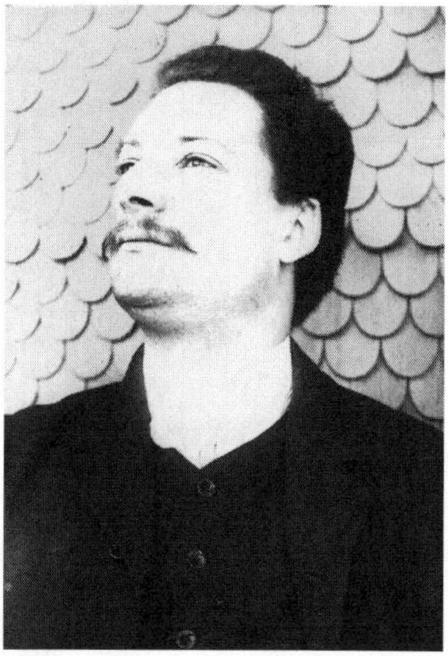

Rudolf Grossmann, a.k.a. Pierre Ramus, ca. 1905. (International Institute for Social History, Amsterdam)

Justus H. Schwab Jr., son of the saloon keeper, ca. 1901. Photographed in New York, with a dedication: "To my friend Emma Goldman, Justus H. Schwab, March 18, 1901." (International Institute for Social History, Amsterdam)

Anna Riedel. (Special Collections Library, Labadie Collection, University of Michigan)

Hans Koch. (Special Collections Library, Labadie Collection, University of Michigan)

*Anarchist flag hanging in the Chicago Historical Society building. (*Chicago Daily News *negatives collection, DN-0003451. Courtesy of the Chicago Historical Society)*

6 *German Anarchists in Progressive New York*

From the 1870s on, socialists and anarchists in the United States had been part of a larger working-class protest movement. Confronted with the pressures of industrial capitalism, workers and farmers launched the first national opposition movement, marking the last quarter of the century with class conflict, militancy, and violence. By the late 1890s, however, much of this movement was broken and scattered. The renewed prosperity of the new century shifted the country's attention to mass production, mass culture, and progressive reform. Anarchists continued their efforts to organize working people, distribute propaganda, nurture a movement geography, and challenge the emerging ethos of efficiency. This chapter chronicles the frustrations and achievements of German anarchists living in the world's mightiest city. One of the frustrations was the noticeable dissolution of the once-vibrant spatial organization of the German movement. The associational structures and discipline of the 1880s and 1890s slowly gave way to a more casual and intellectual community of radicals. In light of the shifting location of radical discourse from meeting hall to countercultural magazine, the various periodical projects launched by the few remaining German-speaking radicals obtain meaning. A look at the movement during the first decade of the new century also reveals the results of a nearly invisible process: the transmission of anarchist ideas from one generation to the next, a shift from old customs to new lifestyles, and it reveals novel ways anarchists thought about revolution and utopia. This narrative is set against the background of the wider anarchist movement in which Germans grew increasingly invisible due to shifting immigration patterns.

From 1900 to 1915, New York was inundated by a new wave of eastern and southern Europeans. From 1901 to 1910, two-thirds of all newcomers to the United States came from Italy, Russia, or the Austro-Hungarian Empire.[1] During the first decade of the twentieth century, immigrants from Germany comprised only 4 percent of the total immigration to the United States; during the next decade, this number dropped to 2.5 percent.[2] Not surprisingly, the visibility of the German-born population of New York also shrunk dramatically beginning in 1900. The census of that year showed that one in ten New Yorkers was born in Germany. In 1910, that ratio dropped to one in seventeen, and in 1920, only one in twenty-eight New Yorkers had a German birthplace.[3] Although the influx of Germans nearly came to a halt, the number of German Americans—persons born in New York of one or two German parents—remained high. It was this population that constituted German New York.

No longer replenished by hordes of newcomers from Germany, the German anarchist movement in New York for the most part had to rely on older, settled activists and the sons and daughters of the German-born in New York and New Jersey. The movement at the turn of the century was concentrated in Yorkville instead of the Lower East Side, which now housed most of the new immigrants, creating one the world's most congested urban neighborhoods. The sinking of the excursion steamer *General Slocum* in the East River on 15 June 1904 killed 1,022 people, most of them German American families, and proved another factor in the shift of German immigrants in general to up- or midtown neighborhoods—most of those killed were from German working-class families on the Lower East Side. The German anarchist movement during the turn of the century witnessed the loss of several veteran activists, the folding of a handful of periodicals, and the dissolution of its group network. The decline was even noticed by the *New York Times,* which editorialized in 1908, "So it has come about that the old-time German Anarchists, one after the other, have dropped out of the game in New York City."[4] This desertion inevitably had an effect on anarchist club life. In the 1890s, twenty-seven German anarchist groups were newly established, while only ten groups were formed during the decade of the 1900s—five of them in Yorkville. During the period 1910 to 1914, only three groups were founded. If one looks at the number of groups in existence (as opposed to when they were founded) during these decades, the decline is even more apparent: forty-three groups were in existence at one time in the 1890s, whereas only fifteen remained during the decade of the 1900s, a 65 percent drop.

The movement in New York had become scattered and atomized, suffering not only from a lack of newcomers in the closing years of the nineteenth century but also from complacency among existing members. "'Does something more harmless exist in the whole wide world than a German anarchist in America?'" asked one St. Louis paper rhetorically. "The German anarchist does nothing at all," thundered *Freiheit* in a bout of extraordinary self-criticism. "He has an abundant store of swear words ready that he generously throws around. He curses all governments and feels like a little god when he is elected chairman by the most wretched association. He condemns with a sacred zeal all beasts of property and tells in all bars that he lent a quarter to a needy person. He raves about free love and understands it to be merely cost-free love."[5] Emma Goldman, who had grown tired of the infighting among the Germans, painted a similar picture in 1898: "Well, fortunately, not much is left of a German movement." Alluding to a sharp generational divide, she explained that "the old only belong to singing societies and lodges, they hide away in their beer shops, where they inveigh against the immorality and disobedience of the youth. The young, who have emancipated themselves from the anarchist-communist-autonomist dogmas and petty club mentality, went their own way and are spreading independently the ideas of freedom."[6]

Yet the memories of the militant movement of the 1880s, epitomized by the unrestrained call for armed struggle amidst arrests and police intimidation, were romantically evoked. By the beginning of the twentieth century, violent methods were no longer advocated, making the movement less reckless as a whole. Despite the movement's loss of intrepid zeal and energy, Georg Lutz, a Milwaukee anarchist, urged his compatriots to rebuild former groups and networks and called for renewed activism because "organizations can take better care of agitation, the press, and solidarity than the solitary person."[7] Brooklyn comrades exhorted their fellow members to leave their comfortable households and participate in meetings and social events.[8] Papers reminded the anarchist community of the glory days, to build on its pioneer tradition, not to falter and wither away in disgrace.

The movement in New York also suffered the death of several influential members. The year 1898 marked the passing of two icons of German American radicalism: the Detroit poet-editor Robert Reitzel and the socialist Paul Grottkau. The movement also lost two veteran activists who had lived through the 1848 revolution in Germany, H. R. Weiss and Wilhelm Könnecke. Weiss, who passed away on 14 September 1895, had been active in the German radical circles of Paris.[9] Later he served as one of the New York delegates to the Pittsburgh convention in 1883. He was active in Brooklyn and probably resided there. In the aftermath of Berkman's attempt on Frick's life, Old Weiss was instrumental in cautioning the young communist-anarchist movement in their approval of the individual deed (Einzeltat).[10] Könnecke died suddenly at age seventy-five in the poorhouse on Blackwell's Island in New York on 1 February 1898.[11] His life's journey reflected the trajectory of many German radicals at the time. A veteran forty-eighter, he learned the trade of printer and was active in the Berlin socialist movement, but he was eventually expelled from the capital in 1880 and emigrated in 1883.[12] Könnecke distinguished himself as a speaker and a tireless colporteur for *Freiheit*.[13] With a suitcase full of anarchist literature, running from one event to another, Könnecke became the most recognizable peddler of German radical literature in the New York area. In May 1891, however, he broke with *Freiheit* to join the autonomist anarchists, and three years later he was selling *Der Anarchist* instead.[14]

The death of Justus H. Schwab on 18 December 1900 not only grieved the German anarchist movement but also shook the entire Lower East Side.[15] His death helped disintegrate the close-knit circle of activists that had made Schwab's saloon their second home. "The loss of Justus increased the dullness of my life," confided Emma Goldman. "The small circle of friends who used to meet at his place was now scattered; more and more I withdrew into my own four walls."[16] For decades, Schwab had managed the most popular radical café in Lower Manhattan (his son, Justus Jr., took over after his death). A tireless and selfless supporter of the movement, Schwab was loved throughout the neighborhood. He contracted tuberculosis in the winter of 1895 and was confined to bed from that point on. The anarchist physician Julius Hoffmann, a close friend of Most, cared for him until the end. The funeral was held at the Labor Lyceum on East Fourth Street. "As the hearse started slowly down Second Avenue, followed by a few carriages, nearly 2,000 people, many of them in tears, fell in line behind it," as one *New York Times* reporter witnessed. As heartbreaking as it surely was, the procession succeeded in transforming the neighborhood into a temporary radical space. "The procession," continued the reporter, "passed the little saloon where Schwab had lived and then proceeded slowly to the ferry at the foot of East Houston Street. All along the route the windows of the tenements were filled with people. At the ferry the carriages followed the hearse and the Anarchists on foot dispersed quietly. The body was taken to Fresh Pond, L.I., for cremation."[17] It was a cortege of grief, but at the same time, every mourner felt the collective power of showing their respects to an icon of New York anarchism, a neighborhood hero whose passing was not going to be unnoticed.

Despite all these setbacks and sorrows, the German anarchists of New York and New Jersey managed to maintain a small cultural and political movement until the eve of the First World War. The most striking development within the movement at the threshold of the new century was the predominance of cultural and intellectual activities, often in collaboration with other ethnic and native groups. This shift from militant to more intellectual endeavors began in the mid-1890s, but by the last years of that decade, reading and discussion forums as well as cultural circles and radical bookstores, if few in number, formed an essential part of the movement. In September 1898, a Free Reading Room (Freie Lesezimmer) as well as two workers' reading circles were founded in Yorkville.[18] Periodicals, brochures, and books in several languages were available, and members organized discussions and lectures (every Sunday evening in German) in the main hall, which also featured billiard tables. German anarchists, many from a younger generation, realized that education and exposure to alternative ideas were more effective than the rhetoric of vengeance and insurrection.[19] An intellectual revolution rather than a violent social revolution was needed in a time of the "mind corruption" that was America's emerging consumer culture. George Bauer, an editorial staff member of *Freiheit,* urged anarchists to act as pioneers, breaking through their own small circles and venturing into "the forest of ignorance in order to first revolutionize the minds and then the conditions."[20]

These reading clubs were not exclusively German in character. The term "international" in their names stressed the transnational and multiethnic nature of anarchism. The Irving Hall Reading Club in Brooklyn, for example, hosted lectures in German, but members also solicited the British anarchist William MacQueen, who had recently arrived in America, to speak about anarchism.[21] In 1899, Ernest Howard Crosby, the leading American Tolstoyan anarchist, was invited to lecture on "Evolution and Violence" at one of the Yorkville clubs.[22]

A similar attention to cultural and educational activism inspired the founding of several anarchist propaganda groups in early twentieth-century New York and New Jersey. The International Club "Freiheit," for example, was founded in June 1896 with much optimism. Top priorities included distribution of *Freiheit* and anarchist pamphlets, organizing meetings, and occasional after-hours schooling for the elderly. In addition, members organized a drama and music section. Judging from its many activities, this may have been the most active anarchist group at the end of the 1890s. The Union of the Free (Bund der Freien), a new and decidedly German anarchist group, was formed in November 1904 and organized weekly "social-political lectures." It is noteworthy that no evidence has been found concerning German anarchist groups in New Jersey after 1900, with the exception of Hudson County. Only one group existed for the entire county, an indication of the extent to which the German ranks had been depleted since the 1880s. The decline in anarchist groups in northern New Jersey, an 89 percent drop (from nineteen to two), was even steeper than for the entire greater New York area.

During the closing years of the nineteenth century, German radicals launched an experiment in communal living. This was probably the first attempt by German anarchists to stake a geographic space and create a miniature anarchist society without any intrusion from the outside world. The alternative spaces of beerhalls and picnics had always been exposed to some interaction with the dominant sphere, which made them at times oppositional borderlands. The first of these experiments was the communist-anarchist Liberta Vesta Commune (Liberta Vesta Gemeinde), founded in December 1895 near Killingworth, Connecticut, about five miles from the Madison ferry station on Long Island Sound.[23] It appears to have been a success, though it is unclear how long the commune lasted. To join, participants were required to contribute one or two hundred dollars to the fund, although those fees would increase slightly. By the end of December, twenty members had signed on to start a shared life of "production and enjoyment."[24] The plan was to construct greenhouses before the new year in order to harvest by spring. Livestock, tools, food, and a spacious farmhouse had been offered for purchase to the commune. Finally, by mid-January, five families set off to the Connecticut shore and then to the farm five miles inland to "begin communally the pioneer work of creating for themselves a paradise."[25] Not all German anarchists approved of communal experiments. When the first announcement for the project was printed in *Freiheit,* the editors included a disclaimer in which they disassociated themselves from the project. Some thought the project reckless and utopian, branding the participants as fanatics. Fritz Nadler, one of the initiators, quickly defended the commune idea as a serious attempt to escape the capitalist system by collectively producing and consuming the fruits of their labor. Every member was given complete freedom, as long as he or she did not violate the rationale and welfare of the collective. It was hoped that they could transport their produce to nearby markets to sustain the commune. Critics held that such communal enterprises could never succeed, since they could not compete with a private industry system. In response, Nadler pointed out that no salaries were paid, and that the goal was not to increase profits but to lead an "independent and carefree existence."[26]

During the summer of 1896, another project to build an anarchist colony was launched in northern New Jersey. The International Group Free Initiative consisted of members of several nationalities. They advertised their project in a variety of anarchist papers of all languages. The group seems to have been led by French radicals, and they had an address in Paris and connections with the French anarchists in Paterson. Regular meetings were held at a Greenwich Village apartment, where one could purchase shares and obtain information in several languages, including German. This colony had a specific purpose: to "be a home and school for children of comrades who are in prison or who are not in a position to raise them." Furthermore, since "male and female comrades have the same needs, they will of course enjoy equal rights."[27]

By the end of 1896, the Free Initiative collective was leasing a 225-acre farm with the agreement to purchase it after two years. The estate was located near the village of Campgaw, not far from the town of Franklin Lakes, seven and a half miles north of Paterson. One hundred acres of the estate consisted of arable land; the rest was covered with forest. A large brick house with fifteen rooms as well as other farm buildings in good condition were available. The goal was to set up a community of several nationalities far from any large city (about one hundred members came from Paterson). The colony was seen as a testing ground for practicing anarchist ideals. The organizers stressed that they had no illusion that building anarchist colonies would subvert the capitalist system; they merely aimed to defy it on a small scale. The main purpose, however, remained providing a home for children of incarcerated anarchists and to prevent these youngsters from falling into the hands of guardians in the employ of the government or church.[28] No information exists that would shed light on how many German anarchists participated.

The first years of the new century witnessed deep and often explosive divisions in American social relations. A renewed militancy of an increasingly frustrated and diverse workforce was bound to affect all radical elements, including the depleted German anarchists. It is telling that the initiative to latch onto the labor activism of the day did not come from members of the local anarchist community but from a young recent immigrant from Austria. Rudolf Grossmann was born in Vienna on 15 April 1882, the son of a Jewish merchant and a Catholic mother. At an early age he was involved with Social-Democratic propaganda and as a result severed ties with his parents and school. In 1895, he was sent to relatives in New York. Three years later he entered the socialist movement there, first as an associate at the *New Yorker Volkszeitung* then at the *Groß-New-Yorker Arbeiterzeitung.*[29] Not surprisingly, he made the acquaintance of Johann Most, who seems to have been impressed by the young radical and allowed him to publish in *Freiheit.*[30] Strongly influenced by Kropotkin (whom he translated) and Tolstoy, Grossmann wrote extensively on antimilitarism, anarchosyndicalism, and communist-anarchism.

In April 1901, the eighteen-year-old Grossmann and some friends decided to publish a new monthly anarchist magazine, *Der Zeitgeist.* Grossmann called himself an editor "from the new literary underworld." He clarified that his magazine sought to present "the blending of all honest, unfanatical, and studious social-revolutionary elements."[31] Biedenkapp's humorist supplement *Der Tramp* would be inserted in *Der Zeitgeist.* The first issue appeared on 1 May 1901 and featured, among other things, a poem on the late poet Robert Reitzel by Biedenkapp and an article by Most. The paper advocated a strongly anticapitalist stance and laid out a mission to overthrow the exploitative system by any effective means. The youthful Grossmann infused his magazine with a spirit of revolution, a romanticism reminiscent of *Sturmvogel* or *Freiheit* during the turbulent 1880s. "And so may this paper find its way in the cottages and homes of all those who feel the pressure, the subjugation, the wage slavery that reigns today."[32] Another editorial declared, "The revolutionary principle, the revolution as means and tactic, communist-anarchism as goal, these disciplines must be planted in the bosom of every worker."[33]

Apart from revolutionary editorials, *Der Zeitgeist* also addressed literary topics. It published short book reviews—for example, of a novel by Maxim Gorki, Eduard Bernstein's history of the socialist movement, and Tomasso Campanello's utopian novel *The City of the Sun. Der Zeitgeist* folded in July 1901, but its supplement *Der Tramp* continued for two more issues until it ceased publication in November.[34] *Der Zeitgeist* was the last of the fiery, revolutionary, Gilded Age anarchist periodicals published in German in the New York City area. According to *Freiheit,* Grossmann, with the help of friends, soon began work on a new "Austrian-Hungarian paper," but nothing more is known about it.[35]

The sudden collapse of Grossmann and Biedenkapp's periodical venture may have had something to do with the anti-anarchist climate after the assassination of William McKinley on 6 September 1901 (he died eight days later) by a deranged American of Polish descent named Leon Czolgosz, who claimed to be an anarchist. The resulting period of repression was intense but relatively short. Most and Goldman were arrested, the former eventually receiving one year in prison—his last stay behind bars and arguably his toughest. "'Throughout the proceedings Herr Most had stood at the bar visibly affected,'" reported the *Jewish Daily Forward.* "'When sentence was pronounced he clutched the railing and only by an effort saved himself from a collapse.'"[36] Numerous anarchist meetings were prevented from taking place in New York and New Jersey. In Newark, police clubbed two anarchists, while the city's Board of Excise stopped granting saloon licenses to "disturbers."[37] "The country was in a panic," wrote Emma Goldman. "Judging by the press, I was sure that it was the people of the United States and not Czolgosz that had gone mad. Not since 1887 had there been evidenced such lust for blood, such savagery of vengeance. 'Anarchists must be exterminated!'"[38]

One of the significant effects of the McKinley assassination and the following months of hysteria was the introduction, for the first time, of national legislation specifically targeting anarchists and the anarchist movement. Czolgosz's deed had propelled anarchism into the national limelight. Mainstream Americans, who were ill-informed about the movement, demanded draconian measures to curb the threat of anarchism. The State of New York, for instance, passed the Anarchy Act in 1902, which made it a crime to advocate "criminal anarchy" by speech or writing, punishable by no more than ten years imprisonment or a five-thousand-dollar fine, or both. Two provisions of the act were devastating for the movement: First, it was now illegal to form a group advocating such doctrines, or for two or more persons to meet and discuss those doctrines. Any proprietor of a hall permitting the advocacy of criminal anarchy on the premises could be thrown in jail for two years or fined up to two thousand dollars, or both. For politicians, however, it was not enough to crush the domestic anarchists. Congress started debates for a new immigration-restriction bill that eventually passed both houses as the Alien Immigration Act, signed by Theodore Roosevelt on 4 March 1903. The content of this federal law was closely modeled on the New York statute and prohibited entry into the country for anybody advocating anarchy. This legislation hit at the nerve center of the anarchist movement: the groups and the meeting places. Such repression had prompted some European activists in the 1870s up to the 1890s to go it alone and commit acts of political violence.

The anarchist movement, however, refused to go underground. Meetings and publications continued, often resulting in harassment or even litigation. It is important to note that some legitimization of anarchism among New York intellectuals had already been under way, and the

McKinley assassination did nothing to halt this. Many liberal intellectuals were horrified at the sweeping legislation, which came close to ending freedom of speech altogether. The anarchist movement itself did change in the light of these new developments. Anarchists went out of their way to explain and repudiate revolutionary violence and individual terrorist acts. "In the years after 1901," wrote the historian Terry Perlin, "the thrust of the anarchist movement moves steadily away from political heroism into the intellectual milieu of criticism and agitation."[39]

Around the time that New York and New Jersey passed so-called criminal anarchy laws, a huge strike broke out among the silk workers of Paterson in the spring of 1902. Beginning in the 1890s, Paterson's anarchist community had grown rapidly and consisted of many nationalities, including Germans. The majority, however, were Italian textile workers, the latest arrivals to be exploited for cheap labor by the booming silk industry. Their presence grew from less than thirty families in 1879 to about eighteen thousand in 1911.[40] Anarchism arrived along with the newcomers, many of whom had worked in textile mills in northern Italy. The Italian anarchist movement in New Jersey had lately been upset by an internal schism and by police repression following Gaetano Bresci's killing of King Umberto I of Italy in July 1900. Bresci was a Paterson silk weaver who had traveled to Europe to accomplish his mission. In October 1901, Luigi Galleani, a syndicalist-leaning anarchist, became the editor of *La Questione Sociale,* the main anarchist organ in Paterson. He believed in the revolutionary potential of the general strike and encouraged workers to unionize. The silk workers' strike was remarkably well organized, with bonds of solidarity extending across state lines. If the Italians comprised the largest contingent, German, French, and American workers also joined in what one newspaper labeled "mob law."[41]

Rudolf Grossmann traveled to Paterson to assist the German strikers, along with William MacQueen, who worked with the English speakers. Galleani and Grossmann did not content themselves with immediate demands, such as improved salaries or conditions, but sought to establish a general strike that would bring the entire system to a halt. By May, however, solidarity with Pennsylvania plants had withered, and workers in Paterson began to return to work. Still, a core group of militants persevered. Grossmann spoke in Paterson on 6 and 14 June.[42] A large meeting was called on 18 June to rally the downtrodden workers; Grossmann had already left town.[43] After the meeting, the crowd filed out and marched through the mill district, where they battled a large police force. Grossmann, Galleani, and MacQueen were arrested for inciting to riot and rioting.

Grossmann was released on bail in August 1902; the New York anarchists had already organized a defense fund. The Austrian and the Scotsman were sentenced to five years hard labor, despite the fact that Grossmann had not been at the meeting. After the conviction in October, Grossmann and MacQueen appealed their case to the New Jersey Supreme Court, but despite numerous witnesses corroborating his alibi, Grossmann's sentence of five years hard labor was upheld. Wasting no time, he fled the country. According to the *New York Times,* Grossmann made his way to Canada first and then to England, where he resided under the pseudonyms Friedrich Stürmer, Klarent Morleit, and Pierre Ramus.[44] Grossmann remained active in London, Berlin, and Vienna, received a doctorate in economics in 1910, and became a sex reformer, editor, and antimilitarist activist in Austria until 1938, when he fled once again to Switzerland, France, and Morocco. To join his family, who had already fled to America, he boarded a ship to Vera Cruz, Mexico, only to die a week after departure in May 1942.[45]

The events of 1901 to 1903 marked an intensification of anti-anarchist mobilization and repression not seen since 1887. Meetings, lectures, and recreational events organized by anarchists were prohibited, thwarted, and subjected to intimidation. The Paterson trial, however, inadvertently brought many anarchists together, including Germans, who together with Italian, French, and Jewish comrades engaged in joint organizing.

Anarchists as a whole continued their mission of education and agitation while adapting to new currents in radical philosophy. It is worthwhile to illustrate some of the work done by German anarchists after 1900 to elucidate this statement. Indeed, much of the historiography of German radicalism portrays the anarchists as unchanging followers of outdated Mostian revolutionary ideas. In fact, the generation after Most was far more creative and innovative than we have been led to believe. Many read the latest theories by German and American authors about revolution, gender, sexuality, and education. For the most part, the voices of these younger radicals have never been heard. One illustration of how German anarchists absorbed new ideas was the anarchist convention in St. Louis in September 1904. Anarchists used the opportunity of the World Exhibition to travel at reduced prices to the city on the Mississippi. There, in the shadow of the fanfare and glamour, thirteen anarchists of different nationalities convened from 5 to 10 September across the river in East St. Louis.[46] The central issue was the tactic of the general strike—an indication of the growing influence of anarchosyndicalism on the international anarchist movement. The delegates also agreed to continue the distribution of pamphlets among American workers, an ever-recurring issue. The St. Louis convention had little effect on the movement in New York. Johann Most disliked the convention, and no delegate from New York or New Jersey attended. Most German anarchists in New York were simply not in the forefront of union activism. Indeed, the Germans within the movement had lost their leading role. It was primarily Jewish, Italian, and American socialists, reformers, and anarchists who embarked on a union-organizing drive among New York's hard-driven garment workers. The result was a particularly intense decade of labor activism in the city. There is little information about the extent to which Germans participated in the labor struggles of early twentieth-century New York.

It seems that German anarchists at this time occupied themselves with small intellectual and educational projects. For the past two decades, from 1880 to 1900, the movement culture of German anarchists in New York had resided in an extensive geographical network of hundreds of conceptualized meeting places across the metropolitan area—participation in the movement was very much a physical, or spatial, experience. The anarchist press was the other pillar in the movement, but in general it tended to fulfill an auxiliary function, providing members with news items and announcements. With the noticeable decline in membership and group infrastructure after 1900, the German anarchist press took up the role of intellectual forum, a different kind of meeting place that sought to compensate for the decline in face-to-face gatherings of radicals.

On the first day of the twentieth century, *Freiheit* was the only German-language anarchist periodical in New York. It is possible that the poet Georg Biedenkapp's small sheet, *Der Tramp,* which he started in 1888, was still running in 1900.[47] Also, on 1 October 1898, a new labor paper, *Groß-New-Yorker Arbeiterzeitung,* appeared out of a Yorkville beerhall. The eight-page paper initially came out once a week and was designed to be nonpartisan and "proletarian-revolutionary."[48] The goal was to provide an alternative outlet for workers' organizations that were denied a voice in the socialist *New Yorker Volkszeitung.* It is not certain when this paper folded.

The next ventures in German anarchist periodical literature in New York reflected not only the shift from physical space to periodical space as the location for radical discourse but also steered away from pure labor activism. The movement after 1901 clearly rejected the Marxist notion of revolution as an apocalyptic act and regarded anarchism as a process of total liberation in which the individual or group played an active role by building new relationships and new organizations and ways of living. One of the first publications came from a group of young activists affiliated with the Yorkville-based reading circles. In May 1907, fifty members decided to launch *Menschenspiegel* (Mirror of humanity), a "freethinking, monthly discussion paper in the German language."[49] The editorial steering group appealed to all comrades to support this venture. In addition to discussions about the social questions of the day, this new publication was to give particular attention—for the first time in German American anarchist periodical literature—to the contemporary and historical conditions of women and the cultural significance of gender. Its goal was to enlighten and revolutionize the hearts and minds of its readers. This educational and literary stance bears witness to the new tendency toward an intellectual anarchist movement in Progressive-era America.

The editorial group included several prominent anarchist personalities, including Hans Koch, Anna Riedel, and Abe Isaak. Born in Hatzfeld, a German enclave in the Banat district of Romania, Hans Koch was a young anarchist poet and master builder who would play an important role in the years leading up to the First World War, including at the Modern School at Stelton, New Jersey, an anarchist-inspired educational undertaking. By the mid-1890s, Koch was in New York, where he attended lectures and was once described as "a very intelligent man and an ardent anarchist."[50] Suzanne Avins, a teacher at the Stelton school, remembered him as "very competent, very German, dignified with a long mustache."[51] Nellie Dick, a pioneer in the English Modern School movement, thought Koch "a handsome fellow with a shock of white hair."[52] Sometime before 1910, Koch met Anna Riedel, an anarchist with skills in gardening and basketry who would become an instructor at Stelton and later his wife. By December 1906, Riedel was a supporter of Emma Goldman's *Mother Earth*.[53]

Abraham Isaak and Mary Isaak exemplified the kind of practicing anarchist family living by the principles of gender equality and anti-authoritarian child rearing. They were pacifist Mennonites from Ekaterinoslav (now Dnepropetrovsk) in the Ukraine who moved to Oregon in 1889. By 1895 they launched *The Firebrand*, which became quite influential. Abe Isaak was soon arrested for publishing the allegedly obscene Walt Whitman poem "A Woman Waits for Me." They moved to San Francisco and renamed the paper *Free Society*, but in 1900 they moved again to Chicago. In 1901, Isaak received a visit from Czolgosz, before his assault on the president, who asked to join the movement. Czolgosz expressed his enthusiasm for terrorist acts, but Isaak was suspicious of him and warned the movement of a possible agent provocateur. The

Isaaks were nevertheless locked up in the aftermath of the assassination. After the affair, they (and their three children) moved to an apartment in the Bronx, where they reissued the paper until 1904.[54] Emma Goldman admired their lifestyle: "[T]he comradeship between the parents and the complete freedom of every member of the household were novel things to me."[55] "'If you can't establish freedom in your own home,'" Abe Isaak used to say, "'how can you expect to help the world to it?'"[56]

This group of young, countercultural anarchists attempted to launch *Der Menschenspiegel,* but the project did not start without problems. More than a year after Most's death, the Freiheit Publishing Association was still not keen to endorse a new German-language magazine in New York. It had printed the announcement for the new project but again attached a disclaimer warning of a reckless venture about to fail. The young editors were surprised; they had specifically stated that they did not wish to compete with *Freiheit* but rather to supplement it with the publication of free anarchist literature unavailable elsewhere. It was supposed to "come to the aid of an old paper," as the editors later put it.[57] Apparently, *Der Menschenspiegel* was immediately seen as *Freiheit*'s "nemesis," and the entire project was aborted.[58] It was then decided to start a whole new paper unattached to *Freiheit.*

In July 1907, the first issue of the monthly *Das freie Wort* (The free word) came out at five cents a copy, published at Hans Koch's residence in Yorkville. More than fifty activists gathered around the paper in the Freie Wort Group, by far the most active German anarchist collective. The paper recognized the transition from the old generation of anarchists to the next, from social revolution to intellectual revolution. In this sense, *Das freie Wort* was a product of its time, when the "new" was celebrated in every form. An opening statement appealed to the old guard of revolutionaries to share their memories with the new generation, because "not all idealism is dead."[59] Inspired by Isaak, the paper urged the young to express their opinions and live their ideals. The editors sought to create an open forum to "hasten toward beauty, to want and dare the great, to give attention to human love, and to enrich ourselves with knowledge."[60] A new interpretation of revolution found its way into the pages. Abe Isaak Jr., for instance, rejected the notion of revolution as a single cataclysmic event; instead, he saw it as a long process of liberation. His father championed free schools and voluntary associations in which children as well as adults could cultivate a sense of initiative and independence. The best way to achieve a free society was not "waiting for the millennial kingdom, but rather the practice of freedom in the present."[61] Attesting to the transnational character of radicalism, this new view was adopted from the philosophy of Gustav Landauer, a contemporary anarchist in Germany who spoke of revolution as regeneration, a spiritual renewal, a process rather than an event. Behaving differently and defiantly in relation to the state, Landauer pointed out, is itself a revolutionary act. Therefore, an anarchist society is always present and can be perfected at any time. This idea would emerge again in the works of Paul Goodman and later Colin Ward. In a sense, the German anarchist movement in America had from the start unwittingly adhered to this view by forging a separate sphere of autonomy while still advocating the necessity for social revolution.

Similar to the discussions in Schwab's saloon two decades earlier, exponents of German philosophy received attention in print. Anna Riedel discussed Max Stirner's ideas of extreme individualism and sought to integrate them with current anarchist thinking. Stirner, whose real name was Johann Kaspar Schmidt, was familiar among anarchists because of his book *Der Einzige und sein Eigenthum* (The ego and his own), published in 1845, in which he made the most extreme case for the affirmation of the self against any form of abstraction or authority. "I can make very little of myself," he stated, "but this little is everything, and is better than what I allow to be made out of me by the might of others, by the training of custom, religion, the laws, the State."[62] The book influenced Friedrich Nietzsche, and even Marx and Engels devoted some attention to it. Stirner's egoism found disciples especially in the Anglo-American world, specifically with American individualist anarchists such as Benjamin Tucker. Steven Byington, an associate of Tucker, translated the book into English. Stirner was less revered among social anarchists, although Goldman acknowledged the book's importance. Kropotkin, however, was irritated by Stirner's cold, indifferent egoism, in which he detected a "'superficial negation of morality.'"[63] When Riedel reviewed Stirner, she cautioned that egoism alone is not enough. "Altruism is also necessary for the individual," she wrote. "If the former [altruism] awakens both a deep understanding for all living things and a tolerance in the most beautiful and purest sense, then the latter [egoism] presents the eternal right of self-assertion on the part of the individual."[64]

Issues of sexuality, marriage, and gender received much more attention than in previous German-language anarchist papers—another indication of the creativity of the post-Mostian movement. The Isaaks had made a lifelong commitment to gender equality, and Abe Isaak published a favorable review of *Die sexuelle Frage* (The sexual question), by the physician and social reformer August Forel.[65] Citing Forel's book, Isaak denounced the widespread prudishness and ignorance of men and women toward sexuality, pregnancy, and childbirth. What was needed, he believed, was early sex education and a willingness to let children explore their own sexuality. Ideals and principles in the realm of personal behavior, Isaak argued, have fewer roadblocks than those in the public realm. One must therefore embrace a progressive sexual and social ethics in one's own life before one can change society as a whole. He furthermore advocated free love and instruction in birth control, rejecting the notion that human love is somehow subjected to regulation or institutions. Another example of the attention devoted to new scholarship in personal relations was the publication of *Ursachen der Ehe* (Origins of marriage) by the Finnish social anthropologist Edvard Westermarck, who had published an acclaimed study, *The History of Human Marriage,* in 1890.[66] He was also among the first anthropologists to speak tolerantly about homosexuality. Only six issues of *Das freie Wort* appeared, the last in December 1907. The paper clearly styled itself as an intellectual, avant-garde, and freethinking magazine.

If *Das freie Wort* presented topics of gender and sexuality for the first time to German-speaking New York anarchists, it was by no means a pioneer in this matter within the larger anarchist movement. Libertarian and individualist anarchists had long battled against the regulation of intimacy and morality during the Victorian era. Early American anarchists and reformers such as Josiah Warren, Ezra Heywood and Angela Heywood, Lysander Spooner, Stephen Pearl Andrews, and Victoria Woodhull pioneered a free-love movement, demanding that issues of love and sex be dislodged entirely from state and church. Moses Harman, an anarchist-feminist editor, was among the most important American radicals to openly discuss issues of sex, marriage, and divorce. His journal, *Lucifer, the Light-Bearer,* which appeared from 1883 until 1907, became the most notorious free-love magazine in America, so much so that Harman went to prison for publishing "obscene" material. German revolutionary anarchist journals in the tradition of *Freiheit* and the *Chicagoer Arbeiter-Zeitung,* in general, hardly touched subjects concerning the private lives of individuals; instead, they focused on the larger historical and sociological—some would say objective—issues of injustice, economic relations, and social revolution.

As might be expected, the issue of free love provided a point of contention between two generations of German anarchists, illustrated by a polemic between Johann Most and Abe Isaak, ten years his junior. In September 1903, Most published an article on the free-love movement expressing concern that the practice of such ideas before the abolition of private property—of which he deemed marriage an example—would lead to the destruction of healthy relationships. Free love may flourish in a free society, he reasoned, but it amounted to selfishness and frivolity in a modern society replete with hardships and uncertainties. Most therefore refused to include free-love ideas in the overall program of revolutionary anarchism.[67] Abe Isaak strongly condemned anarchists of Most's type for exempting so-called private matters—religion and marriage, for example—from anarchist scrutiny, as if domination and inequality were irrelevant in the private sphere. "It is indeed curious," Isaak wrote, "that we anarchists, who continuously remind ourselves that marriage is a product of private property, become ecstatic [i.e., alarmed] as soon as others reject this sacred capitalist institution, asserting their freedom-yearning individuality, because it 'causes pain and scandals.'"[68] Isaak insisted that anarchists cannot ignore the individual as a locus for betterment and revolution; the inner self must be liberated from prejudice before a social revolution can be contemplated. "We must not forget," he continued, "that we ourselves have put on many chains . . . and it is especially in our emotional life that we can today enjoy more freedom, provided we're not preoccupied with prejudices."[69]

An important step in anarchist organization in New York—now dominated by Russian Jews and Italians, among others—was the founding of the Anarchist Federation of New York in January 1908. For the first time, a citywide anarchist umbrella organization had been set up "along autonomic lines," as the organizers termed it.[70] It can be assumed that it was mostly Yiddish-speaking groups that took the initiative (Alexander Berkman was treasurer.) The federation's goals—an emphasis on education, syndicalism, and self-reliance—are emblematic of the general philosophy of the American anarchist movement at this time. A quick comparison with the principles of the Pittsburgh Manifesto of a quarter century ago will attest to the changing times. The federation's goals were as follows:

1. Participation in the everyday social life of the people.
2. Self-educational clubs and lecture bureau.
3. Participation in the labor movement with the specific propaganda of Direct Action and the General Strike.
4. An Anarchist Home; i.e., hall, club, and library.
5. Defence Bureau for imprisoned comrades, and for other political prisoners, if possible. (The Federation considers the defense of comrades a duty, irrespective of the Federation's attitude toward the particular cause of arrest.)

6. School for Children.
7. Declaration of Principles. (After a greater number of groups and individuals have joined the Federation, the latter will call a Convention to work out a Declaration of Principles.)
8. Joining the American Federation of the International.[71]

The fourth point in particular illustrates again the need for anarchists to forge a "sphere of free action," a thread that runs throughout the history of the anarchist movement in urban America, specifically in New York. "The Anarchist Home" is a free space, a place of comfort, communality, and defiance. The old methods of agitation and outreach were not abandoned. The immediate goals of the federation included the organization of a mass meeting of the unemployed and the arrangement of a lecture series "to popularize Anarchism."[72]

Little information exists about the number of Germans or German groups within the federation. It is certain that the Internationale Arbeiter Lese-Zirkel, the group whose members started *Das freie Wort,* joined alongside several Jewish groups.[73] Germans were not heavily represented, however, and it is interesting that in an announcement for a Commune Festival organized by the federation, German was listed last among languages in which speeches would be given (after English, Italian, Spanish, Bohemian, and Yiddish).[74] At the 1908 May Day demonstration in Union Square, organized by the Industrial Workers of the World and the Anarchist Federation of New York, it was Alexander Berkman—recently released from prison—who attracted the most attention, especially from nervous New York police officers. Three thousand mostly unemployed New Yorkers attended. August Lott, a German activist also on the podium, specifically noticed the absence of the Germans. "Conspicuous was the 'large number' of German comrades who did NOT show up, although they too are represented in the Federation." He continued with a revealing suggestion. "It seems that the 'Jews,' who in certain circles are often 'not taken seriously,' are better people when it comes to taking it to the streets for our principles. To follow their example would be better than to reflect, in certain 'clubrooms' and bars, on views regarding 'über- or untermensch,' or to lament about 'bad times.'"[75]

Lott seems to suggest that certain German comrades held anti-Semitic opinions, which may explain partly why more Germans did not participate in the anarchist movement during the years in which Jewish radicals played a dominant role. Much earlier, in July 1891, Germans had been conspicuously absent from a mass meeting of Jewish anarchists in Paterson.[76] Still, it is not apparent that anti-Semitism was widespread among German anarchists—it most likely was not. In fact, speakers of both ethnicities presented lectures together or attended each other's. The early Jewish anarchists in New York were generous supporters of *Freiheit,* and many had arrived at anarchism through the speeches of Johann Most, who, incidentally, had chosen a Jewish midwife as partner. In the end, it is not clear how long the Anarchist Federation of New York remained operative and what role the Germans played in it.

On 18 March 1910, Hans Koch and Anna Riedel—now married—rekindled their interest in journalism and published another German-language monthly, *Der Strom: Ein Organ frei-sozialistischer Richtung* (The current: A free socialist organ), with an editorial office in the Bronx. The editors proclaimed the paper to be a nonpartisan vehicle for the unfettered truth. "It will go its own way" became somewhat of a motto, and the articles breathed a strong individualistic air. The paper was almost entirely written, edited, and published by Koch and Riedel, with the help of the poets Hans Stromer and Claire and Richard Freund. At one point, the editors called on all poets to submit their work and mailing address and to join a Community of Worker-Poets (Gemeinschaft der Arbeiter-Dichter). If enough addresses were collected, a meeting of the labor bards would be organized.[77] Koch also used the paper to foster a relationship between fellow German Americans born in the Banat District, straddling Hungary and Romania.[78] *Der Strom* folded in May 1912 after more than two years of cultural and literary journalism covering, among other things, Leo Tolstoy, Friedrich Nietzsche, and libertarian education. Meanwhile, in February 1911, another little-known periodical, *Junge Erde* (Young earth) saw the light of day in New York. The magazine was advertised as a "social-aesthetic organ" and was edited by the poet Otto Sattler at his address in Yorkville. It was a radical-literary paper with anarchistic tendencies; at least two issues appeared, and it certainly adds to the largely untapped source of radical German American literature.[79]

In March 1911, the month of the disastrous Triangle Shirtwaist factory fire, a new German group was formed with the mission to publish yet another paper, *Der Anti-Autoritär* (The anti-authoritarian), with Hans Koch as secretary and G. Rahmlow as chairman.[80] Koch, like in *Das freie Wort,* appealed to older comrades and the younger generation for their solidarity. In its first article, in which anarchism and its mission were explained, the editors echoed the subtitle of Benjamin Tucker's journal, *Liberty:* "Freedom is not the daughter but the mother of order."[81] The years 1910–11 were eventful ones for the anarchist movement in New York. Early on, New York anarchists and freethinkers established a Ferrer

Association in June in honor of the murdered Spanish libertarian educator Francisco Ferrer. Josef Peukert, the veteran Austrian anarchist who could not resolve his quarrel with Most, passed away in Chicago. On 17 August 1910, after more than thirty years, *Freiheit*, the chief exponent of German American anarchist journalism, folded for good. The paper had become an emblem of turn-of-the-century radicalism in New York and the entire East Coast. Moreover, it was one of the longest running anarchist periodicals in the United States. This was perceived as a major blow to the German American anarchist movement. *Der Strom* and *Der Anti-Autorität* emerged in the wake of *Freiheit*'s demise.

Nearly thirty years had passed since *Freiheit*, the pioneer paper of the German radicals, came to New York, sparking a row over autonomy and the role of the editor within the movement. Over the course of three decades, Johann Most sought to hold his paper above water, often forgetful of the fact that *Freiheit* was as much the property of the movement as it was his own. Now that *Freiheit* was gone, it was still possible for old wounds to open. *Der Anti-Autorität*, the new kid on the block, could not take advantage of the old mailing list comprising addresses going back to 1879. At least that is what one old-timer, Carl Nold, knew from hearsay. It was, of course, extremely risky to publicize such a mailing list, but sharing information among various papers within the movement had not been a hallmark of the Germans in New York. The new periodical therefore was forced to build a list of subscribers from scratch. Nold also warned that serious fundraising must accompany editorial duties, or else the new paper would fold after only six or twelve issues. "We have already seen this so many times in the last 25 years," wrote Nold, "either you learn from the past or 'hands off!'"[82] A Milwaukee anarchist feared there would be considerable reluctance to support a new paper because many German comrades were still angry at *Freiheit* for suddenly folding without reimbursing or prorating their subscriptions. A prominent activist from Chicago was more optimistic: "With the greatest joy I look forward to the re-awakening of the revolutionary spirit within the German circles." He cautioned, however, that "something old and decaying won't be young again, and enthusiastic young comrades are too scarce to warrant big hopes."[83] One of those younger comrades, Georg Stine, supported the paper wholeheartedly and deplored the flood of pessimism that sought to dampen the spirits of Koch and Rahmlow. Stine believed that even if such ventures were short-lived, it was a comfort to know that new talent and initiative would invariably present themselves. In the end, much of the warning signals proved to be prophetic. *Der Anti-Autorität* folded that same year and possibly ran for only two issues.[84]

Hans Koch and Anna Riedel did not despair. Putting stock in the renewed value for anarchists of cultural and educational activism, they became involved in the Modern School project at Stelton, New Jersey. The Modern School movement in New York began with the founding of the Ferrer Modern School on New Year's Day 1911 at 6 St. Mark's Place on the Lower East Side. Suffering from lack of funds, the Ferrer Association decided to move the school to Stelton, a small hamlet in Piscataway Township, twenty-six miles southwest of Manhattan. This school was the longest-running Modern School in the United States, operating for four decades. As a master builder, Koch helped construct the schoolhouse and instructed children in carpentry and metalworking. Clara Solomon, a New York anarchist, however, remembered Koch as a "ne'er-do-well" who "never worked and was basically a phoney." She did admit that he was an educated conversationalist "full of German culture."[85] Koch later left the school to take a job with Frank Lloyd Wright, who was building Taliesin West in Scottsdale, Arizona. Koch died in Los Angeles in 1948.[86] At some point, he and Riedel separated. They had a son, Inko, and a daughter, Gerda, both of whom attended the Stelton school.[87] Riedel also taught at Stelton. She first took lessons in weaving and became an expert artist. At the colony she coedited a small paper, *Action*, that appeared in 1921. "Anna Riedel was a remarkable woman," remembered Solomon, "and a good influence on the children."[88] Four years later, she left New Jersey to become a teacher at Antioch Preparatory School in Ohio. The Russian anarchist Abraham Blecher, a resident at Stelton, attested that aside from Koch and Riedel, "there were also a few other Germans at the colony."[89]

The involvement of German anarchists in libertarian education goes back to the 1890s, with the founding of Free Schools. In April 1891, a Free German School (Freie deutsche Schule) existed in Ridgewood, a neighborhood in Brooklyn. In 1892 a similar school operated in Jersey City Heights and organized a school festival attended by the local German anarchist group.[90] These schools were an integral part of the German anarchist movement, as much participants in as organizers of recreational events. For example, the Women's Association (Frauen-Verein) of one of the schools organized an annual Sunday chowder party and dance gathering with children's games and beer for adults; every child received a prize.[91] Pupils and teachers showed up at a May Day gathering in Cooper Union, while the neighborhood comrades supported school activities as they would their own. Educational projects were often joined by Jewish anarchists, who in 1892 endorsed the idea of libertarian free schools, whereupon a committee was to look into closer cooperation with the

Germans.[92] As part of the wider anarchist movement, these schools occasionally received prominent visitors. On 3 March 1901, for example, Johann Most gave a lecture at the Ridgewood Free School on Darwinism, a topic regarded as controversial in large segments of American society.[93] In 1910, Josef Jülich, a writer for *Freiheit* and a former actor, founded the first German Modern School in New York.[94] The school offered evening and Sunday classes and lasted at least a few years after Jülich's death in 1918.[95]

Max Baginski, a veteran journalist and former editor of *Freiheit,* launched the last German-language anarchist periodical produced in New York. He was born in 1864 in East Prussia, only a few years older than Rudolf Rocker and Gustav Landauer, two preeminent exponents of German anarchism. Trained as a shoemaker, Baginski entered the labor movement as a Social-Democrat but veered quickly toward the left. When in January 1890, the Antisocialist Law was scrapped from the books, ending twelve years of persecution in Germany, a renewed socialist and anarchist movement began to blossom. A group of dissident Marxists emerged within the Socialist party calling themselves the Young Ones (Die Jungen). These radicals were partly influenced by the individualism and voluntarism of Nietzsche, and it became clear that after years of fierce polemics with party leaders, the young activists had rejected Marxism altogether. Landauer was particularly skillful in arriving at some kind of Nietzschean anarchism, thereby ignoring Nietzsche's loathing for progressive ideals such as equality and solidarity. Baginski was in the forefront of this new movement, which later established its own journal, *Der Sozialist,* with members who referred to themselves as "independent socialists."[96] In 1890, Baginski lived in Langenbielau, an industrial town in Silesia, where he edited *Der Proletarier aus dem Eulengebirge,* a journal that inspired the playwright Gerhard Hauptmann to chronicle the lives of local weavers. In 1891 he was imprisoned for more than two years for distributing radical propaganda, after which, at age twenty-nine, he traveled to Zürich, Paris, and London and ultimately immigrated to America. He was particularly impressed by Johann Most, whom he had always admired. In August 1893, Baginski met Emma Goldman, five years his junior. It was the start of a long friendship (they were lovers for a brief period), despite their differences of opinion regarding Most. Baginski "was of medium height, spiritual-looking, and frail, as if he had just been through a long illness," Goldman recalled. "His blond hair stood up in defiance of the persuasions of a comb, his intelligent eyes appearing small through the thick glasses he wore. His pronounced features were an unusually high forehead and a face contour that looked as Slavic as his name sounded. I tried to engage him in conversation, but he seemed depressed and indisposed to talk."[97] Baginski fell in love with and later married Emilie (Millie) Schumm, the daughter of Emma and George Schumm, a German American individualist anarchist and associate of Benjamin Tucker.

In 1894 Baginski went to Chicago to take over the editorship of the ailing *Chicagoer Arbeiter-Zeitung,* a paper once edited by August Spies.[98] To supplement his income, he solicited for his trade of shoemaker in New York through a system of mail ordering.[99] During the 1890s Baginski lived in Chicago, where he was a member of the drinking club the Damp Corner (Die feuchte Ecke) and in April 1896 he launched *Sturmglocken* (Tocsin), an anarchist weekly that quickly folded.[100] Baginski wrote satirical pieces about the Social-Democrats in Germany and published on syndicalism, humor, Jonathan Swift, and other literary topics.[101] "Max showed greater breadth, sympathy, and understanding than I had found among even the best of the German anarchists," Goldman recalled. She also noted that Baginski had sided with Berkman during the controversy, even though he refused to discard Most as a sellout.[102]

Baginski seems to have been able to transcend some old rivalries within the movement. "There was nothing petty about him, no trace of rancour or desire to censor, no vestige of a partisan," remembered Goldman. "To be with him was like breathing the pure air of green fields."[103] When Johann Most died on 17 March 1906, Baginski moved to New York, where he assumed the editorship of *Freiheit.* This, however, was not his initial wish. He agreed with Helene Minkin and others that the paper should be buried along with Most; anarchist propaganda would soon find another German-language outlet, he reasoned.[104] But in November 1907 Henry Bauer devised a plan in which *Freiheit* would appear fortnightly under the editorship of Baginski, beginning on 4 January 1908.[105] Almost simultaneously, he acted as coeditor of and prolific contributor to *Mother Earth.* His limited knowledge of the English language was sometimes a hindrance, so his articles were translated from German.[106] He also continued lecturing around New York, the Northeast, and the Midwest and was chosen with Goldman to be a delegate at the International Anarchist Congress in Amsterdam in August 1907.[107] Baginski seems to have consistently applied anarchism in all aspects of life, including gender equality. For Emma Goldman, he was an exception among the Germans. "I have met only two Germans in all my life," she wrote in 1929, "who are free, our own Max [Baginski] and Rudolf [Rocker]."[108]

An accomplished writer and thinker with years of experience as an editor in Germany and the United States, Max Baginski seems to have been the best candidate to attempt another journalistic venture in the German language in New York. On 30 March 1914, he launched *Internationale Arbeiter-Chronik* (International worker-chronicle), a monthly published at 751 East 181st Street in the Bronx. Among the financial supporters were members of the Freie Wort Group.[109]

Baginski's intellectual maturation in Germany as a member of the "Jungen" who sought to bridge socialism and individualism shone through in the content of his paper. He believed that conflict between ideological camps and the tenacity with which one holds fast to a doctrine harbored a certain kind of tyranny. "In the past they used to say Communism or Individualism," he wrote. "Today many a sensible person recognizes the existence of an intimate connection between the two. We even consider economic communism as a prerequisite for individual freedom. It no longer is unusual to hear: Freedom and Cooperation, Anarchism and Organization, Labor movement and independent local and individual action."[110] In stating the goal of his paper, one can detect an inkling of Nietzschean voluntarism: "To unify the working class in solidarity in order to transform a society [Gesellschaft] full of ignominy into an independent, anxiety-free existence in communist community [Gemeinschaft] under the principle of fundamental equality of all humans."[111]

Baginski also invoked the thought of Ferdinand Tönnies, one of Germany's best-known sociologists, although his seminal work was not widely read when it came out. That work was *Gemeinschaft und Gesellschaft*, first published in Leipzig in 1887.[112] In it, Tönnies distinguishes between a community and a society, arguing that Gemeinschaft societies prevailed in ancient times, and Gesellschaft societies dominated during the modern era. However, he carefully avoids any unilinear or teleological interpretation of human evolution. Every human society necessarily contains elements of both models, which differ in economic organization and even in psychology. Baginski called on his readers to reverse what he perceived as a trend toward more rigid models of Gesellschaft and to return to a romantic notion of Gemeinschaft, or community.

Johann Most received more attention in the pages of the *Internationale Arbeiter-Chronik* than in any other paper apart from *Freiheit*. This can be explained by the fact that Max Baginski and August Lott, the two most active German anarchists in New York, had been close friends of Most and still admired him greatly. Lott wrote a lengthy article defending him against insinuations made by Landauer that Most was an alcoholic. Lott even resurrected the old Neve affair.[113] Baginski was also irritated with Landauer when he learned that he had claimed he received the information about Most's drinking habits from Baginski. Despite a strong disagreement between Most and Baginski on the issue of Berkman's assassination attempt, Baginski always retained a respect and understanding for Most. In fact, the men were similar in their inability to adjust to life in America. "I believe I understand to a large extent Most's tragic situation and isolation in this country," Baginski wrote. "I do not want to make a saint out of him, but I won't let him be degraded or besmirched."[114] Incidentally, Landauer was not impressed with Baginski's new paper; he thought it decadent and dull. The extent to which the late Most was admired by older German anarchists was illustrated in 1913. Alexander Berkman had just finished his autobiographical account *Prison Memoirs of an Anarchist,* one of the best pieces of prison literature ever written, in which he criticized Johann Most. The book was first published in 1912 by the Mother Earth Publishing Association, and Berkman had been in contact with Rudolf Grossmann to arrange a German translation. One of the issues was whether the name "Most" should be changed to "Müller," a pseudonym Most had used. "It is not a question of antagonizing the German comrades," Berkman wrote to Grossmann, "but of relating historic events. As there is quite an element of the old German comrades, who, though not very active in the movement, would be anxious to read the book in German."[115] Frederic Thaumazo (whose real name was Frederic Loevius) took offense and vented his disgust in a pamphlet, *The Martyrdom of Berkman,* in which he painted the ex-convict as an emotional martyr looking for appreciation. Thaumazo also accused Goldman of being hypocritical by attending Most's memorial gathering because she had publicly humiliated him in 1892. Berkman simply ignored Thaumazo, and so did Grossmann, apparently. "I agree with you," wrote Berkman, "that the man is not quite well balanced. The malice of his pamphlet is too apparent and deserves no attention."[116]

The First World War loomed large over the German radical community in America. Hostilities began on 1 August, when Germany declared war on Russia. This set in motion a mechanism of treaties that would bring every major power into a worldwide conflict, resulting in massive numbers of casualties. By mid-September, the war stalemated in an immensely murderous trench warfare. Nearly every article in the last two issues of the *Internationale Arbeiter-Chronik* (23 August and 23 September) was devoted to the war. One article strongly denounced the socialists in Germany for endorsing patriotism, calling them sellouts.[117]

Baginski did not hesitate to announce his antiwar stance and urged a "war against war."[118] That anarchists should be against this war, which many saw, like Lenin, as an imperialist conflict waged by capitalists and aristocrats, was not at all self-evident. Peter Kropotkin, the preeminent anarchist thinker, proclaimed his support for the allies, especially France, a country he greatly admired for its revolutionary tradition. Kropotkin viewed the conflict as a mission to preserve France's heritage against the blunt militarism of the kaiser. But Kropotkin became instantly isolated from the mainstream anarchist movement. Errico Malatesta was furious and went so far as to label Kropotkin and Jean Grave, a well-known French anarchist editor, as "Pro-government Anarchists."[119] The majority of immigrant anarchists in America were fiercely antimilitarist, and Goldman, Berkman, and others threw themselves in the vanguard of a relatively noisy antiwar movement, especially in the months leading up to the U.S. declaration of war on 6 April 1917. However, pro-German sentiment pervaded much of the Yiddish press. Jewish radicals hated the czar and saw the eastern front as a battlefield of German civilization against Russian barbarism. Still, a great number of Jews equally opposed President Wilson's appeal to unquestioned patriotism.[120] At the time of the trenches, a German anarchist from Buffalo wrote that "the war itself is the crime of all crimes. It is impossible to train and command armies to their highest killing potential, and at the same time impregnate them with kindness and respect for human life. The assertion that modern warfare only engages soldiers and is not conducted against the population of the besieged areas is a vain falsehood and deceit, as anyone can already witness daily. Surely, it is impossible to persuade the poor villagers of this, whose houses are set on fire while they flee like beggars, homeless."[121]

But even among American radicals there was disagreement. The war issue became so divisive that it tore apart old bonds, leaving the socialist and anarchist movements in shatters. Ben Lieberman, a teacher at the Stelton Modern School, lived through those times. "I am convinced that the First World War was the great watershed of the modern period. The result of the split in the radical ranks was an irreconcilable legacy of bitterness and enmity. A line of blood was drawn between them, with charges of 'traitor' and 'renegade.'"[122]

America's entry into World War I was followed by a climate of chauvinism and anti-German feelings that pushed older and second-generation German radicals outside any national attachment. Suddenly, these anarchists could image themselves standing in No Man's Land between the German and American states—between abstract loyalties of nationalism they sought to transcend. The German anarchists opposed war in 1914 and distanced themselves from what one New Jersey anarchist called the "German patriots." Caught between two states, the anarchists resorted once again to their proud status of "citizens of the world"; as the French anarchist Victor Drury once proclaimed, "'I am a patriot of the universe.'"[123]

In the end, it is telling that three of the most public figures in the declining German anarchist movement in New York from 1900 to 1914 were young immigrant activists and not German Americans born in New York. Rudolf Grossmann and Max Baginski, like Most and other German radicals, could not adjust to life in America. Both returned to their homelands after active duty abroad. The *New York Times* reported that Most expressed a desire to return to Germany in the autumn of 1890, the year the Antisocialist Law was repealed; he never did.[124] Baginski remained on a farm in Pennsylvania before returning to Germany in the 1920s, but he did not stay there. He returned to New York, where he lived in the Bronx. Fermin Rocker, the son of Rudolf Rocker, thought that Baginski "was a man without a country, a frustrated person, in contrast to Father's buoyant optimism."[125] To a large extent, the experiences of Most and Baginski resemble the larger story of German anarchists in the United States. Anarchism came as a foreign import and withered away unnoticed. Their public rhetoric of social revolution was ridiculed at first, then silenced and maligned. Their community life in the immigrant neighborhoods throughout the city was either feared or misunderstood. That said, immigrant anarchism was a part of urban culture in America, a visible, audible, and physical presence that sheds light on how radical space can exist and give meaning to one's life.

At this point, one conclusion emerges: the German anarchist movement in the New York metropolitan area from 1880 to 1914 was a diverse community with much infighting, but it was also home to a rich associational life that fostered enduring friendships and creative projects. Aside from a common language, many personalities differed greatly in character from their comrades, only shaking hands based on a common anarchist philosophy. One thing they all shared, however, was the experience of migration and adaptation to a new culture. Whether naturalized citizens or newly off the boat, all German anarchists had at one point or another the need to reflect on their new environment and to evaluate their beliefs, their tactics, and their choices. The anarchists' view of the American reality of life is unique, especially when one acknowledges that they were also wage earners and consumers in a society they sought to change. How did they view the United States? Did it affect the movement? Did it affect American culture?

Much is known about what mainstream America thought of immigrant anarchists, but less well known is the German anarchists' view of America, and in particular of the multicultural metropolis where many lived and worked. Foreign radicals who immigrated during the 1880s and 1890s arrived largely ignorant of American customs and conditions. In the case of Germans, most harbored feelings of bitterness and defeat because of nationwide suppression of socialism in their homeland. This condition of an uprooted psyche, landless but pregnant with moral and political idealism, underlay immigrant anarchism's public voice in America.

To some extent, German immigrant revolutionaries held the same preconceptions about America as most working-class immigrants at the end of the nineteenth century. While political liberties and higher wages in the United States were seen as invaluable benefits, these were offset by realities of higher living costs and a faster work pace. Gilded Age immigrants often regarded neither Germany nor the United States as particularly free countries. They simply wanted to escape the old in search for independence elsewhere. The historian Dirk Hoerder has argued that "migrants do not move to a 'free' society, they 'free' themselves from the old."[126] In this sense, German anarchists had few illusions about power relations in America, although most believed that building a labor movement was still possible in the United States.

What is striking about the anarchist viewpoint is its lack of meaningful affiliations with traditional concepts and institutions. German exile anarchists could not identify with the United States as a political entity; they harbored a militant antistatism and criticized any form of domination. They loathed capitalism and the ethos of private property and thus could not agree with the American economic system. Nationalist and religious affiliations, which helped shape the identity of millions of other immigrants, offered little meaning to atheistic anarchists. Furthermore, they refused to participate in electoral politics, which distinguished them from the socialists. German anarchists sought a radical transformation of the established order and advocated armed self-defense against the brutality of guardsmen and police. Their viewpoint was that of the outsider, removed and certainly oppositional. This is not to say that German anarchists were without locality or culture in the United States. They did not hide ethnic pride, and, above all, they cultivated their own autonomous sphere with family picnics, barroom discussions, theater, and lectures.

If their political idealism alienated them from the reality of American society, German anarchists lived in America and helped build the America they criticized. Political convictions often crystallize through personal encounters with reality, and it is precisely in those moments that immigrant anarchists confronted what some historians call "the dominant patterns of Victorian America's middle-class and largely Anglo-Saxon culture."[127] Anarchists mobilized against the Puritanism of the Anti-Saloon League and the Sunday closing laws, for instance. Beer drinking and family gatherings on Sunday were German customs, and anarchists continued to schedule meetings and picnics on any day they liked. Saloons would appear closed from the street, but one could find an entrance in the back of an adjoining alley.

German anarchists profiled themselves as watchdogs of the state of American freedom and were quick to challenge the country's claim to democracy. They reminded the American public that venerable democratic traditions, which they admired, were being eroded by big industry. German anarchists celebrated American independence as much as native patriots, and the Fourth of July was always an occasion for a picnic. The Pittsburgh Manifesto of 1883 and the Chicago Conference Manifesto a decade later invoked Jefferson's call for overthrowing a tyrannical government in the Declaration of Independence to bolster their arguments for revolution.[128] The *Freiheit* editing room was adorned with portraits of Thomas Paine, John Stuart Mill, and Jean-Jacques Rousseau.[129] The nationwide uprising of workers during the 1870s was common knowledge among German anarchists, and to them it seemed proof that indigenous revolt was possible. (Bakunin himself contemplated coming to America after he heard of the uprising, but he fell ill.) In August 1884, Johann Most believed American workers were simply fed up. "The workers have a strong desire," he wrote to a friend, "to smash everything to pieces at the first appropriate occasion."[130]

Despite these antagonisms, American civil liberties remained an obvious advantage over Germany's and Austria's repressive regimes, and German anarchists who had lived in America for more than a decade—men like Justus Schwab or Moritz Bachmann—were especially aware of this. Newcomers, however, had been so affected by Bismarck's ruthless politics that they were blind to differences in political culture on the western shores of the Atlantic. They rejoiced at freedom of speech, but they were astonished when "inciting to riot" overruled the First Amendment. Johann Most attracted large crowds to hear his stunning oratory, but he was frequently reprimanded by German American anarchists for dramatizing his condemnation of the "bourgeois-republic." "'You don't understand,'" one anarchist retorted during a discussion in a Milwaukee saloon. "'You've only been here for two years—I have four.'"[131] The fact that length of residency was invoked by anarchists to tone down the ranting of newcomers suggests that some integration into American society had occurred.

Optimism turned to disillusion and isolation when German anarchists were unjustly executed in Chicago on 11 November 1887 after being implicated in a bomb explosion in Chicago's Haymarket Square. The judge openly stated that they were sentenced for their beliefs, not for any involvement in a crime; their guilt was never proven. The Haymarket hangings shocked the entire labor movement, and the anarchists retreated to mourn in obscurity. Haymarket had enormous repercussions for the way any radical viewed America, especially immigrants with memories of Old World repression. The hope that America would not renege on its promise of democracy had vanished completely, and for anarchists, this new country would require as much, if not more, vigilance from people with an opinion critical of capitalism or Christian morality.

Repression took its toll on anarchists' daily lives: nearly all anarchist meetings were shadowed, anarchist saloons were forced to close or denied a license, while several leading speakers were arrested and imprisoned. But the attention and widespread condemnation of anarchism was for some a badge of honor. Rather than seeking to redress unfair imagery of anarchists, Johann Most, in a spirit of defiance, proudly pinned offending cartoons from *Punch* and *Puck* magazines on his apartment wall.

Isolation turned the anarchist movement inward and arguably strengthened its self-righteous posturing as a martyred counterculture. This post-Haymarket state of affairs, the combination of isolation and repression, profoundly influenced the anarchists' view of America. Emboldened by this status, anarchists continued to publish pamphlets and editorials and to deliver speeches in which not only "America" was lambasted but increasingly ordinary Americans themselves, who had so rashly and heartlessly demanded the death penalty for their comrades. "The Americans . . . are on average entirely without Idealism," wrote *Freiheit* in 1887.[132] Similar sentiments appeared in other papers. "All their dealings are determined by an unparalleled Egoism."[133] Most's paper offered an historical explanation for America's rugged individualism: opportunistic settlers who emigrated and devoured the land like "hyenas on a corpse" eventually passed on their predatory instincts to the present generation. Editorials painted Americans as lagging behind in intellectual matters and described their "fundamental trait" as "a most blatant instinct of acquisition."[134] The poet Georg Biedenkapp summed it up in a poem, "Amerika":

America, beautiful land,
needs no thinkers or poets
With so many men of standing
like the boodler and the judge.

America, beautiful land,
needs no poets and thinkers
With so many men of standing
like the clubber and the hangman.[135]

To some, American individualism could be fertile ground to sow the seeds of anarchism. One obstruction, however, was a seemingly irrational fear of socialism that killed any sympathy for solidarity-based movements. "The introduction of the teachings of Socialism, esp. of communist-anarchism to the English-American people," wrote one Brooklyn anarchist, "is very difficult and . . . it will take up a long time."[136] Another paper thought Americans "funny people" for dreading the word "socialism" and pointed out that clubs founded in the wake of Edward Bellamy's popular socialist novel, *Looking Backward,* were called nationalist, not socialist.[137]

Despite these frustrations, German anarchists continued to view the American worker as capable of being revolutionized. It may be an uphill battle, but activists maintained a tireless will to distribute literature among American and German workers. In fact, agitation among English-speaking workers constituted one of the most important items on the anarchists' public agenda, a headline issue at every major anarchist convention in the United States. Many German anarchists feared that unless some support could be won from native workers, they would be discredited as irrelevant outlaws unable to cross ethnic boundaries. In other words, the mission was to extend the "sphere of free action" to non-anarchists and specifically to English-speaking wage earners. Johann Most was keenly aware of this problem. He always believed anarchism should be of the masses, and even though Germans comprised a relatively significant portion of the American population, the fact that the bulk of native-born workers fell outside the anarchist radius was troublesome. "In America, on the other hand, we resemble voices crying in the wilderness, kept unheard," he once wrote to fellow comrades. "Socialism [in America] is German, and anarchism a violet that blooms unnoticed." Most criticized mainstream and socialist labor for condemning anarchism before understanding it. "'The English, American, and Irish labor associations are great in number, meaningless in principles,'" he wrote. "'In those circles they see us as villains and clowns because they don't know us, and don't *want* to know us. Our struggle will be hopeless so long as this situation persists. It would be foolish not to understand this; indefensible to let ourselves bleed to death in isolation, disgraceful to give up hope.'"[138] This remarkable statement comes close to summarizing the raison d'être of revolutionary anarchism—and perhaps of any oppositional movement—in the United States. It radiates passion for the righteousness of one's beliefs but also fear of isolation. It reveals the innermost anxieties of a man who suffered so much the pangs of misunderstanding and ridicule.

A closer look at the ways German-language anarchists disseminated ideas to native workers through the radical press reveals much about their view of America. German anarchists in New York and elsewhere were only too happy to generously support English-language anarchist papers, if only someone would write and publish one. From the conclusion of the Pittsburgh Congress until October 1884, not one English-language paper was included as an official organ of the IWPA; there were, however, seven German and two Czech papers. In April 1884, the English-language paper *Nemesis* came out in Baltimore, but it was not included as an official IWPA organ. German anarchists were encouraged to purchase five to ten issues to distribute later to American workers.[139] *The Alarm* was an IWPA paper that appeared from 1884 until 1889, first in Chicago then in New York. It was first edited by Albert Parsons, who was executed as one of the Haymarket defendants, and later by Dyer D. Lum, an American anarchist embracing individualist and communist-anarchist tenets. The paper failed to gain a healthy circulation. Moreover, it turned out that most subscribers were Germans. "It is said in the circles of German-speaking anarchists," reported *Freiheit* in 1889, "that it is a problematic beginning when German revolutionaries publish English papers that are only read or purchased by German workers anyway."[140] Johann Most had been one of the most adamant supporters of *The Alarm,* although he was not known for ideological tolerance. He bluntly attacked Lum for including individualist-anarchist views in his paper and even urged German subscribers to withdraw their support.[141] In November 1890, German and American anarchists launched a new English-language IWPA organ, *Freedom,* in Chicago.[142] Three of the most active German anarchist groups in New York decided to order 145 copies to distribute on the streets.[143] Another paper that was welcomed by German anarchists was *Solidarity,* a communist-anarchist fortnightly that appeared from 1892 until 1898 in New York and was edited by Francesco Saverio Merlino and John H. Edelmann. As can be expected, the autonomists and not the Mostians supported this paper, as did William Himmler, who became secretary of the Solidarity Group. Interestingly, Edelmann once suggested Johann Most publish *Freiheit* in English.[144]

Anarchist pamphlets translated into English rolled of the press by the thousands. Nearly all German anarchist propaganda groups in New York and New Jersey approved of the production and distribution of English-language literature. Especially Johann Most's pieces, such as *Die Gottespest,* at one time translated as *God, Heaven, Hell: An Appeal to Pious Men and Infidels* and published by the Committee of Agitation, were translated. The original Pittsburgh Proclamation, the primer of revolutionary anarchism in America, was quickly made available in English and could be ordered in bulk—usually one thousand copies—for further distribution and sale at three cents a copy.[145]

Despite these efforts, it remained extremely difficult to reach native-born workers with the written message of anarchism. By 1890, the deficiency in English-language propaganda was deemed the "greatest difficulty that all this time has stood in the way of communist-anarchist agitation in this country"—not to mention the fact that printing and publishing material in English was a costly affair.[146] The New York Committee of Agitation complained that not a single well-established "Anglo-American branch" of the IWPA was in existence.[147] American workers were simply not receptive to anarchism, at least not in a lasting way.

If German anarchists deplored the apparent complacency of native-born workers, the knife cut both ways: a large number of German anarchists could not speak English and therefore could not participate in English-language agitation. The boundaries of language and politics coincided. Most American workers did not respond to revolutionary anarchism, while many Germans struggled with a new language to convey an impossible dream. This situation amounted to a cultural collision of a transnational ideal and the reality of ethnic identity abroad. It was Babel in New York. It was not anarchism itself that was inadequate, but its bearer. Still, many German activists did speak English. Claus Timmermann, for instance, delivered speeches in English and during the 1890s decided to devote his time to the production of English translations of Kropotkin and Elisée Reclus. Translation of documents was seen as the key to minimizing language boundaries. During the 1890s, an initiative to set up a Bureau of Translation (Übersetzungs-Anstalt) circulated among anarchists. Documents were to be sent to this bureau, where they would be translated into English, Dutch, German, French, Spanish, and Portuguese before being sent out to various periodicals.[148]

Few older German orators mastered the English language. If some tried, many others were simply set in their ways. In June 1889, a meeting was called for American workers at which Johann Most haphazardly improvised a speech in English, but it turned out that nearly all attendants were immigrants.[149] On several occasions, Most refused to render his speeches in English because he could not employ the German (or Bavarian) idiom and familiar expressions that otherwise spiced his declamations.[150]

As a result, the German movement contented itself with lending logistical and financial support to a host of English and American speakers. Thomas Hamilton Garside, a mathematics professor from Scotland, became for a short time a prolific speaker within the German movement. His biography is sketchy, but he was born in 1855, the son of a railroad contractor. Compliant with his father's wishes, he became a preacher and moved to northern Ireland, where he remained for seven years. Sometime in the late 1880s, Garside immigrated to Baltimore, where he worked as a tutor and later moved to Philadelphia, where he joined the Socialist Labor party. He also became a lecturer for the Knights of Labor, and in January 1889 he attended a meeting in Chicago where Lucy Parsons spoke. Garside expressed concerns about the methods of revolutionary anarchism but at the same time ridiculed the idea of the ballot box.[151] Garside had veered toward anarchism, and it was at this meeting that the party leader Thomas Morgan proclaimed, "'Garside has disgusted all the socialists while the anarchists roared with delight.'" He was promptly ostracized from the SLP.[152] Goldman remembered him as "tall, pale, and languid-looking. His manner was gentle and ingratiating, and he resembled somewhat the pictures of Christ. He was always trying to pacify conflicting elements, to smooth things over."[153] By 1889, Garside was living in New York, where he spoke at IWPA meetings alongside Johann Most. He authored a pamphlet, *A Critique of the Present Industrial System,* with a circulation of fifteen thousand copies.[154] In the summer of 1891, Garside's name showed up in a sensational *New York Times* story revealing him as a police detective in pursuit of a fraudulent banker. It is not possible to verify this story, but after the affair, Garside disappears from the anarchist record.

Hugh O. Pentecost was another middle-class radical who was sympathetic to the German movement and willing to spread the word of anarchism. Pentecost, a largely neglected figure in the annals of American radicalism, had been a minister in New York from 1886 to 1888, but he abandoned the church to become a prominent lawyer, single-taxer, freethinker, socialist, and later anarchist.[155] He was an autodidact and never attended law school, but that did not prevent him from lending legal services to the defense of Berkman in 1893 and later in the case against the English anarchist John Turner in 1903. He seems to have been a generous man, extremely conscious of the plight of others, especially the poor, which was partly a product of a deep—if misunderstood—spiritual side. Pentecost was above all a brilliant speaker and attracted large crowds—mostly Americans—in New York. In 1888, he launched *Twentieth Century,* a radical magazine in which the anarchist movement received much attention, including the German movement. In 1892 he published an anthology, *Why I Am's,* to which Most contributed "Why I Am a Communist," and Lum, "Why I Am a Social Revolutionist."[156] German anarchists hailed his lectures in Brooklyn and Newark to crowds of Americans, in which he condemned the Haymarket trial and executions, as the best and most effective to date.[157] But like Garside and others, Pentecost's sojourn among New York's radical community did not last; his ambition led him to seek a job as assistant district attorney of New York. He still gave a speech with Most and Goldman on 22 January 1906, probably his last one; he died shortly after it.[158] American liberals in New York during the 1890s had organized numerous clubs, such as the Manhattan Liberal Club, the Newark Liberal League, and the Brooklyn Ethical Association, in which anarchism and freethought were discussed and to which immigrant anarchists like Goldman and Most were occasionally invited.

Language was a significant player in the transfer of radical ideas from European immigrants to an American public. Germans in particular were loyal to their mother tongue, and the language barrier prompted German anarchists to view the United States as something other in the first place. Communication among various immigrant anarchists was facilitated by multilingual festivities and probably benefited from some form of shared European or immigrant identity. Typically, large meetings featured several speakers in different languages, mostly German, English, Yiddish, and Italian. Interestingly, some German anarchists proposed to eliminate German from a future lecture tour by Peter Kropotkin, who was rumored to visit America soon; the Russian ended up not visiting Canada and the United States until 1897.[159] To improve American relations, it was deemed more practical in terms of propaganda effectiveness to stick to English addresses. "Everybody who knows the English-speaking public knows the reason for this," one writer tells us, "as soon as another speaker begins in a different language (German, for example) the public becomes bored, impatient, and runs away from it."[160] Perhaps for this reason the editors of *Der Anarchist* objected to highly publicized speechmaking and lecture tours that were only attended for their theatrical value. "As long as comrades do not regard the creation of a viable press as being of the first order, everything will be useless in America."[161]

For German anarchists, the fact remained that communist-anarchism would at best gain only a toehold in Anglo-America, that the country's working class (including immigrant workers) could not be convinced of the validity of anarchism. "No apostle or missionary coming from Europe will do wonders through oral propaganda," warned one editorial in 1895, "because Americans look at a meeting as a theatre performance."[162] Some activists proposed a more direct method of propaganda rather than theorizing about anarchism. "We always bring in speeches and writings that were distributed in other countries and among people that have enjoyed a decade-long development of ideas within the labor movement," complained one anarchist.[163] This view of a discrepancy in the evolution of revolutionary consciousness was not uncommon with German anarchists. In many instances, a whiff of cultural chauvinism is evident in anarchists' analyses of American society. "All previous propaganda among the Americans, with their crass materialistic nature, was much too theoretical," wrote a Brooklyn anarchist.[164]

Emma Goldman also alluded to misplaced pride among German radicals who seemed to revel in an impractical insularity despite efforts to break out of the ethnic shell and "go to the people." As a reaction to the prevailing pessimism (and arrogance) among the Germans, Goldman recognized America's libertarian heritage. As late as 1898, having read Paine, Thoreau, and Emerson, she held that "'the fuss . . . about America not being the soil for anarchism, is ridiculous and false. . . . The Americans are by nature independently disposed, and are more than any other people, equipped to understand the ideas of anarchism.'"[165] The fault for the slow progress of the dissemination of anarchist ideas did not lie with Americans, but with those "who practiced the 'movement' only in German and have used every possible means to hinder the instruction in the English language. The pursuit of anarchist propaganda in the English language was and remains the main task."[166] It is important to note that Goldman by this time had abandoned the confines of the ethnic movements—German and Jewish—and embarked on a nationwide lecture tour. She may also have retained some bitterness after breaking with Most in the mid-1890s.

In 1907, when progressivism was in full swing and immigrant anarchists had become more bohemian (though still political), the anarchist George Bauer appealed to his comrades to style themselves as avant-garde educators: "As anarchists we have to present ourselves as pioneers, especially in this land of corruption and dissolution of the mind. Pioneers who don't endlessly turn around in their own little circle, but instead push forward into the forest of ignorance, in order to revolutionize the minds first, then the conditions."[167] This essentially nonviolent strategy stands in contrast to the militant rhetoric of a generation earlier. Intellectual activism and revolution of the mind, ideas later appropriated by the New Left, found expression in radical bookstores and reading and discussion rooms.

In 1911, Max Baginski, one of the last German anarchist editors, wrote somewhat condescendingly that "the atmosphere of this country is not very conducive to the mental development of the Germans; as a rule, they lose here all incentive to intellectual pursuit."[168] He was referring to the growing commercialism and consumerism of early twentieth-century America. Baginski also criticized German anarchists for abandoning their ideals and being swept up in commercial opportunities by becoming "successful business men."[169] This missionary attitude, illustrated by Bauer and Baginski, was not uncommon among the German American community as a whole. Many Germans were better educated than their American neighbors, and it was not unusual for Americans to be deemed naive or uncultured. The social linguist Joshua Fishman wrote that German Americans "looked upon Americans as spiritually dormant worshippers of the golden calf. They looked upon themselves and upon others of German stock as the leaven that would bring about the spiritual awakening and maturing of the Yankee loaf."[170]

As outsiders, German anarchists found themselves in a position to deconstruct or demythologize the so-called exceptionalist interpretation of the United States, in which America is seen as unique in its classless egalitarianism. This campaign of challenging America's claim to democracy and equality was not merely a defensive reaction. Anarchists sought to educate the disaffected about the lies and myths upheld by the media and the elite, lies that were exposed by Haymarket. German anarchists spiced their speeches and writings with provocative and muckraking analyses of how wage slavery had replaced chattel slavery in Gilded Age America. Like in Europe, a privileged elite had emerged, they argued, an elite unwilling to hear the demands of working people that instead demanded law and order in the face of human injustice. "So, the laws are there to strangle freedom. And yet, there are certain people who still scream for more laws," remarked *Der Kämpfer.* "Isn't this the height of nonsense?"[171] One St. Louis anarchist paper reported on the appalling conditions in Chicago's slaughterhouses and questioned how free American workers really were. *Freiheit* urged that "the American workers must finally realize what kind of 'freedom' theirs really is." "It is then," the paper reasoned, "that America's labor movement will become revolutionary."[172] Here, the paper alluded to the inherent corruptness of the system. No reformist strategies could change the status quo; only a fundamental readjustment would be fruitful.

In summary, German anarchists believed that the spirit of America's revolutionary generation of the 1770s had long vaporized into thin air, while their sons and daughters were either lured by the continent's riches or had become victims of the new creed of the dollar. Gilded Age Americans, including the working classes, had resigned themselves to the pragmatic pursuit of wealth. As a result, the exploited American worker only joined a union when immediate gains could be won. As one writer in *Freiheit* remembered, "Sometimes we talk to an American for a while. If he is a poor devil, he'll listen eagerly to the way we reason about the rich. We guide him step by step through our train of thought. He follows by nodding. Occasionally we throw in the remark that we have for years devoted ourselves entirely to revolutionary propaganda by word and writing. And surely, our listener blurts out the question: Must be well-paying?"[173]

This attitude, according to the anarchists, was also prevalent in the politics of the labor movement. While socialists believed the American political system could be a vehicle for success, the anarchists abhorred electoral politics: power corrupts anybody who attempts to gain it, even for honorable or righteous purposes. Politics, no matter how democratic or socialist, always contains the seeds of tyranny.

The anarchists' cultural text was unique in turn-of-the-century America. It was as much a making of America as an unmaking. It was also a foreign making of America, but one that occurred inside its borders. The authors of this text were immigrants who were also atheists and internationalists. As immigrants, they participated in the dominant culture; as atheists and internationalists they excluded themselves from it. This dichotomy created a distance between them (the observers) and American society (the subject). Although, perhaps this distance only existed in the realm of ideas and not so much in the daily lives of German anarchists as citizens and consumers.

Multiple identities intersected within the movement and its members. German American anarchists did not deny their German heritage perhaps precisely because they lived elsewhere, and they also embraced America's revolutionary ideals, contrasting it with the oppression in the land they had left for good. And finally, they celebrated the anarchist identity of freedom and internationalism to indicate their allegiance to no one. To put it more colorfully, one gathering of German anarchists in Philadelphia in 1883 featured one small German flag, a medium-sized Stars and Stripes, and an enormous red flag.[174]

Conclusion

The story of the German anarchist movement in New York and New Jersey from 1880 to the First World War reveals an important dimension of turn-of-the-century radicalism, ethnic history, and the history of urban America. New York radicalism did not consist only of the better-known socialists and communists but also produced a strong left-libertarian undercurrent, of which immigrant anarchism was one manifestation.

The German anarchists of New York and northern New Jersey anchored their movement in the seabed of Lower Manhattan, the dirt-ridden streets of the Lower East Side, Yorkville, Brooklyn, and Newark. Countless saloons and the much-frequented Germania Assembly Rooms became the spaces for an oppositional movement. From 1880 to 1914, the German anarchists organized clubs, agitation groups, discussion circles, theater groups, picnics, lecture evenings, mass protest meetings, demonstrations, fundraising events, and children's games in the parks lining the Hudson River. They combined a German working-class conviviality with principles of freedom and anarchy.

Social and political circumstances in the United States and Germany served as a catalyst for the emergence of anarchism in urban America. New York City was the final destination for the transatlantic liners filled with Europe's malcontents. This impersonal behemoth provided the backdrop for the German anarchists and their movement, even creating rivalry with its midwestern sister city on the lake. The first anarchistic club in America was formed on the Lower East Side and consisted of German social revolutionaries. Many of those early members were German Americans who had lived in New York since the 1870s, such as the colorful saloon keeper Justus Schwab and the journalist Moritz Bachmann.

During the early 1880s, the movement rose to its apex in membership and notoriety. Johann Most, the leading figure of that time, and the 1883 Pittsburgh Congress, a little-known episode in U.S. labor history, sought to "institutionalize" the movement and set up a loose infrastructure. Most's politics engendered strong opposition within the movement, causing internal strife along ideological and even ethnic lines. His opponents, the autonomists, became the foremost representatives of communist-anarchism among German-speaking radicals in America. They raised questions about autonomy and exclusivity within a radical movement that are still being debated by anarchists today. These divisions were not unique to Germans, or to anarchism; they are a product of the anxieties of a high-minded marginal movement within an unreceptive dominant culture.

The German anarchists' public campaign consisted of antistatist and anticapitalist propaganda disseminated through lectures and the printed word. At first geared mostly toward events in central Europe, German anarchists quickly confronted conditions in America as well. They sharply censured what they saw as America's departure from its original revolutionary ideals. The activism of German anarchists in New York was hampered not only by police surveillance but also by factionalism, ethnic insularity, and a widening gulf between the anarchists' message and the view of the majority of American workers. During the 1890s, New York anarchism began to drift toward an intellectual movement, in contrast to the emphasis on propaganda by deed during the previous decade.

The German anarchists' relationship with the dominant culture resulted in an element of confrontation as well as an element of defiance. The former amounted to an oppositional attitude expressed in strong language and posture, including some rhetoric of insurrectionary violence; the latter resulted in the creation of an alternative, peaceful countercommunity. Rather than relying on political parties and elections to bring about social change, German anarchists simply lived by their beliefs as much as possible. They fashioned an alternative space in which their ideals could be practiced in places such as beerhalls, picnics, singing societies, and theater groups.

The German anarchist countercommunity was instrumental for the rise of subsequent radical movements in the city, particularly the Jewish and Italian. The early days in the careers of Emma Goldman and Alexander Berkman were spent among German anarchists of New York. Jewish radicalism and Yiddish-language culture came to define New York's

Lower East Side for decades to come. The bohemian and multicultural image of this neighborhood carries through even today, despite the dual effects of gentrification and urban decay in the area. German anarchists in New York were also in the forefront of fashioning an American bohemian culture in New York long before the days of Greenwich Village. To some degree, the ideas of the Germans spilled over into the emerging guild of Anglo-American liberal intellectuals. Not only anarchism but also the ideas of Stirner, Nietzsche, and other exponents of German culture found a receptive ear among some of New York's middle-class liberals. Undoubtedly, the Germans laid some of the groundwork for the extraordinary energy of American anti-institutional progressivism during the 1910s and the subsequent counterculture that still exists today in New York.

If anarchism as a philosophy and movement has not vanished, one must concede that the German element, or the memory of German radicals, has faded. The First World War abruptly—and unjustly—damaged the respectability and credibility of anything German in America. Second-generation immigrants from Germany promptly changed their names, or lay low for the duration of the war. In the atmosphere of 100-percent Americanism, radicals of all stripes were targeted, and some one hundred anarchists were simply shipped to Russia. The success of the Russian Revolution further diminished the influence of anarchism, as American radicals turned their hopes to communism or syndicalism. But unlike in Europe, any hint of socialism was firmly suppressed in the United States following the armistice, a red scare that lasted until at least 1925. A return to prosperity and the rise of consumer capitalism in the 1920s effectively silenced the voices of protest until 1929, when capitalism was struck by its own overindulgence.

By the mid-1930s, the German anarchist movement in America had all but disappeared. In 1933, Rudolf Rocker traveled from New York to Los Angeles and then to Canada to see for himself what had happened to the movement. In February 1934, while in Vancouver, he wrote to the historian Max Nettlau that not a single German anarchist group survived; only individuals such as Max Baginski, Max Metzkow, Carl Nold, Georg Bauer, and Alfred Sanftleben were still alive.[1] However, like the rise of Bismarckian realpolitik in the 1860s and 1870s and chauvinistic militarism of Wilhelm II in 1914, the threat of Nazism in the late 1930s mobilized German radicals and exiled intellectuals in Europe and America. Anarchist ideas once again found an audience, mostly within the tiny anti-Stalinist Left who had lost their sympathy for communists in Europe and America. Once more, German anarchists resurfaced in

New York. Sometime in 1938, a group published *Der Antifaschist*, but it folded shortly after. On 1 March 1938, about two weeks before Hitler announced the Anschluss (joining) with Austria, the Deutsch-Amerikanischen Kulturverband (DAKV; German-American Cultural Alliance) launched *Gegen den Strom* (Against the current), a monthly published and edited by Rudolf Rocker and Robert Bek-gran. Rocker had fled Europe, while Bek-gran had been in New York during the 1910s. Other contributors included Fritz Gross and Ernst W. Mareg. This journal was explicitly antifascist and anti-Stalinist and offered anarchist perspectives. The paper lasted until 2 November 1939, a month after Hitler's invasion of Poland.[2] The unexpected resurgence of anarchist ideas in the late 1950s and 1960s resulted in the appearance of several histories of anarchism, reprints of classics, and new biographies of icons such as Landauer, Goldman, and Kropotkin. However, the German pioneer anarchists remain elusive in the literature.

One enduring reminder of the role of German radicalism is a somber one: the Haymarket Martyrs' Monument. The Pioneer Aid and Support Association, a group started by Lucy Parsons, erected this granite shaft with two figures in bronze in 1893. It was dedicated in the presence of a crowd of eight thousand. On 2 May 1971, Irving Abrams, the last surviving member of the association, presented the deed of the monument to the Illinois Labor History Society. To this day, every Sunday nearest 4 May, activists and sympathizers gather at the monument to commemorate the anarchists.

Incidentally, in 1889, another Haymarket monument was built, this one dedicated to the police. It featured the inscription: "In the name of the people I command peace." This monument was moved several times due to traffic circulation, and in October 1969 it was dynamited by left-wing radicals, causing extensive damage. After restoration, another bomb exploded near it a year later. Ultimately, the statue moved to the Police Academy building, where it can be viewed only after making arrangements. It is perhaps ironic that explosives vandalized the Haymarket police monument. Even more ironic is the fact that New Left radicals succeeded in denying a police memorial a public space the same way the elite had denied a public voice for the anarchists less than a century earlier.

In recent times, anarchist activists have reappeared on the streets of European and American cities. In 1999, a demonstration against the World Trade Organization in Seattle launched a worldwide anticorporate-globalization movement in which anarchists have a strong presence. Subsequent demonstrations in Washington, D.C., Philadelphia, New York,

London, and Genova attracted media attention. Anarchists were well represented at large demonstrations against the U.S. invasion of Iraq in 2003 and are always present at rallies of a new abolitionist movement to end the death penalty in the United States. Insurrectionist methods have not disappeared entirely, either. Groups such as Direct Action Network, Anarchist Dance Bloc, and the Anarchist Black Bloc occasionally engage in directed vandalism such as the smashing of windows of the coffee chain Starbucks in Seattle. What is remarkable about the new movement—activists and infoshops—is that the past is never forgotten. On 12 May 2001, for instance, during an anti–death penalty demonstration, a masked anarchist was dressed as a large puppet with the text: "August Spies: Hanged by the State 1887."[3]

All things considered, anarchism did not become a large protest (or proletarian) movement. Perhaps this expectation is unfair, as it comes not out of an anarchist philosophy but rather a Marxist notion of mass politics. The debate over whether anarchism is best suited as a lifestyle or as a grassroots political movement is still ongoing. Still, anarchist ideals linger and occasionally well up in American social ideology. Anarchism's uncompromising critique of capitalism and parliamentary politics and its call for revolutionary measures alienated it from the larger American society even as it influenced other social critics. In an essay on the abolitionist movement, Martin Duberman pointed to the powerfully engrained optimism of the American mainstream, which caused it to discard any radical attack on institutions. "And so the majority has generally found it necessary," Duberman writes, "to label 'extreme' any measures that call for large-scale readjustment."[4] An insight that is equally relevant for the nineteenth, twentieth, and for our own centuries.

NOTES

Introduction

1. See www.infoshop.org/directory_namerica.html.
2. Morris, "Germans in Baltimore," 12–13.
3. Wiebe, *Search for Order.*
4. Zinn, *People's History of the United States,* 206.
5. Wiebe, *Search for Order,* 156.
6. Duberman, *Left Out,* xx.
7. *The Rebel,* 20 October 1895.
8. This term comes from Gemie, "Counter-Community."
9. Foucault, "Question of Geography"; Foucault, "Of Other Spaces"; Lefebvre, *Production of Space;* Soja, *Postmodern Geographies.*
10. Park, "The City," 126.
11. Soja, *Postmodern Geographies,* 6.
12. Pile and Keith, *Geographies of Resistance.*
13. Quoted in ibid., 15.
14. Ward, *Anarchy in Action,* 11; Parisi, *Artist of the Actual,* 26.
15. Scott, *Domination and the Arts of Resistance.*
16. Chauncey, *Gay New York.*

Chapter 1: Radical Geography.

The subtitle of this chapter is taken from Scott, *Domination and the Arts of Resistance,* 108.

1. Speed, "Anarchists in New York," 798.
2. Trachtenberg, *Incorporation of America,* 126.
3. Lang, *Tomorrow Is Beautiful,* 41.
4. Certeau, *Practice of Everyday Life,* 91.
5. Dinnerstein and Reimers, *Ethnic Americans,* 206–8.
6. Claghorn, *Reports of the Industrial Commission,* 465–92.
7. Lapham. "German-Americans of New York City," 14.
8. Quoted in ibid., 70.
9. Rosenwaike, *Population History of New York City,* 67; Claghorn, *Reports of the Industrial Commission.*
10. Rosenwaike, *Population History of New York City,* 95; Adams, Lewis, and McCrosky, *Regional Survey of New York and Its Environs,* 93.

11. Quoted in Dinnerstein and Reimers, *Ethnic Americans,* 29.
12. Sante, *Low Life,* 15–16.
13. Maffi, *Gateway to the Promised Land,* 85.
14. Jackson, *Encyclopedia of New York City,* 1284–85.
15. Burrows and Wallace, *Gotham,* 741.
16. Lidtke, *Alternative Culture,* 87.
17. *Freiheit,* 22 February 1890. Unless otherwise noted, all translations are by the author.
18. *Freiheit,* 16 May 1891.
19. Burrows and Wallace, *Gotham,* 933.
20. *Brooklyn Daily Eagle,* 9 May 1885.
21. Rosenwaike, *Population History of New York City,* 70.
22. Dinnerstein and Reimers, *Ethnic Americans,* 28.
23. Rosenwaike, *Population History of New York City,* 70.
24. Ibid., 83; *Brooklyn Daily Eagle,* 9 May 1885.
25. Lapham, "German-Americans of New York City," 65.
26. *Brooklyn Daily Eagle,* 9 May 1885.
27. *Lain's Brooklyn Directory, 1897–98.*
28. Sanders, *Downtown Jews,* 65, 74.
29. Jackson, *Encyclopedia of New York City,* 171–72.
30. *Freiheit,* 17 August 1901 and 2 May 1903.
31. Lapham, "German-Americans of New York City," 157.
32. Quoted in ibid., 156.
33. Burrows and Wallace, *Gotham,* 992, 994.
34. *Freiheit,* 5 January 1884.
35. Lapham, "German-Americans of New York City," 135.
36. Ibid., 136.
37. Jackson, *Encyclopedia of New York City,* 733, 966.
38. Ibid., 966. One source (based on the census) claims that in 1890, about one-third of Long Island City's population was German-born or of German parentage. Morris, "Germans in Baltimore," 13.
39. *Freiheit,* 24 October 1891.
40. Rosenwaike, *Population History of New York City,* 56.
41. Quoted in ibid., 52, 56.
42. *Freiheit,* 24 July 1886.
43. *Freiheit,* 15 March 1890.
44. Jackson, *Encyclopedia of New York City,* 922–23.
45. Adams, Lewis, and McCrosky, *Regional Survey of New York and Its Environs,* 93.
46. Ibid., 103.
47. Dinnerstein and Reimers, *Ethnic Americans,* 28; Morris, "Germans in Baltimore," 13.
48. Quoted in Cunningham, *Newark,* 198.
49. Mehring, *Geschichte des deutschen Sozialdemokratie,* vol. 2, 80, 171, 182; Na'aman, *Lassalle,* vol. 6, 890.
50. *Freiheit,* 10 October 1891.
51. Adams, Lewis, and McCrosky, *Regional Survey of New York and Its Environs,* 93.

52. Ibid., 103.

53. Hudson County contains the towns of Jersey City, Jersey City Heights, Hoboken, West Hoboken, Union Hill (now Union City), Secaucus, West New York, Guttenberg, North Bergen, Weehawken, Woodcliff, Bayonne, Kearny, Harrison, and East Newark.

54. Shaw, *Immigration and Ethnicity in New Jersey History,* 19.

55. Dinnerstein and Reimers, *Ethnic Americans,* 28.

56. Adams, Lewis, and McCrosky, *Regional Survey of New York and Its Environs,* 93.

57. Ibid., 103.

58. Ibid., 93, 103.

59. Morris, "Germans in Baltimore," 13.

60. Johann Most to Victor Dave, 19 September 1884, Max Nettlau Archives, "Most und Neve: Briefe deutscher Anarchisten, 1884–1887; Aus Victor Dave's Nachlass," 18; Manuscript dated 12 October 1925, Internationaal Instituut voor Sociale Geschiedenis, Amsterdam (hereafter IISG).

61. Adams, Lewis, and McCrosky, *Regional Survey of New York and Its Environs,* 93, 103.

62. Waltershausen, *Der moderne Socialismus,* 364.

63. Adams, Lewis, and McCrosky, *Regional Survey of New York and Its Environs,* 93.

64. Ibid., 103.

65. Dinnerstein and Reimers, *Ethnic Americans,* 28.

66. *Freiheit,* 6 September 1890.

67. *Freiheit,* 9 January 1892.

68. A detailed discussion on the individualist anarchists in America is beyond the scope of this study. However, it is important to mention that these anarchists did not only base their philosophy on early American libertarian thinkers such as Thomas Paine, Thomas Jefferson, Josiah Warren, or Elihu Palmer but also on European philosophers like Max Stirner and Pierre-Joseph Proudhon. Several German radicals were or became individualist anarchists, including Georg Schumm, Moritz Bachmann, and to some extent Justus Schwab. They gathered around Benjamin Tucker's *Liberty* magazine, the foremost exponent of individualist anarchism in the United States.

69. Lidtke, *Alternative Culture,* 21.

70. Quoted in Roberts, "Wirtshaus und Politik," 127.

71. Ensslen, "German-American Working-Class Saloons in Chicago," 159.

72. Kolb, *Als Arbeiter in Amerika,* 75.

73. Quoted in Ensslen, "German-American Working-Class Saloons in Chicago," 164.

74. Powers, *Faces along the Bar.*

75. Schumacher, *Small Is Beautiful.*

76. Speed, "Anarchists in New York," 799.

77. Jacoby, *Last Intellectuals,* 21.

78. *Brooklyn Standard Union,* 13 March 1877 and 5 December 1882.

79. *Freiheit,* 26 March 1887.

80. Jacoby, *Last Intellectuals,* 29.

81. Ibid.

82. Quoted in Ensslen, "German-American Working-Class Saloons in Chicago," 170.

83. Speed, "Anarchists in New York," 798–99.

84. Berkman, *Prison Memoirs of an Anarchist,* 238.

85. Quoted in McLean, *The Rise and Fall of Anarchy in America,* 240–41 and 244–45.

86. *New York Times,* 24 November 1887.

87. *Freiheit,* 15 May 1886.

88. Quoted in Powers, *Faces along the Bar,* 176.

89. Quoted in ibid., 179.

90. Huneker, *New Cosmopolis,* 5.

91. McCabe, *History of the Great Riots,* 298–99.

92. Goldman, *Living My Life,* vol. 1, 119.

93. McCabe, *History of the Great Riots,* 299.

94. "Heimath und Werkstatt aller Reimschmiede, die ihren Pegasus versohlen wollen." (Pegasus is the symbol of poetic inspiration.) *Sturmvogel,* 15 June 1898.

95. *Freiheit,* 5 December 1891.

96. Huneker, *New Cosmopolis,* 5.

97. "Sammelplatz aller feuchtfröhlichen, freiheitlich gesinnten Geister." *Sturmvogel,* 15 June 1898.

98. Drinnon, *Rebel in Paradise,* 62. The reporter Nellie Bly visited Schwab's saloon; her report appeared in the *New York World,* 17 September 1893.

99. Goldman, *Living My Life,* vol. 1, 145.

100. Lidtke, *Alternative Culture,* 181.

101. *Freiheit,* 1 November 1890.

102. Ibid.

103. Ibid.

104. *Freiheit,* 9 February 1889.

105. Ek, "Historical Study of the Speechmaking at Cooper Union."

106. *Freiheit,* 21 January 1893.

107. *Freiheit,* 23 September 1905.

108. Burrows and Wallace, *Gotham,* 1139.

109. *Freiheit,* 24 September 1887.

110. *Sturmvogel,* 16 January 1899.

111. *Freiheit,* 12 December 1891.

112. *Freiheit,* 26 March 1887.

113. Hecker hats (Heckerhüte) are named after Friedrich Hecker, a revolutionary who, together with Gustav Struve, led an armed uprising in the principality of Baden in March 1848. He later immigrated to America and became an anticlerical, liberal Republican opposed to slavery. He fought in the Civil War and remained active as speaker in Republican circles. Hecker hats became a symbol of freedom, equality, and the early days of German democracy.

114. Kolb, *Als Arbeiter in Amerika,* 94–95.

115. Quoted in Avrich, *Haymarket Tragedy,* 411.

116. Goldman, *Living My Life,* vol. 1, 43.

117. Ek, "Historical Study of the Speechmaking at Cooper Union," 360.

118. *Freiheit,* 30 October 1886.

119. Scott, *Domination and the Arts of Resistance,* 65–66.

120. Ibid., 9.
121. Ibid., 37.

Chapter 2: From Heimat to Exile

1. Nadel, *Little Germany,* 42.
2. The law's official title was "Gesetz gegen die gemeingefährlichen Bestrebungen der Sozialdemokratie" (Law against the dangerous aspirations of Social-Democracy). Thümmler, *Sozialistengesetz §28.*
3. Nomad, *Apostles of Revolution,* 267.
4. Quoted in Lidtke, *Outlawed Party,* 111.
5. Auguste Blanqui was a French activist and law student. He adhered to socialist republican ideas and believed the class divide revolutionized the proletariat. Imprisoned numerous times, he nevertheless organized small cells (or "families") and planned armed insurrections throughout the 1830s. Blanqui's notion of a "vanguard party" made him a recognized forerunner of Lenin.
6. Lidtke, *Outlawed Party,* 109.
7. [Schneidt], *Die Hintermänner der Socialdemokratie,* 3. Schneidt's book was originally published anonymously, as "von einem Eingeweihten," or "by an initiate."
8. Thümmler, *Sozialistengesetz §28.*
9. Auer, *Nach zehn Jahren,* 285.
10. Ibid., 289.
11. Thümmler, *Sozialistengesetz §28,* 171–244, 149. Thümmler revised earlier inquiries made by the socialist Ignaz Auer, who obtained the information by way of questionnaires sent to the expatriates. A New York committee then sent the manuscripts back. Auer, *Nach zehn Jahren.*
12. Linse, "Der deutsche Anarchismus," 513–19.
13. Lidtke, *Outlawed Party,* 122.
14. Quoted in Becker, "Johann Neve," 105.
15. Ibid., 104.
16. [Schneidt], *Die Hintermänner der Socialdemokratie,* 34.
17. Ibid.
18. Ibid., 38.
19. Quoted in Becker, "Johann Neve," 104.
20. Quoted in Becker, "Johann Most in Europe," 299.
21. Quoted in ibid., 300.
22. Dinnerstein and Reimers, *Ethnic Americans,* 16.
23. Commons et al., *History of Labour in the United States,* vol. 2, 282.
24. Ibid., 284.
25. Waltershausen, *Der moderne Socialismus,* 162.
26. Rocker, *Johann Most,* 469.
27. Commons et al., *History of Labour,* vol. 2, 286.
28. Quoted in Avrich, *Haymarket Tragedy,* 48.
29. Avrich, *Haymarket Tragedy,* 48.
30. Waltershausen, *Der moderne Socialismus,* 170.
31. Keil, *German Workers' Culture in the United States,* 7.
32. Kautsky, "Johann Most," 555.

33. Bers, *Wilhelm Hasselmann,* 38.
34. Quoted in ibid.
35. Mehring, *Geschichte des deutschen Sozialdemokratie,* vol. 2, 299.
36. [Schneidt], *Die Hintermänner der Socialdemokratie,* 57.
37. Bers, *Wilhelm Hasselmann,* 10.
38. Quoted in ibid., 12–13.
39. Quoted in ibid., 13, 15.
40. Ibid., 29.
41. Quoted in ibid., 31.
42. Thümmler, *Sozialistengesetz §28,* 195.
43. [Schneidt], *Die Hintermänner der Socialdemokratie,* 59.
44. Bers, *Wilhelm Hasselmann,* 55.
45. Quoted in ibid.
46. [Schneidt], *Die Hintermänner der Socialdemokratie,* 55.
47. Quoted in Bers, *Wilhelm Hasselmann,* 13.
48. Bernstein, *Die Geschichte der Berliner Arbeiter-Bewegung,* vol. 2, 348–55.
49. [Schneidt], *Die Hintermänner der Socialdemokratie,* 106.
50. Ibid.
51. *New Yorker Volkszeitung,* 16 September 1880.
52. [Schneidt], *Die Hintermänner der Socialdemokratie,* 66.
53. *New Yorker Volkszeitung,* 19 September 1880.
54. Ibid.
55. *New York Times,* 14 January 1874.
56. *New York Times,* 19 December 1900.
57. "Defense of Justus Schwab."
58. Speed, "Anarchists in Hard Times," 840–41.
59. *New York Times,* 14 January 1874.
60. Gutman, "Tompkins Square 'Riot,'" 55.
61. 1880 U.S. Census, New York, New York (Manhattan).
62. *New York Times,* 19 December 1900.
63. *New York Times,* 8 June 1876.
64. *New York Times,* 9 April 1877.
65. Avrich, *Haymarket Tragedy,* 50; *Freiheit,* 22 December 1900.
66. [Schneidt], *Die Hintermänner der Socialdemokratie,* 99.
67. Goldman, *Living My Life,* vol. 1, 320.
68. Deleon, *Party Ownership of the Press,* 15.
69. *New York Times,* 16 April 1883.
70. "Defense of Justus Schwab."
71. Creagh, *L'anarchisme aux Etats-Unis,* vol. 1, 622.
72. Quoted in ibid., 602.
73. Quoted in Avrich, *Haymarket Tragedy,* 50.
74. *Freiheit,* 22 December 1900.
75. Waltershausen, *Der moderne Socialismus,* 170.
76. Ibid.
77. *New Yorker Volkszeitung,* 16 November 1880.
78. *Freiheit,* 17 March 1888.
79. *Freiheit,* 9 April 1881.
80. Ibid. The pamphlet was entitled *Sic temper tyrannis* (So it goes for all tyrants).

81. *New York Times,* 30 November 1880.
82. *New York Times,* 6 December 1880.
83. *New Yorker Volkszeitung,* 30 November 1880.
84. Thümmler, *Sozialistengesetz §28,* 243.
85. Waltershausen, *Der moderne Socialismus,* 171; Hoerder, *Plutokraten und Sozialisten,* 107.
86. The German-language paper *Philadelphia-Demokrat* captured this rendition of his speech on 27 September 1880. Quoted in Bers, *Wilhelm Hasselmann,* 60–61.
87. Quoted in Avrich, *Haymarket Tragedy,* 50.
88. Waltershausen, *Der moderne Socialismus,* 170.
89. *New Yorker Volkszeitung,* 19 November 1880.
90. *Freiheit,* 11 December 1880.
91. *Freiheit,* 19 February 1881.
92. *Freiheit,* 17 December 1881.
93. *Freiheit,* 14 May 1887.
94. Johann Most to Victor Dave, 28 April 1885, Max Nettlau Archives, "Most und Neve," 43, IISG.
95. Bers, *Wilhelm Hasselmann,* 58–59.
96. *Freiheit,* 2 February 1907.
97. Bers, *Wilhelm Hasselmann,* 60.
98. Linse, "'Propaganda by Deed' and 'Direct Action,'" 207.
99. Quoted in ibid., 210.
100. Rocker, *Johann Most,* 142.
101. Quoted in Becker, "Johann Neve," 107.
102. Nettlau, *Anarchisten und Sozialrevolutionäre,* 188.
103. Creagh, *L'anarchisme aux Etats-Unis,* vol. 1, 612; Nettlau, *Anarchisten und Sozialrevolutionäre,* 187–201.
104. Cahm, *Kropotkin and the Rise of Revolutionary Anarchism,* 155.
105. Quoted in Nettlau, *Anarchisten und Sozialrevolutionäre,* 222. Nettlau's source was the paper *Le Révolté;* note that the word "political" was put in parentheses.
106. Quoted in ibid., 213.
107. Ibid., 216.
108. Nomad, *Apostles of Revolution,* 276.
109. Agents' Report (Washington, D.C., 22 April 1881) quoted in Hoerder, *Plutokraten und Sozialisten,* 94.
110. Waltershausen, *Der moderne Socialismus,* 177.
111. Quoted in Avrich, *Haymarket Tragedy,* 59. The representatives from the New York City area included Justus Schwab (New York City), Adolph Herber (by proxy: Jersey City Heights, Hoboken, Union Hill, Jersey City), and John P. Dusey (by proxy: Paterson).
112. Quoted in Creagh, *L'anarchisme aux Etats-Unis,* vol. 1, 629.
113. Quoted in ibid., vol. 2, 994. The original German text reads: "Haben wir uns in den Ver. Staaten in Gemässheit mit den Zuständen und Verhältnissen, welche hier herrschen, organisirt." *Freiheit,* 19 November 1881.
114. Commons et al., *History of Labour,* vol. 2, 293.
115. Hoerder, *Plutokraten und Sozialisten,* 98.

116. Creagh, *L'Anarchisme aux Etats-Unis,* vol. 1, 638.
117. Linse, "'Propaganda by Deed' and 'Direct Action,'" 207.
118. Creagh, *L'Anarchisme aux Etats-Unis,* vol. 1, 639.
119. Tcherikower, *Early Jewish Labor Movement,* 204.
120. Sanders, *Downtown Jews,* 74.
121. Rocker, *Johann Most,* 143.

Chapter 3: Johann Most and the Pittsburgh Congress

1. According to the anarchist free-love magazine *Lucifer, the Light-Bearer,* reporters for the *New York Journal* and *New York World* were instructed to mark any interview with or "story" about Most with the initials "P.F.," for pure fake, and "C.S.," for color strongly. *Lucifer, the Light-Bearer,* 12 December 1901.
2. Quoted in Avrich, *Haymarket Tragedy,* 62.
3. Becker, "Johann Most in Europe," 291;Most, *Memoiren, erlebtes, erforschtes, und erdachtes.*
4. Quoted in Becker, "Johann Most in Europe," 291.
5. Quoted in ibid.
6. Tscherikower, *Early Jewish Labor Movement,* 220–21.
7. Nomad, *Apostles of Revolution,* 262.
8. Quoted in ibid.
9. Becker, "Johann Most in Europe," 297.
10. Rocker, *Johann Most,* 444.
11. Ibid., 453.
12. *Briefe und Auszüge aus Briefen von Joh. Phil. Becker,* 169.
13. Letter from 1 July 1883, in *Sozialistische Briefe aus Amerika.*
14. Nomad, *Apostles of Revolution,* 259.
15. Quoted in Rocker, *Johann Most,* 20.
16. Waltershausen, *Der moderne Socialismus,* 194.
17. Quoted in Becker, "Johann Most in Europe," 295.
18. [Schneidt], *Die Hintermänner der Socialdemokratie,* 26.
19. Creagh, *L'anarchisme aux Etats-Unis,* vol. 1, 569.
20. Becker, "Johann Most in Europe," 304.
21. [Schneidt], *Die Hintermänner der Socialdemokratie,* 28.
22. Ibid., 41.
23. *Freiheit,* 26 December 1903.
24. Quoted in Becker, "Johann Most in Europe," 299.
25. Johann Most to Victor Dave, 10 August 1884, Max Nettlau Archives, "Most und Neve," 13, IISG.
26. [Schneidt], *Die Hintermänner der Socialdemokratie,* 99.
27. Waltershausen, *Der moderne Socialismus,* 199; *New York Times,* 19 December 1882.
28. Quoted in Creagh, *L'anarchisme aux Etats-Unis,* vol. 1, 449.
29. *New York Times,* 19 December 1882.
30. Goldman, *Living My Life,* vol. 1, 6.
31. *Freiheit,* 23 December 1882.
32. *Freiheit,* 10 February 1883 and 16 February 1884.
33. *Freiheit,* 3 July 1886.
34. Max Nettlau Archives, "Most und Neve," 2, IISG.

35. *Lucifer, the Light-Bearer,* 12 December 1901.
36. Grottkau and Most, *Discussion über das Thema "Anarchismus oder Communismus?"*
37. Goldman, *Living My Life,* vol. 1, 77.
38. Avrich, *Anarchist Voices,* 18.
39. *Freiheit,* 21 April 1906.
40. Helene Most, "An die Leser der 'Freiheit'" (To the readers of *Freiheit*), *Freiheit,* 21 April 1906.
41. Avrich, *Anarchist Voices,* 18.
42. Lucifer Most to Rudolf Grossmann, n.d. [after 1906]. Pierre Ramus Archives, IISG.
43. *Freiheit,* 11 August 1883.
44. *Freiheit,* 31 March 1883.
45. *Freiheit,* 20 January 1883.
46. *Freiheit,* 26 May 1883.
47. *Freiheit,* 14 July 1883.
48. *Freiheit,* 8 September 1883.
49. *Freiheit,* 15 September 1883.
50. *Liberty,* 1 May 1886.
51. Waltershausen, *Der moderne Socialismus,* 213. According to Paul Avrich, delegates from Boston and New Orleans attended. Avrich, *Haymarket Tragedy,* 71.
52. Quoted in Avrich, *Haymarket Tragedy,* 75.
53. "Manifesto of the International Working People's Association, 1883," in Fried, *Socialism in America,* 212.
54. Ronald Creagh makes this observation in *L'anarchisme aux Etats-Unis,* vol. 1, 646.
55. The German text can be found in Rocker, *Johann Most,* 146–49. An English version appeared in Ely, *Labor Movement in America,* 358–63, and in Fried, *Socialism in America,* 208–12.
56. Quoted in Fried, *Socialism in America,* 208.
57. Creagh, *L'anarchisme aux Etats-Unis,* vol. 1, 652.
58. Waltershausen, *Der moderne Socialismus,* 236.
59. *Liberty,* 1 May 1886.

Chapter 4: Beyond Most

1. Quoted in Peukert, introduction to *Erinnerungen eines Proletariers aus der revolutionären Arbeiterbewegung,* 9.
2. Rocker, *Johann Most,* 144.
3. Ibid.
4. *Freiheit,* 21 April 1883 and 21, 28 June, and 5 July 1884; *Liberty,* 6 September 1884 and 3 January, 18 July 1885.
5. Carlson, *Anarchism in Germany I,* 236.
6. Johann Most to Victor Dave, 13 January 1885, Nettlau Archives, "Most und Neve," 41, IISG.
7. *Freiheit,* 13 June 1891 and 11 January 1890.
8. See the annual reports in *Freiheit,* 11 January 1890 and 6 January 1894.

9. *Freiheit,* 15 June 1895.
10. Peukert, *Erinnerungen,* 16.
11. Josef Peukert to Victor Dave, 20 September 1880, Nettlau, "Most und Neve," 7–8, IISG.
12. Peukert, *Erinnerungen,* 112.
13. Johann Most to Victor Dave, 7 October 1884, Nettlau, "Most und Neve," 23, IISG.
14. *Freiheit,* 29 August 1891.
15. Johann Most to Victor Dave, 7 October 1884, Nettlau Archives, "Most und Neve," 23, IISG.
16. Johann Most to Victor Dave, 8 November 1884, Nettlau Archives, "Most und Neve," 26, IISG.
17. Nettlau Archives, "Most und Neve," 31 n.57, IISG.
18. Johann Most to Victor Dave, 10 January 1885, Nettlau Archives, "Most und Neve," 37, IISG.
19. *Liberty,* 3 January and 25 April 1885.
20. *Freiheit,* 12 April 1884.
21. *Freiheit,* 11 August 1883.
22. *Freiheit,* 26 April 1884.
23. *Freiheit,* 5 February 1887.
24. Rocker, *Johann Most,* 298.
25. *Amerikanische Arbeiter-Zeitung,* 2 January 1886.
26. Ibid.
27. Reprinted in *Liberty,* 17 April 1886.
28. Quoted in Anderson, *All-American Anarchist,* 175.
29. Quoted in *Liberty,* 1 May 1886.
30. *Liberty,* 8 October 1892.
31. *Freiheit,* 20 July 1889.
32. *Die Autonomie,* 17 August 1889.
33. *Freiheit,* 20 July 1889.
34. *Freiheit,* 11 April 1891.
35. *Freiheit,* 21 December 1889.
36. *Freiheit,* 9, 16, 23, and 30 August 1890; Rocker, *Johann Most,* 336.
37. *Freiheit,* 3 September 1892.
38. *Liberty,* 22 May 1886.
39. *Liberty,* 1 May 1886.
40. Linse, *Organisierter Anarchismus im deutschen Kaiserreich von 1871,* 23–24.
41. Nettlau, *Anarchisten und Sozialrevolutionäre,* 384.
42. Ibid., 317.
43. Quoted in Rocker, *Johann Most,* 154.
44. Goldman, *Living My Life,* vol. 1, 75.
45. [Schneidt], *Die Hintermänner der Socialdemokratie,* 93.
46. Speed, "Anarchists in New York," 799.
47. Johann Most to Victor Dave, 7 May 1885, Nettlau Archives, "Most und Neve," 47, IISG.
48. Carlson, *Anarchism in Germany,* 343–93.
49. Peukert, *Erinnerungen,* 199.

50. Huneker, *New Cosmopolis,* 27.
51. *Der Anarchist,* 3 September 1892.
52. Goldman, *Living My Life,* vol. 1, 217.
53. *Die Anarchist,* 3 September 1892.
54. *Solidarity,* 9 February 1893.
55. Esteve, *Memoria de la Conferencia Anarquista Internacional,* 26–27.
56. *Mother Earth* 5.2 (April 1910).
57. Berkman, *Prison Memoirs of an Anarchist,* 82.
58. *New York Times,* 14 January 1889.
59. Johann Most to Victor Dave, 13 January 1885, Nettlau Archives, "Most und Neve," 40, IISG.
60. *Die Autonomie,* 11 August 1888.
61. *Der Anarchist,* 27 February 1892.
62. *Freiheit,* 25 September 1897.
63. *New York Times,* 4 May 1892.
64. *Der Anarchist,* 5 March 1892.
65. *Der Anarchist,* 26 March 1892.
66. *Der Anarchist,* 10 March 1894.
67. *Der Anarchist,* 8 August 1891.
68. Goldman, *Living My Life,* vol. 1, 86.
69. *Der Anarchist,* 1 February 1890.
70. Quoted in Avrich, *Anarchist Voices,* 56.
71. Staudacher, *Sozialrevolutionäre und Anarchisten,* 303–4; Peukert, *Erinnerungen,* 84.
72. *Der Anarchist,* 8 August 1891.
73. *Der Anarchist,* 23 January 1892.
74. Nicolaus Mauer to Josef Peukert, undated [ca. 1895], Josef Peukert Archives, IISG.
75. *Der Anarchist,* 12 December 1891.
76. *Der Anarchist,* 18 February 1893.
77. Ibid.
78. *Der Anarchist,* 22 June 1895.
79. Datenbank des deutschsprachigen Anarchismus (DadA), Abteilung Periodica, "Die Brandfackel."
80. *Die Brandfackel,* 1 July 1893.
81. *Die Brandfackel* 3.1 (January 1895).
82. *Sturmvogel,* 1 November 1897.
83. *Sturmvogel,* 15 January 1898.
84. *Sturmvogel,* 16 January 1899.
85. *Freiheit,* 10 July 1886.
86. *Freiheit,* 12 January 1889.
87. Goldman, *Living My Life,* vol. 1, 76, 77.
88. *Freiheit,* 15 October 1887.
89. Goldman, *Living My Life,* vol. 1, 380.
90. *Freiheit,* 27 April 1895.

Chapter 5: Facing America

1. Pierson, "The Spirit of Anarchy and the Weapon of Assassination," 804.
2. Deville, *Der Anarchismus,* 4.
3. Waltershausen, *Der moderne Socialismus,* 204–5.
4. Bakunin, *Political Philosophy of Bakunin,* 380.
5. Sullivan, "Is Homestead Portentous of a General Class War?"
6. *New York Times,* 16 April 1883.
7. [D. H.] *Socialismus und Anarchismus,* 145.
8. *Freiheit,* 12 June 1886.
9. Speed, "Anarchists in Hard Times," 840.
10. Nelson, *Beyond the Martyrs,* 104.
11. *Freiheit,* 24 September 1887.
12. *Freiheit,* 27 April 1889.
13. *Freiheit,* 1 November 1890; *Freiheit,* 23 January 1892.
14. Dinnerstein and Reimers, *Ethnic Americas,* 16.
15. Kautsky, "Johann Most," 557.
16. Burrows and Wallace, *Gotham,* 1186.
17. *Freiheit,* 29 May 1897.
18. Waltershausen, *Der moderne Socialismus,* 218.
19. *Freiheit,* 19 January 1884.
20. Waltershausen, *Der moderne Socialismus,* 361.
21. Ibid., 218.
22. *Freiheit,* 27 June 1891.
23. The monthly balance sheets were published in *Freiheit,* 14 September 1889, 12 October 1889, 23 November 1889, 14 December 1889, 18 January 1890, 15 February 1890, 22 March 1890, 19 April 1890, 17 May 1890, 14 June 1890, 12 July 1890, 2 August 1890, 18 October 1890, 15 November 1890, 27 December 1890, and 14 March 1891.
24. *Freiheit,* 12 February 1898.
25. Goldman, *Living My Life,* vol. 1, 115.
26. Most, *Free Society,* 10.
27. Marsh, "Anarchist-Feminist Response," 543.
28. *Freiheit,* 2 March 1889.
29. Rocker, *Johann Most,* 193.
30. *Freiheit,* 11 April 1903; *Der Anarchist,* 5 November 1892.
31. Goldman, *Living My Life,* vol. 1, 115.
32. Quoted in ibid., 151.
33. Ibid., 151 (italics added).
34. Emma Goldman to Alexander Berkman, St. Tropez (France), 20 February 1929, in Goldman and Berkman, *Nowhere at Home,* 145.
35. *Freiheit,* 6 September 1890.
36. *Freiheit,* 25 June 1892.
37. *Freiheit,* 25 October 1884.
38. *Freiheit,* 13 June 1896.
39. *Freiheit,* 8 November 1884.
40. *Freiheit,* 24 September 1887.
41. *Freiheit,* 30 March 1889.

42. *Freiheit,* 18 October 1890.
43. *Sturmvogel,* 16 January 1899.
44. *New York Times,* 29 May 1886.
45. Waltershausen, *Der moderne Socialismus,* 243.
46. Quoted in ibid.
47. *Der Anarchist,* 23 July and 10 December 1892.
48. Rocker, *Johann Most,* 392.
49. *Freiheit,* 21 December 1889.
50. Schneider, *Trade Unions and Community,* 119.
51. Waltershausen, *Der moderne Socialismus,* 167, 264.
52. *Freiheit,* 15 January 1887.
53. *Freiheit,* 4 June 1887.
54. *Freiheit,* 6 September 1890.
55. Waltershausen, *Der moderne Socialismus,* 376.
56. *Freiheit,* 27 July 1889.
57. Waltershausen, *Der moderne Socialismus,* 385–86.
58. *Freiheit,* 31 August 1889.
59. Schlereth, *Victorian America,* 52.
60. *Freiheit,* 7 September 1889.
61. *Freiheit,* 6 September 1890.
62. *Amerikanische Arbeiter-Zeitung,* 8 May 1886.
63. Bonsal, *Heyday in a Vanished World,* 13.
64. Nelson, *Beyond the Martyrs,* 240–41.
65. *Freiheit,* 25 May 1889.
66. *Der Anarchist,* 2 April 1892.
67. *Freiheit,* 25 May 1889.
68. *Freiheit,* 26 April 1890.
69. *Freiheit,* 15 February 1908.
70. *Der Anarchist,* 26 March 1892.
71. Most, *Social Monster,* 20.
72. *Freiheit,* 10 December 1904 and 15 February 1908.
73. *Freiheit,* 18 May 1889.
74. *Freiheit,* 21 September 1889.
75. *Der Anarchist,* 12 August 1893.
76. Pierre Ramus Archives, no. 438, p. 125, scrapbook, IISG.
77. King, *King's Handbook of New York City,* 604.
78. Haenni, "Constituting a Public," 223.
79. *Freiheit,* 19 March 1887.
80. *Freiheit,* 22 and 29 October 1887.
81. *Freiheit,* 15 December 1894 and 20 October 1894.
82. Blankenagel, "Early Reception of Hauptmann's *Die Weber,*" 335.
83. *Freiheit,* 22 September 1894.
84. Blankenagel, "Early Reception of Hauptmann's *Die Weber,*" 336–37.
85. *Freiheit,* 24 November 1894.
86. Quoted in Blankenagel, "Early Reception of Hauptmann's *Die Weber,*" 338.
87. Ibid., 338–39.
88. *Liberty,* 17 November 1894.

89. Pierre Ramus Archives, no. 438, p. 155, scrapbook, IISG.
90. *New York Times,* 21 March 1895.
91. *Sturmvogel,* 15 January 1898.
92. Nelson, *Beyond the Martyrs,* 132.
93. *Freiheit,* 22 April 1905.
94. *Freiheit,* 11 April 1891.
95. *Freiheit,* 22 October 1898.
96. *Freiheit,* 24 August 1895.
97. *New York Times,* 5 July 1896.
98. *Sturmvogel,* 16 May 1899.
99. *Freiheit,* 22 October 1898.
100. *Der Anarchist,* 1 October 1892.
101. *Freiheit,* 18 June 1887.
102. *Freiheit,* 15 October 1898 (italics added).
103. Park, "The City," 126.
104. Quoted in Nelson, *Beyond the Martyrs,* 127.
105. Ibid., 138.
106. *Freiheit,* 18 June 1887.

Chapter 6: German Anarchists in Progressive New York

1. Dinnerstein and Reimers, *Ethnic Americas,* 208.
2. Ibid.
3. Rosenwaike, *Population History of New York City,* 95; Adams, Lewis, and McCrosky, *Regional Survey of New York and Its Environs,* 93.
4. *New York Times,* 8 March 1908.
5. Quoted in *Freiheit,* 16 February 1901.
6. *Sturmvogel,* 15 February 1898.
7. *Freiheit,* 4 March 1899.
8. *Freiheit,* 17 August 1901.
9. An obituary appeared in *Freiheit,* 14 September 1895; Carlson, *Anarchism in Germany,* 328.
10. *Freiheit,* 24 September 1892.
11. Obituaries appeared in *Freiheit,* 12 February 1898, and *Sturmvogel,* 1 February 1898.
12. Thümmler, *Sozialistengesetz §28,* 206.
13. Bernstein, *Die Geschichte der Berliner Arbeiter-Bewegung,* vol. 2, 348.
14. *Freiheit,* 1 October 1892 and 27 May 1893; *Der Anarchist,* 1 September, 27 October, and 24 November 1894
15. An obituary appeared in *Freiheit,* 22 December 1900.
16. Goldman, *Living My Life,* vol. 1, 321.
17. *New York Times,* 21 December 1900.
18. *Sturmvogel,* 15 September 1898.
19. *Freiheit,* 15 December 1900.
20. *Freiheit,* 13 April 1907.
21. *Freiheit,* 22 February 1902.
22. *Sturmvogel,* 16 April 1899.
23. *Freiheit,* 7 December 1895.

24. *Freiheit,* 28 December 1895.
25. *Freiheit,* 1 February 1896.
26. *Freiheit,* 22 February 1896.
27. *Freiheit,* 11 July 1896.
28. *Freiheit,* 31 December 1896.
29. See the Pierre Ramus Gesellschaft website: www.ramus.at.
30. Nettlau, *Anarchisten und Syndikalisten,* 289; *Freiheit,* 23 March 1901.
31. *Freiheit,* 27 April 1901.
32. *Der Zeitgeist,* 1 May 1901.
33. Ibid.
34. *Der Tramp,* November 1901.
35. *Freiheit,* 13 June 1903.
36. Cahan, "We Find the Defendant Guilty," 345.
37. *New York Times,* 16 and 20 September 1901.
38. Goldman, *Living My Life,* vol. 1, 304.
39. Perlin, "Anarchist-Communism in America," 145.
40. Carey, "The Vessel, the Deed, and the Idea," 50. See also Carey, "*La Question Sociale,*" 289–98; Nichols, "Anarchists in America," 859–63.
41. Carey, "The Vessel, the Deed, and the Idea," 54.
42. *Freiheit,* 18 October 1902.
43. Ibid.
44. *New York Times,* 20 October 1903; Nettlau, *Anarchisten und Syndikalisten,* 289.
45. Carey, "The Vessel, the Deed, and the Idea," 55; Nettlau, *Anarchisten und Syndikalisten,* 289–90.
46. *Freiheit,* 25 September 1904; *New York Times,* 29 November 1904.
47. Arndt and Olson, *Deutsch-amerikanische Zeitungen und Zeitschriften,* 402.
48. *Freiheit,* 17 September 1898.
49. *Freiheit,* 18 May 1907.
50. Avrich, *Modern School Movement,* 277–78.
51. Avrich, *Anarchist Voices,* 247.
52. Ibid.
53. *Mother Earth* 1.10 (December 1906) and 1.12 (February 1907).
54. See the interview with Grace Umrath, Isaak's granddaughter, in Avrich, *Anarchist Voices,* 23–27.
55. Goldman, *Living My Life,* vol. 1, 224.
56. Quoted in ibid., 224.
57. *Das freie Wort,* July 1907.
58. Ibid.
59. Ibid.
60. Ibid.
61. Ibid.
62. Stirner, *Ego and His Own,* 182.
63. Quoted in Marshall, *Demanding the Impossible,* 221.
64. *Das freie Wort,* July 1907.
65. *Das freie Wort,* August 1907.
66. *Das freie Wort,* November 1907.

67. *Freiheit,* 26 September 1903.
68. *Freiheit,* 3 October 1903.
69. Ibid.
70. *Mother Earth* 2.11 (January 1908).
71. Ibid.
72. Ibid.
73. *Mother Earth* 2.12 (February 1908).
74. *Freiheit,* 14 March 1908.
75. *Freiheit,* 9 May 1908.
76. *Freiheit,* 1 August 1891.
77. *Der Strom,* 17 December 1910.
78. *Der Strom,* 15 June 1910.
79. *Der Strom,* 18 February and end of March 1911.
80. *Der Anti-Autoritär,* 15 March 1911.
81. Ibid.
82. Ibid.
83. Ibid.
84. *Der Anti-Autoritär,* 15 April 1911.
85. Avrich, *Anarchist Voices,* 447.
86. Avrich, *Modern School Movement,* 337.
87. Avrich, *Anarchist Voices,* 247, 287–88.
88. Ibid., 247, 287–88, 447.
89. Ibid., 352.
90. *Freiheit,* 9 July 1892.
91. *Freiheit,* 17 August 1901.
92. *Freiheit,* 2 January 1892.
93. *Freiheit,* 2 February 1901.
94. *Freiheit,* 17 October 1896.
95. Avrich, *Modern School Movement,* 66.
96. Nettlau, *Anarchisten und Syndikalisten,* 188–89.
97. Goldman, *Living My Life,* vol. 1, 216.
98. Avrich, *Anarchist Voices,* 479 n.35.
99. *Freiheit,* 29 September 1894.
100. Avrich, *Anarchist Voices,* 13; *Freiheit,* 4 April 1896.
101. Rocker, *Johann Most,* 421.
102. Goldman, *Living My Life,* vol. 1, 217.
103. Ibid., 218.
104. *Freiheit,* 21 April 1906.
105. Rocker, *Johann Most,* 432.
106. Wexler, *Emma Goldman in America,* 125.
107. *Freiheit,* 14 September 1907 and 26 September 1908.
108. Emma Goldman to Alexander Berkman, St. Tropez (France), 20 February 1929, in Goldman and Berkman, *Nowhere at Home,* 145.
109. *Internationale Arbeiter-Chronik,* 30 March 1914.
110. Ibid.
111. Ibid.
112. Tönnies, *Gemeinschaft und Gesellschaft.*
113. *Internationale Arbeiter-Chronik,* 30 March 1914.

114. *Internationale Arbeiter-Chronik*, 23 July 1914.

115. Berkman to Grossmann, 28 February 1913, Pierre Ramus Archives, IISG.

116. Ibid.

117. *Internationale Arbeiter-Chronik*, 23 August and 23 September 1914.

118. *Internationale Arbeiter-Chronik*, 23 September 1914.

119. Marshall, *Demanding the Impossible*, 332.

120. Howe, *World of Our Fathers*, 538–39.

121. *Internationale Arbeiter-Chronik*, 23 September 1914.

122. Avrich, *Anarchist Voices*, 269–70.

123. Quoted in Creagh, *L'anarchisme aux Etats-Unis*, vol. 1, 449.

124. *New York Times*, 16 October 1890.

125. Avrich, *Anarchist Voices*, 40.

126. Hoerder, "German Immigrant Workers' View of 'America' in the 1880s," 18.

127. Keil and Ickstadt, "Elements of German Working-Class Culture in Chicago," 90.

128. Esteve, *Memoria de la Conferencia*, 25.

129. McLean, *Rise and Fall of Anarchy in America*, 240–41, 244–45.

130. Johann Most to Victor Dave, 10 August 1884, Nettlau Archives, "Most und Neve," 11, IISG.

131. Quoted in Waltershausen, *Der moderne Socialismus*, 206.

132. *Freiheit*, 26 February 1887.

133. Ibid.

134. *Freiheit*, 4 September 1880.

135. *Freie Wacht!* 24 August 1895 ("Amerika, du schönes Land / Brauchst keine Denker und Dichter / Du hast so manchen Mann von Stand / Die Boodler und die—Richter. / Amerika, du schönes Land / Brauchst keine Dichter und Denker / Du hast so manchen Mann von Stand / Die Knüppler und die Henker").

136. *Freiheit*, 16 February 1889.

137. *Der Anarchist*, 1 November 1889.

138. Quoted in Rocker, *Johann Most*, 332.

139. *Freiheit*, 19 April 1884.

140. *Freiheit*, 21 December 1889.

141. *Freiheit*, 27 April 1889.

142. *Freiheit*, 1 November 1890.

143. *Freiheit*, 13 December 1890 and 3 January 1891.

144. *Solidarity*, 9 July 1892 and 9 February 1893; *The Rebel*, 20 November 1895.

145. *Freiheit*, 24 August 1889.

146. *Freiheit*, 16 August 1890.

147. *Freiheit*, 3 August 1889.

148. *Der Kämpfer*, 25 July 1896.

149. *Freiheit*, 8 June 1889.

150. Rocker, *Johann Most*, 372.

151. *New York Times*, 23 June 1891; Ashbaugh, *Lucy Parsons*, 170.

152. Quoted in Ashbaugh, *Lucy Parsons*, 171.

153. Goldman, *Living My Life*, vol. 1, 57.

154. *Freiheit,* 1 June 1889 and 30 November 1889.
155. Boase, *Rhetoric of Protest and Reform,* 37.
156. Rocker, *Johann Most,* 365.
157. *Freiheit,* 16 November 1889.
158. *Freiheit,* 20 January 1906; Goldman, *Living My Life,* vol. 1, 393–94.
159. Avrich, *Anarchist Portraits,* 79–106; *Der Anarchist,* 26 December 1891.
160. *Der Anarchist,* 26 December 1891.
161. *Der Anarchist,* 22 June 1895.
162. Ibid.
163. Ibid.
164. *Freiheit,* 16 February 1889.
165. Quoted in *Sturmvogel,* 15 February 1898.
166. *Sturmvogel,* 15 February 1898.
167. *Freiheit,* 13 April 1907.
168. *Mother Earth* 6.1 (March 1911): 13.
169. Ibid.
170. Fishman, *Language Loyalty in the United States,* 227.
171. *Der Kämpfer,* 22 August 1896.
172. *Freiheit,* 18 June 1887.
173. *Freiheit,* 26 February 1887.
174. *Philadelphia Times,* 6 February 1883.

Conclusion

1. Nettlau, "Anarchisten und Syndikalisten," band 7, 76, unpublished manuscript, Max Nettlau Archives, IISG.
2. DadA, Abteilung Periodika, "Gegen den Strom."
3. *Insubordination* 2 (2002): 12.
4. Duberman, *Left Out,* 5–6.

BIBLIOGRAPHY

Archival Material

Internationaal Instituut voor Sociale Geschiedenis, Amsterdam
Victor Dave Archives, 1873–1914
Max Metzkow Archives, 1880–1945
Josef Peukert Archives, 1880–1910 (–1914)
Max Nettlau Archives, 1885–1944
Pierre Ramus Archives, (1826, 1872–) 1882–1936 (–1991)

The Labadie Collection at the University of Michigan at Ann Arbor
Voltairine de Cleyre Collection, 1876–1914
Cassius V. Cook Papers, 1908–1950
James B. Elliott Papers, 1853–1912
Emma Goldman Collection of Papers, 1909–1940
Max Metzkow Papers, 1881–1934
George Schumm Papers, 1878–1940
Johann Most, Miscellaneous Pamphlets
Online Photograph Collection

The Southwest Collection/Special Collections Library at Texas Tech University, Lubbock
Boeer/Wolf Families Papers (letters by George Bauer, Georg Biedenkapp, Martin Drescher, Helene Most)

State Historical Society of Wisconsin, Madison
Johann Most, letter, 1888

Anarchist Periodicals

Amerikanische Arbeiter-Zeitung (American labor journal). New York, 1886. Ed. Wilhelm Hasselmann.

Der Anarchist: Anarchistisch-Communistisches Organ (The anarchist: Anarchist-communist organ). St. Louis and New York, 1889–95. Ed. Claus Timmermann, Karl Mazur, Nicolaus Mauer.

Der Anti-Autorität (The anti-authoritarian). New York, 1911. Ed. G. Rahmlow, Hans Koch.

Die Autonomie (Autonomy). London, 1886–93. Ed. Josef Peukert, P. Wallhausen.

Die Brandfackel (The torch). New York, 1893–94. Ed. Claus Timmermann.

Freie Wacht! (Free watch!). Philadelphia, 1894–95.

Das freie Wort (The free word). New York, 1907. Ed. Hans Koch, Georg Stine.

Freiheit (Freedom). London and New York, 1879–1906. Ed. Johann Most, Max Baginski.

Insubordination. Philadelphia, 1999–. Ed. Arthur Stamoulis, Herb Avram, Hans Bennett.

Internationale Arbeiter-Chronik (International labor-chronicle). New York, 1914. Ed. Max Baginski.

Der Kämpfer (The fighter). St. Louis, 1896. Ed. Otto Rinke.

Liberty. Boston, 1881–1908. Ed. Benjamin R. Tucker.

Man! San Francisco, 1933–40. Ed. Marcus Graham.

Mother Earth. New York, 1906–18. Ed. Emma Goldman, Alexander Berkman.

New Jersey Freie Presse (New Jersey free press). Newark, 1889–90. Ed. Julius Adolf Grunzig.

The Rebel. Boston, 1895–96. Ed. Charles W. Mowbray, Harry Kelly.

The Social Question. Paterson, N.J., 1902 (English-language version of *La Questione Sociale*).

Solidarity. New York, 1892–98. Ed. F. Saverio Merlino, John H. Edelmann.

Der Strom: Ein Organ frei-sozialistischer Richtung (The current: A free socialist organ). New York, 1910–12. Ed. Hans Koch, Anna Riedel.

Der Sturmvogel (The storm petrel). New York, 1897–99. Ed. Claus Timmermann.

Der Tramp (The tramp). New York, 1901. Ed. Rudolf Grossmann (supplement of *Der Zeitgeist*).

Twentieth Century. New York, 1888–98. Ed. Hugh O. Pentecost.

Der Zeitgeist. New York, 1901. Ed. Rudolf Grossmann.

Other Newspapers

Harper's Weekly. New York, 1857–1976.

The Masses. New York, 1911–17. Ed. Piet Vlag, Max Eastman.

New Yorker Volkszeitung (New York people's journal). 1878–1932. Ed. Alexander Jonas, Sergius E. Schewitsch, Julius Adolf Grunzig, Ludwig Lore, Siegfried Lipschitz.

New York Times. 1861–.

Philadelphia Press. 1880–85.

Philadelphia Times. 1877–1902.

Published Sources

Adams, Thomas, Harold Lewis, and Theodore McCrosky. *Regional Survey of New York and Its Environs, Volume II: Population, Land Values and Government.* New York: Committee on Regional Plan of New York and Its Environs, 1929.

Anderson, Carlotta R. *All-American Anarchist: Joseph A. Labadie and the Labor Movement.* Detroit: Wayne State University Press, 1998.

Arndt, Karl, and May Olson, eds. *Deutsch-amerikanische Zeitungen und Zeitschriften, 1732–1955: Geschichte und Bibliographie* (German-American newspapers and periodicals, 1732–1955: History and bibliography). Heidelberg: Quelle und Meyer, 1955.

Ashbaugh, Carolyn. *Lucy Parsons: American Revolutionary.* Chicago: Charles H. Kerr, 1976.

Auer, Ignaz. *Nach zehn Jahren: Material und Glossen zur Geschichte des Sozialistengesetzes* (After ten years: Material and annotations on the history of the Antisocialist laws). Nürnberg: Verlag der Fränkischen Verlagsanstalt, 1913.

Avrich, Paul H. *Anarchist Voices: An Oral History of Anarchism in America.* Princeton, N.J.: Princeton University Press, 1995.

———. *The Haymarket Tragedy.* Princeton, N.J.: Princeton University Press, 1984.

———. *The Modern School Movement: Anarchism and Education in the United States.* Princeton, N.J.: Princeton University Press, 1980.

Bakunin, Mikhail. *The Political Philosophy of Bakunin: Scientific Anarchism.* Ed. G. P. Maximoff. New York: Free Press, 1953.

Becker, Heiner. "Johann Most in Europe." *The Raven: Anarchist Quarterly,* 1.4 (March 1988): 291–321.

———. "Johann Neve (1844–1896)." *The Raven: Anarchist Quarterly* 1.2 (August 1987): 99–114.

Berkman, Alexander. *Prison Memoirs of an Anarchist.* 1912; reprint, New York: New York Review of Books, 1999.

Bernstein, Eduard. *Die Geschichte der Berliner Arbeiter-Bewegung* (History of the labor movement in Berlin). 3 vols. Berlin: Buchhandlung Vorwärts, 1907.

Bers, Günter. *Wilhelm Hasselmann, 1844–1916: Sozialrevolutionärer Agitator und Abgeordneter des Deutschen Reichstages* (Wilhelm Hasselmann, 1844–1916: Social-revolutionary agitator and member of the German Parliament). Köln: Einhorn-Presse, 1973.

Blankenagel, John C. "Early Reception of Hauptmann's *Die Weber* in the United States." *Modern Language Notes* 68 (May 1953): 334–40.

Briefe und Auszüge aus Briefen von Joh. Phil. Becker, Jos. Dietzgen, Friedrich Engels, Karl Marx u.A. an F. A. Sorge und Andere (Letters and excerpts from letters of Joh. Phil. Becker, Jos. Dietzgen, Friedrich Engels, Karl Marx, and others to F. A. Sorge and others). Stuttgart: Verlag von J. H. W. Dietz, 1921.

Boase, Paul H., ed. *The Rhetoric of Protest and Reform, 1878–1898.* Athens: Ohio University Press, 1980.

Bonsal, Stephen. *Heyday in a Vanished World.* New York: W. W. Norton and Co., 1937.

Burrows, Edwin G., and Mike Wallace. *Gotham: A History of New York City to 1898.* New York: Oxford University Press, 1999.

Cahan, Abraham. "We Find the Defendant Guilty." In *Grandma Never Lived in America: The New Journalism of Abraham Cahan.* Ed. Moses Rischin. Bloomington: Indiana University Press, 1985. 345.

Cahm, Caroline. *Kropotkin and the Rise of Revolutionary Anarchism, 1872–1886.* Cambridge: Cambridge University Press, 1989.

Carey, George W. "*La Questione sociale,* an Anarchist Newspaper in Paterson, N.J. (1895–1908)." In *Italian Americans: New Perspectives in Italian Immigration and Ethnicity.* Ed. L. F. Tomasi. New York: American Italian Historical Association, 1985. 289–98.

———. "The Vessel, the Deed, and the Idea: Anarchists in Paterson, 1895–1908." *Antipode: A Radical Journal of Geography* 10.11 (1979): 46–58.

Carlson, Andrew R. *Anarchism in Germany I: The Early Movement.* Metuchen, N.J.: Scarecrow Press, 1972.

Certeau, Michel de. *The Practice of Everyday Life.* Berkeley: University of California Press, 1984.

Chauncey, George. *Gay New York: Gender, Urban Culture, and the Making of the Gay Male World, 1890–1940.* New York: Basic Books, 1994.

Claghorn, Kate H. *Reports of the Industrial Commission.* Vol. 15. Washington, D.C.: Government Printing Office, 1901.

Commons, John, et al. *History of Labour in the United States.* Vol. 2. New York: Macmillan, 1946.

Creagh, Ronald. *L'anarchisme aux Etats-Unis* (Anarchism in the United States). 2 vols. New York: Peter Lang, 1983.

Cunningham, John T. *Newark.* Newark: New Jersey Historical Society, 1988.

"A Defense of Justus Schwab." *The Outlook,* 25 November 1893.

Deleon, Daniel. *Party Ownership of the Press: Historic Documents Relating to the Establishing of the Principles Involved.* New York: New York Labor News Company, 1931.

Deville, Gabriel Pierre. *Der Anarchismus* (Anarchism). New York: National Executive Committee of the Socialist Labor Party, 1886.

[D. H.] *Socialismus und Anarchismus in Europa und Nordamerika während der Jahre 1883 bis 1886: Nach amtlichen Quellen* (Socialism and anarchism in Europe and North America from 1883 to 1886: From official sources). 1887; reprint, Berlin: Leutershausen, 1974.

Dinnerstein, Leonard, and David M. Reimers. *Ethnic Americans: A History of Immigration.* New York: Harper Collins, 1988.

Drinnon, Richard. *Rebel in Paradise: A Biography of Emma Goldman.* New York: Harper and Row, 1961.

Duberman, Martin. *Left Out: The Politics of Exclusion; Essays, 1964–1999.* New York: Basic Books, 1999.

Ek, Richard Almo. "A Historical Study of the Speechmaking at Cooper Union, 1859–1897." Ph.D. dissertation, University of Southern California, 1964.

Ely, Richard T. *The Labor Movement in America.* New York: Macmillan, 1905.

Ensslen, Klaus. "German-American Working-Class Saloons in Chicago: Their Social Function in an Ethnic and Class-Specific Cultural Context." In *German Workers' Culture in the United States, 1850 to 1920.* Ed. Hartmut Keil. Washington, D.C.: Smithsonian Institution Press, 1988. 157–80.

Esteve, Pedro. *Memoria de la Conferencia Anarquista Internacional, Celebrada en Chicago en septiembre de 1893: A los anarquistas de España y Cuba* (Memoir of the International Anarchist Conference, held in Chicago in September 1893: To the anarchists of Spain and Cuba). Paterson, N.J.: El Despertar, 1900.

Fishman, Joshua. *Language Loyalty in the United States: The Maintenance and Perpetuation of Non-English Mother Tongues by American Ethnic and Religious Groups.* The Hague: Mouton, 1966.

Foucault, Michel. "Of Other Spaces." *Diacritics* 16.1 (1986): 22–27.

———. "The Question of Geography." In *Power/Knowledge: Selected Interviews and Other Writings, 1972–1977.* Ed. and trans. Colin Gordon. New York: Pantheon Books, 1980. 63–77.

Fried, Albert, ed. *Socialism in America from the Shakers to the Third International: A Documentary History.* New York: Anchor Books, 1970.

Gemie, Sharif. "Counter-Community: An Aspect of Anarchist Political Culture." *Journal of Contemporary History* 29 (April 1994): 349–67.

Goldman, Emma. *Living My Life.* 2 vols. London: Knopf, 1931.

Goldman, Emma, and Alexander Berkman. *Nowhere at Home: Letters from Exile of Emma Goldman and Alexander Berkman.* Ed. Richard Drinnon and Anna Maria Drinnon. New York: Schocken Books, 1975.

Grottkau, Paul, and Johann Most. *Discussion über das Thema "Anarchismus oder Communismus?" Geführt von Paul Grottkau und Joh. Most, am 24. Mai 1884 in Chicago* (Debate about the theme "anarchism or communism?" by Paul Grottkau and Joh. Most, on 24 May 1884 in Chicago). Chicago: Das Central-Comite der Chicagoer Gruppen der I.A.A., Office of the 'Chicagoer Arbeiter-Zeitung' und der 'Vorbote,' 1884.

Gutman, Herbert G. "The Tompkins Square 'Riot' in New York City on January 13, 1874: A Re-Examination of Its Causes and Its Aftermath." *Labor History* 6.1 (Winter 1965): 44–70.

Haenni, Sabine. "Constituting a Public: German Jewish Contact, German American Theater, and the Formation of German American Ethnicity in the 1890s." In *German? American? Literature? New Directions in German-American Studies.* Ed. Winfried Fluck and Werner Sollors. New York: Peter Lang, 2002. 217–48.

Hoerder, Dirk. "German Immigrant Workers' View of 'America' in the 1880s." In *In the Shadow of the Statue of Liberty: Immigrants, Workers, and Citizens in the American Republic 1880–1920.* Ed. Marianne Debouzy. Vincennes: Presses Universitaires Françaises, 1988. 17–33.

———, ed. *Plutokraten und Sozialisten: Berichte deutscher Diplomaten und Agenten über die amerikanische Arbeiterbewegung 1878–1917* (Plutocrats and socialists: Reports by German diplomats and agents on the American labor movement, 1878–1917). München: Saur, 1981.

Howe, Irving. *World of Our Fathers: The Journey of East European Jews to America and the Life They Found and Made.* New York: Harcourt Brace Jovanovich, 1976.

Huneker, James Gibbons. *New Cosmopolis: A Book of Images.* New York: Charles Scribner's Sons, 1915.

Jackson, Kenneth, ed. *The Encyclopedia of New York City.* New York: Yale University Press, 1995.

Jacoby, Russell. *The Last Intellectuals: American Culture in the Age of Academe.* New York: Basic Books, 1987.

Kautsky, Karl. "Johann Most." *Die Gesellschaft: Internationale Revue für Sozialismus und Politik* 1.6 (1924): 515–64.

Keil, Hartmut, ed. *German Workers' Culture in the United States, 1850 to 1920.* Washington, D.C.: Smithsonian Institution Press, 1988.

Keil, Hartmut, and Heinz Ickstadt. "Elements of German Working-Class Culture in Chicago, 1880 to 1890." In *German Workers' Culture in the United States 1850 to 1920.* Ed. Hartmut Keil. Washington, D.C.: Smithsonian Institution Press, 1988.

Keith, Michael, and Steve Pile, eds. *Place and the Politics of Identity.* London: Routledge, 1993.

King, Moses, ed. *King's Handbook of New York City, an Outline History and Description of the American Metropolis.* Boston: Moses King, 1893.

Kolb, Alfred *Als Arbeiter in Amerika: Unter deutsch-amerikanischen Großstadt-Proletariern* (As a worker in America: Among German-American urban proletarians). Berlin: K. Siegismund, 1904.

Lain's Brooklyn Directory, 1897–98. Brooklyn: Lain and Healey, 1898.

Lang, Lucy Robins. *Tomorrow Is Beautiful.* New York: Macmillan, 1948.

Lapham, James Sigurd. "The German-Americans of New York City 1860–1890." Ph.D. dissertation, St. John's University, 1977.

Lefebvre, Henri. *The Production of Space.* 1974; reprint, Oxford: Blackwell, 1991.

Lidtke, Vernon L. *The Alternative Culture: Socialist Labor in Imperial Germany.* New York: Oxford University Press, 1985.

———. *The Outlawed Party: Social Democracy in Germany, 1878–1890.* Princeton, N.J.: Princeton University Press, 1966.

Linse, Ulrich. "Der deutsche Anarchismus 1870–1918: Eine politische Bewegung zwischen Utopia und Wirklichkeit" (German anarchism, 1870–1918: A political movement in between utopia and reality). *Geschichte in Wissenschaft und Unterricht* 20 (1969): 513–19.

———. *Organisierter Anarchismus im deutschen Kaiserreich von 1871* (Organized anarchism in the German empire since 1871). Berlin: Duncker and Humbolt, 1970.

———. "'Propaganda by Deed' and 'Direct Action': Two Concepts of Anarchist Violence." In *Social Protest, Violence, and Terror in Nineteenth- and Twentieth-Century Europe.* Ed. Wolfgang Mommsen and Gerhard Hirschfeld. New York: St. Martin's Press, 1982. 201–29.

Maffi, Mario. *Gateway to the Promised Land: Ethnic Cultures in New York's Lower East Side.* New York: New York University Press, 1995.

Marsh, Margaret. "The Anarchist-Feminist Response to the 'Woman Question' in Late Nineteenth-Century America." *American Quarterly* 30 (Fall 1978): 533–47.

Marshall, Peter. *Demanding the Impossible: A History of Anarchism.* London: Fontana Press, 1992.

McCabe, James Dabney. *History of the Great Riots, Being a Full and Authentic Account of the Strikes and Riots on the Various Railroads of the United States and in the Mining Regions.* Philadelphia: National Publishing Co., 1877.

McLean, George N. *The Rise and Fall of Anarchy in America: From Its Incipient Stage to the First Bomb Thrown in Chicago, a Comprehensive Account of the Great Conspiracy Culminating in the Haymarket Massacre, May 4th, 1886.* 1890; reprint, New York: Haskell House, 1972.

Mehring, Franz. *Geschichte des deutschen Sozialdemokratie* (History of social democracy in Germany). 2 vols. Berlin: J. H. W. Dietz, 1922.

Most, Helene. "An die Leser der 'Freiheit'" (To the readers of *Freiheit*). *Freiheit,* 21 April 1906.

Morris, J. G. "The Germans in Baltimore." In *8th, 9th, and 10th Annual Reports of the Society for the History of Germans in Maryland.* Baltimore: n.p., 1894–96.

Most, Johann. *August Reinsdorf und die Propaganda der That* (August Reinsdorf and propaganda by deed). New York: Selbstverlag des Verfassers, 1885.

———. *Die Eigenthumsbestie* (The beast of property). New York: Internationale Druckerei Freiheit, 1883.

———. *The Free Society: Tract on Communism and Anarchy.* New York: Internationale Bibliothek, 1891.

———. *Die freie Gesellschaft: Eine Abhandlung über Principien und Taktik der kommunistischen Anarchisten* (Treatise on principles and tactics of the communist-anarchists). New York: Selbstverlag des Verfassers, 1884.

———. *Die Gottespest und Religions-Seuche* (The god pestilence and religion-disease). New York: Internationale Bibliothek, 1883.

———. *Die Lösung der sociale Frage: Ein Vortrag, gehalten vor Berliner Arbeitern* (The solution to the social question: A lecture for Berlin workers). Berlin: Allgemeine deutsche Associations-Buchdruckerei, 1876.

———. *Memoiren, erlebtes, erforschtes, und erdachtes* (Memoirs, experienced, explored, and invented). New York: Selbstverlag des Verfassers, 1903.

———. *Revolutionäre Kriegswissenschaft: Ein Handbüchlein zur Anleitung betreffend Gebrauches und Herstellung von Nitro-Glycerin, Dynamit, Schießbaumwolle, Knallquecksilber, Bomben, Brandsätzen, Giften u.s.w.* (The science of revolutionary warfare: A manual of instruction in the use and preparation of nitroglycerin, dynamite, gun cotton, fulminating mercury, bombs, fuses, poisons, etc.). New York: n.p., 1885.

———. *The Social Monster: A Paper on Communism and Anarchism.* New York: Bernhard and Schenck, 1890.

———. *Unsere Stellung in der Arbeiterbewegung* (Our position in the labor movement). New York: John Müller, 1890.

Na'aman, Shlomo. *Lassalle.* Hannover: Verlag für Literatur und Zeitgeschehen, 1970.

Nadel, Stanley. *Little Germany: Ethnicity, Religion, and Class in New York City, 1845–80.* Urbana: University of Illinois Press, 1990.

Nelson, Bruce C. *Beyond the Martyrs: A Social History of Chicago's Anarchists, 1870–1900.* New Brunswick, N.J.: Rutgers University Press, 1988.

Nettlau, Max. *Anarchisten und Sozialrevolutionäre: Die historische Entwicklung des Anarchismus in den Jahren 1880–1886* (Anarchists and social revolutionaries: The historical development of anarchism, 1880–1886). Berlin: Asy Verlag, 1931.

———. *Anarchisten und Syndikalisten* (Anarchists and syndicalists). Vaduz: Topos Verlag, 1984.

Nichols, Francis H. "Anarchists in America." *The Outlook,* 10 August 1901, 859–63.

Nomad, Max. *Apostles of Revolution.* Boston: Little, Brown, 1939.

Parisi, Peter, ed. *Artist of the Actual: Essays on Paul Goodman.* Metuchen, N.J.: Scarecrow Press, 1986.

Park, Robert E. "The City: Suggestions for the Investigation of Human Behavior in the Urban Environment." In *Classic Essays on the Culture of Cities.* Ed. Richard Sennett. New York: Appleton-Century-Crofts, 1969. 91–130.

Perlin, Terry M. "Anarchist-Communism in America, 1890–1914." Ph.D. dissertation, Brandeis University, 1970.

Peukert, Josef. *Erinnerungen eines Proletariers aus der revolutionären Arbeiterbewegung* (Memoirs of a proletarian from the revolutionary labor movement). 1913; reprint, Frankfurt a.M.: Verlag Edition AV, 2002.
Pierson, Arthur T. "The Spirit of Anarchy and the Weapon of Assassination." *Missionary Review of the World* 24.11 (November 1901): 804.
Pile, Steve, and Michael Keith, eds. *Geographies of Resistance.* London: Routledge, 1997.
Powers, Madelon. *Faces along the Bar: Lore and Order in the Workingman's Saloon, 1870–1920.* Chicago: University of Chicago Press, 1998.
Roberts, James S. "Wirtshaus und Politik in der deutschen Arbeiterbewegung" (Tavern and politics in the German labor movement). In *Sozialgeschichte der Freizeit* (Social history of leisure). Ed. Gerhard Huck. Wuppertal: Hammer, 1980.
Rocker, Rudolf. *Johann Most: Das Leben eines Rebellen* (Johann Most: Life of a rebel). Foreword Alexander Berkman. 1924; reprint, Glashütten im Taunus: Detlov Auvermann, 1973.
Rosenwaike, Ira. *Population History of New York City.* Syracuse, N.Y.: Syracuse University Press, 1972.
Roskolenko, Harry. *The Time That Was Then: The Lower East Side, 1900–1914; An Intimate Chronicle.* New York: Dial Press, 1971.
Sanders, Ronald. *The Downtown Jews: Portrait of an Immigrant Generation.* New York: Harper and Row, 1969.
Sante, Luc. *Low Life: Lures and Snares of Old New York.* New York: Vintage Books, 1991.
Schaack, Michael J. *Anarchy and Anarchists: A History of the Red Terror and the Social Revolution in America and Europe.* Chicago: F. J. Schultze and Co., 1889.
Schlereth, Thomas J. *Victorian America: Transformations in Everyday Life, 1876–1915.* New York: HarperCollins, 1992.
Schneider, Dorothee. *Trade Unions and Community: The German Working Class in New York City, 1870–1900.* Urbana: University of Illinois Press, 1994.
[Schneidt, Karl.] *Die Hintermänner der Socialdemokratie: Von einem Eingeweihten* (Rear-guard supporters of social democracy: From an initiate). 2d ed. Berlin: Conitzer's Verlag, 1890.
Schumacher, E. F. *Small Is Beautiful: Economics as if People Mattered.* New York: Harper, 1973.
Scott, James C. *Domination and the Arts of Resistance: Hidden Transcripts.* New Haven, Conn.: Yale University Press, 1990.
Shaw, Douglas V. *Immigration and Ethnicity in New Jersey History.* Trenton: New Jersey Historical Commission, Department of State, 1994.
Soja, Edward. *Postmodern Geographies: The Reassertion of Space in Social Critical Theory.* London: Verso, 1989.
Sozialistische Briefe aus Amerika (Socialist letters from America). München: C. Merhoff, 1883.
Speed, John Gilmer. "Anarchists in Hard Times." *The Outlook,* 11 November 1893, 840–41.
———. "Anarchists in New York." *Harper's Weekly,* 20 August 1892, 798–99.
Staudacher, Anna. *Sozialrevolutionäre und Anarchisten: Die andere Arbeiterbe-*

wegung vor Hainfeld; Die Radikale Arbeiter-Partei Österreichs (1880–1884) (Social revolutionaries and anarchists: The other labor movement before Hainfeld; The Radical Workers' party of Austria, 1880–1884). Wien: Verlag für Gesellschaftskritik, 1988.

Stirner, Max. *The Ego and His Own.* Trans. Steven Byington. London: Rebel Press, 1982.

Sullivan, J. W. "Is Homestead Portentous of a General Class War?" *Twentieth Century,* 8 December 1892.

Tcherikower, Elias, ed. *The Early Jewish Labor Movement in the United States.* Trans. Aaron Antonovsky. New York: Yivo Institute for Jewish Research, 1961.

Thümmler, Heinzpeter. *Sozialistengesetz §28: Ausweisungen und Ausgewiesene, 1878–1890* (Anti-socialist law §28: Expulsions and exiles, 1878–1890). Berlin: Akademie-Verlag, 1979.

To the Workingmen of America. New York: IWPA Committee of Agitation, 1883.

Tönnies, Ferdinand. *Gemeinschaft und Gesellschaft: Abhandlung des Communismus und des Socialismus als empirischer Culturformen.* Leipzig: Fues, 1887.

Trachtenberg, Alan. *The Incorporation of America: Culture and Society in the Gilded Age.* New York: Hill and Wang, 1982.

Waltershausen, August Sartorius von. *Der moderne Socialismus in den Vereinigten Staaten von Amerika* (Modern socialism in the United States of America). Berlin: Hermann Bahr, 1890.

Ward, Colin. *Anarchy in Action.* New York: Harper and Row, 1973.

Wexler, Alice. *Emma Goldman in America.* Boston: Beacon Press, 1984.

Wiebe, Robert. *The Search for Order, 1877–1920.* New York: Hill and Wang, 1967.

Zinn, Howard. *A People's History of the United States.* New York: HarperPerennial, 1980.

Internet Sources

Anarchy Archives: An Online Research Center on the History and Theory of Anarchism. Ed. Dana Ward. http://dwardmac.pitzer.edu/anarchist_archives/archivehome.html.

Centre International de Recherches sur l'Anarchisme. Lausanne, Switz. (multilingual). www.anarca-bolo.ch/cira/.

Datenbank des deutschsprachigen Anarchismus (DadA). Ed. Ralf Hoerig and Hajo Schmück. Abteilung Periodica, 1798–2000. www.free.de/dada.

Emma Goldman Papers. University of California at Berkeley. http://sunsite.berkeley.edu/ Goldman/project.html.

The Haymarket Affair Digital Collection. Chicago Historical Society. www.chicagohs.org/hadc/index.html.

Kate Sharpley Library. www.katesharpleylibrary.org.

Max Stirner Archiv Leipzig. www.max-stirner-archiv-leipzig.de/.

Pierre Ramus Gesellschaft. Wien. www.ramus.at.

INDEX

TOM GOYENS teaches American history at Salisbury University and is currently writing a biography of Johann Most.

The University of Illinois Press
is a founding member of the
Association of American University Presses.

University of Illinois Press
1325 South Oak Street
Champaign, IL 61820-6903
www.press.uillinois.edu